The How and Why of

Market Democracy

*The Decline of American Ideals
and Rise of a Two Class Society* ©

by
 Rory Blake

Copyright © 1996 by Rory Blake
All rights reserved.

Grateful acknowledgment is made to authors
and copyright holders of works cited in this book.

Cover drawing © 1996 by Pat Clark

Gp10987654321

Printed in the United States of America

Library of Congress Catalog Card Number 96-85861

ISBN 0-9653521-0-2

BC Press   Charlotte

PO Box 4001, 28226

THIS BOOK IS DEDICATED
TO THE MEMORY OF A TRUE PATRIOT:

R. KENNER AMOS
9/17/18 - 7/2/96

Foreword

Leon Uris, in his novel *Redemption*, recounts the political struggles in Ireland at the turn of this century. At that time, an elite owned and controlled the land and most of the valuable assets. These elites encouraged the fighting between Catholics and Protestants because it distracted the poor from what the elites were doing to them both. While the Protestants and Catholics were fighting with one another, they were unable to see they had more in common than they had differences. Their hatred of one another blinded them as to who was gaining and who was losing in the larger picture.

Things are like that again– but in our country. Today, an elite Congressional majority scapegoats others for what they, themselves are doing to the country. Since the Nixon administration and during the previous two administrations, the elites have benefitted from tax and environmental laws designed to help and to protect only them. This period was marked by deficit spending, high real interest rates and low growth, all of which benefit only an elite. Before President Clinton was elected in 1992, a true class war was in the making over who got the crumbs which were left.

The choice for 1996 is clear: To play the red meat politics of hatred– where only the elite benefits, or to find the middle way– where everyone who works hard and follows the rules can get ahead. Most prefer the latter choice. Our system *is* based on the profit motive. Yet, it is in the interest of all, to look out for the common interest along with our own individual interests. *Market Democracy* develops when the narrow and special interests of the marketplace gain more clout and influence with elected officials than do the voters.

Clout and influence is not always solely negative. Yet, today, *too many* politicians have sold us out, to provide favors to corporations and to others who invest in their campaigns. The citizens owe it to themselves to elect as their leaders, individuals who will work for the common interest and not just for their own interest and that of their financial supporters.

Bob Dole in announcing his economic recovery and tax cutting plan, asked, " If the economy really is getting better, why do so many people feel they are much worse off." Mother Jones Magazine reported that Bob Dole received almost $1 million from Archer Daniels Midland Corporation and that it, in turn, gets the bulk of $500 million in annual federal subsidies for ethanol production and up to $2.1 billion a year in total federal subsidies. This is not the only questionable political contribution ever made either. ADM money had earlier been linked to the bank account used by the Watergate burglars.

I have great confidence in our people. We are a great and resourceful nation, our citizens want to do that which is best for all. We have so much more in common than we have which are differences. We all agree that we all benefit from a growing economy and a level playing field for commerce. The Clinton Presidency is now on the right track for us to clear the air between the opposing sides in this debate. All that we need now– is to have that debate between informed voters. I am exceedingly confident that we will, together, make the right choices.

Contents

Foreword		vii
Chapter 1:	Introduction	11
	Trust: Unwritten Agreements	21
	Civilization	43
Chapter 2:	Orderly Society	49
	Democracy	57
	Liberty	67
Chapter 3:	Liberty in Decline	73
	The Principles of Our Government	81
	Developing the Role of Government	87
Chapter 4:	Government's Proper Role	91
	Changing Institutions	95
	The Decline and Fall of Civilizations	105
Chapter 5:	A Nation in Decline	109
	The Role of Religion	115
	Religious Opportunists	119
Chapter 6:	Conservatism	125
	Neo-Conservatism	131
	Divided Americans	137

Chapter 7:	The Influence of Money	145
	Think Tanks	157
	Overpopulation and Growth of Elites	167
Chapter 8:	The Constitution and Fairness	175
	The More Things Change	181
	Anti-Trust Laws	193
Chapter 9:	Profiting from Trust	199
	The Threat to the National Health	207
	Reform and Health Care	213
Chapter 10:	Our Pooled Resources	223
	Social and Economic Policy	229
	The Public Health and Safety	239
Chapter 11:	A National Psychosis	245
	Creeping Barbarianism	251
	A New Dark Ages	255
Chapter 12:	Enlightened Self Interest	259
	Looking Out for One Another	267
	True Patriotism	271
INDEX:		279
ENDNOTES:		283

1. Introduction

Most of us are aware our political system is not working. When seventy to eighty percent of Americans favor reforming health care or increasing the minimum wage, and it doesn't quickly happen, democracy *must* be in decline. It is hard to defend a political system which is rapidly becoming more and more centered on the profit motive. Patronage can never be popular with those outside of the inner circles, just as the benefit to multiple self-interests will never fully equate with the best interests of the entire community. Often as not, programs which are enacted– are not what voters thought we were voting for. As a result, many of us are taking a much harder look at both the political leaders and the political parties which we now support.

The public wants answers and solutions, and cannot understand how we have gotten ourselves into such a mess. By huge margins, voters are demanding more accountability from their elected officials, the reform of campaign financing and election practices, and the institution of term limits. Along with their abandonment of the traditional two-party system– some are even boycotting the constitutionally mandated method for enacting change– their participation in elections. Increasing numbers are using this form of "passive resistance" to stand-up against a system they feel no longer represents them. The end result is that our chances for a truly representative government have plummeted along with the voter turn-out.

People demand strong moral leadership for the country, yet, increasingly the politicians calling for moral leadership are, at the same time, selling-out to narrow interests. They call for personal responsibility and for higher standards, while they, themselves, sell their vote to the highest bidder.

Today, only organized interests wield political clout, to the detriment of anyone else. Americans dislike transfer programs, where wealth is transferred from one group to another. Yet, special interests benefit greatly from these transfer programs and from their close association with political figures. When the special interests win, the rest of us, the taxpayers, consumers, and even as individuals dependent on clean air and water– will all lose. Our America is now a *Market Democracy*. As such, it's government becomes "for-sale" to the highest bidders, and elected officials can advance narrow and special interests over that of the ordinary citizens.

Politics in America now favors the wealthy, and other powerful interest groups

The first rule of American politics is that virtually nothing happens by accident. Often, it only becomes necessary to discover who will benefit– in order to know what will happen politically. A related observation is there is never anything entirely new in politics. Every plan, trick or gimmick has been tried, or even been used successfully, before.

It is also said that history repeats itself. Politics, too, runs in cycles and often tends to go to extremes, usually from one extreme to the other. Since the 1950s, American politics have become increasingly conservative and, with the exception of what President Johnson was able to accomplish due to the martyred JFK, so has government policy. The media and those corporations which control it, mega-business and other special interests have joined together to protect the status quo. Under this increasing conservatism, some individuals have done extremely well, while the majority has done much less well.

There is an increasing unfairness in our system, and conservative economic and tax policies which protect or advance these vested interests are at the very heart of this unfairness. Since Nixon's conservative fiscal policies and the "trickle down" tax cuts of President Reagan there has been a tremendous growth of wealth at the very top, while at the same time, individuals of ordinary means have become much less secure.

The debate in America, today, is actually quite simple. Without the emotional distractions of the left or the right, it clearly becomes "What should be the role of government?" The cold war is over. These external threats to national security have diminished. Any "unifying" effect this common fear once had is also diminished. Instead of unity, there is now increased disunity. Talk of internal enemies has replaced talk of external ones in political rhetoric. We have become further divided, and this *politics of division* has become intensified.

Cooperation with one another and the fusion of ideas which was once so common has been replaced with scapegoating and the derision of the other guy's ideas. Our options *are* limited by a national debt. However, this debate, too, boils down to just one thing: Who gains, or conversely, who loses?– from those functions which are undertaken by government.

What are the answers? Where do we find them? As patriotic Americans, the Constitution must always be the basis for these decisions and others which we make about the role of government. Our American ideals of honesty and fairness are based on Constitutional principles and should be the only basis of our political decision making. We must again return to those beginnings and to our roots– to the original agreements and to the meeting of the minds that first forged our nation. We must once again restore those American ideals of honesty, and fairness, where it is in the interest of all, to protect the interests of each and every one.

As such, the protection and maintenance of a sound economy is a prime governmental function. When government allows the economic pie to expand, all citizens will share, to some degree, in the increase. This never fails to happen in growing economies. When economic opportunity is allowed to shrink, the young and the poor are the first to suffer. In stagnant, slow-growing, or shrinking economies individuals who must labor to earn a living much worse off, as they must rely solely on economic growth to build wealth. This is a prime reason America is becoming a nation of the very rich and the very poor.

During the 1973 to 1993 period, the American economy grew at a rate of over fifty percent less than it had grown, after inflation, since 1870. Certain segments of our economy did not grow at all, some were growing more slowly, and many more were, indeed, shrinking. This lack of growth in our economy only favors those with capital or those with ownership in the means of production. In other entrepreneurial economies during this period, in Asia for example, the annual rate of economic growth often exceeded 8-10 percent– almost four times the rate of growth of the American economy.[1] What factors explain such huge differences in economic growth?

Clearly, the free-enterprise system still works, but does it simply work better in Asia? True, some Asian countries were underdeveloped and, therefore, held more opportunities for growth, accounting for some of this gain. However, the existence of pro-growth economic policies in Asian countries are a major difference between these governments and our own, more conservative one. In Asia, government programs encourage commerce and investment, but will also tend to have little environmental or worker protection.

Many in this country argue that we have too much governmental intrusion in every aspect of our society. Some scapegoat "excessive government regulations" for our lack of economic growth and fairness, while arguing for laws that favor their specific industries or groups, or which would benefit them financially. These arguments totally ignore our own lack of pro-growth economic policies. However, they continue pushing for policies which favor their own and other special interests, even those policies which place America at a disadvantage in world trade.

Our government, under the Constitution, should only become involved in markets in order to keep them honest and fair. Government should be active and supportive of markets but should never involve itself in a market to favor one group over another group. Markets will make themselves, and in a true free-enterprise system, are generally self-leveling. Only when the rules are changed to favor one group over another group, does free enterprise, or any other political system get itself into trouble.

Russian communism failed, in part, because the government tried to use the control of production to accomplish its goals. The Soviet system sought to favor certain segments of the economy, primarily the military, over all of the others. However, by allocating resources in inefficient and unfair ways, many in society were left without having an important role to play. Those who were excluded felt they had job security, yet had less of a stake in the success or the failure of the system. Therefore, many individuals did as little as they could, figuring they would be supported by the state in any event. These individuals were missing that connection between work and reward that is so important to our free enterprise system.

The Japanese government had also manipulated it's economy to benefit certain segments as well. Japan sought to favor manufacturing and export over everything else. In one of the world's richest economies, Japan consistently short-changed workers to benefit industry. The Japanese, too, placed great value on job security. However, Japanese economic-growth policy was funded initially by low wages and later by high government-enforced savings rates. Both policies tended to work against the individual to the benefit of the society.

Risky and unadvisable banking practices were tolerated and even encouraged. Currently, Japan has a looming financial crisis which will greatly overshadow our own S&L crisis. Moody's Investor Services has even rated some top Japanese banks as low as "D" for soundness, yet that economy continues under government control, and the banks are not allowed to take their losses and let the market correct itself.[2]

We, in this country, are not immune to this interference. Here, special interests have been successful in lowering the rate of economic growth and also in changing long held tax policy. However, only a very few have benefitted from these changes. The special interests now wish to further revamp the workings of the free-enterprise system by radically changing or even eliminating other laws which promote fairness. They wish to further change our system in ways that will continue to favor only them. They are, in essence, seeking to legislate opportunity away from others to gain more of it for themselves. They claim these changes are necessary to recapture and preserve the ideological purity of the free market. They say this time things are different. However, this has all been said and done before. Herbert Hoover did not intend to start a depression. He was simply trying to help the bond market.[3]

Any government regulation of the markets is criticized by the vocal few. However, some rules are of necessity. Rules are necessary because not everyone is going to be completely honest all of the time. Rules are also necessary to settle honest disputes between honest people. We will all agree with that. We can also agree that when someone breaks the rules, we are all hurt by it.

Markets depend on fairness and honesty, and they must enforce more than just minimal standards to garner any trust in their stability. When markets are seen as being dishonest, only the dishonest will participate in them. The honest individuals will simply stay away. For markets to be successful, or even to exist, the highest standards must always be maintained. In the end, the public perception of fairness and honesty is what matters the most.

Civilizations are held together in much the same way. Individuals form bonds with one another and then with their communities. These bonds must be quite strong for a society to progress. Our bond as Americans has traditionally been exceedingly strong. Our society and the bonds which hold us together are, however, only as strong as their weakest links.

As has always been typical of America culture, when one person breaks the rules, everyone is punished or is made to suffer for it. This is a lesson taught early in American society. The one child that throws the candy wrapper out of the school bus window, gets the entire bus load of children kept in after school.[4] The individual who misuses guns, compromises the rights of all who own guns. In America, more than any other society, we sink or swim together.

Abraham Lincoln termed it to be the *political religion* of America, "never to violate in the least particular, the laws of the country; and never to tolerate their violation by others."[5] This must always be true in our culture, because our free enterprise system also depends heavily on an orderly society underlying all of our dealings.

We all value freedom. Yet the free interchange of goods and services is seriously impeded by those who would take advantage of others for their own personal gain. Buyers and sellers, alike, need to be protected from those who would cheat, steal, and bend the rules in their favor. We all agree that it is in everyone's best interest to have a smoothly running society, a society based on trust and fairness. Without these two things no market can function efficiently, if it can function at all.

This same principle also applies to politics. The enemies of democracy and of the common man say that they are merely trying to prevent the spread of Socialism. Socialism is a system where the ownership or control of the means of production lies with the government. This is not our system. In our system, the corporations control the means of production. These seemingly "conservative" politicians are not seeking to conserve our system, but would, instead, change it into something else. They wish to have those who control the means of production to also have control of the government. Allowing the means of production to control the government is not simply the opposite of socialism. It is, instead, a de-evolution of our current system, the reversion of capitalism into "something else."

What this "something else" will lead to, can only be imagined. History abounds with examples of free peoples who have followed their leaders into slavery. We may be more in danger than we now realize. Our system has been changed in ways which thwart the power of a majority in favor of an elite. Our political system has been altered to make money more important than votes. Money can buy the advertisements and smear campaigns that will produce the desired voter response.

Even the prospect of economic slavery is no idle threat. Our workers no longer share in the increased production of their labor. The assets of the top 1% of Americans now exceed that of the bottom 95%.[6] The wealthy are getting wealthier, but for most, the standard of living is declining.[7] This may be the first generation since the Civil War to not leave our children a better life than what we enjoyed.

Today, there is very little job or income security in the workplace. American workers are more productive than ever, yet Americans are also working harder than ever, working longer hours, and for lower real wages.[8] Our citizens are increasingly divided into opposing groups– pitting their interests against the interests of others. What has happened to fairness and to the trust that we once had in our system? What has happened to the ideals and to the common vision that we all should share, and one time did share, as Americans?

Today we are seeking to resolve our worst economic crisis in over sixty years. As with Japan and the former USSR, there is a crisis of honesty and fairness in the allocation of resources. Twenty years ago in America, the man on the shop floor, the average worker, made about 3% of what was then the top salary. Today, he makes roughly 0.6% of what the top boss does.[9] Either, today, just 20 years later, the CEO now earns four times what he once did, or our workers are earning a quarter of what they once were. However one chooses to view it, the changes made in our economic policy during this period have placed our middle class in a slow, steep decline.

Money talks, but money should not be allowed to circumvent the will of the majority. America is, again, in need of true patriots, those who will defend the American Ideals of freedom and equality. This inequity can be fixed, however, we need those who will fight for election reform and for the re-birth of common sense in our political systems. We must fight for the most basic concepts of honesty and fairness, because they are fundamental to both our American forms of self-government and to free enterprise.

In a *Market Democracy*, where a price is put on everything and everything has a price, the priceless may ultimately become valueless. Priceless resources such as community, the environment, and our civilization itself, once lost, simply cannot be replaced, at any price. *If you believe that the individual contributions of each of us are important*, and that America is more than merely the sum of our individual self-interests, then the emergence of true patriots, today, is just as essential to the future of America, as was the banding together of those original patriots in 1776.

Trust: the unwritten agreements

There is a general breakdown of trust in the America of today. People don't trust each other the way that they once did, and with good reason. Few individuals, today, are considered to be "as good as their word." In the relatively recent past, at least among the more respectable members of the community, a man's word was as good as his bond. You could count on and feel comfortable in trusting in others. Not too very long ago, deals could be, and were, consummated with a handshake. This expectation of an atmosphere of trust, and of the ability to deal in good faith, is no longer universally true in the America of today. Today, if a deal is not in writing, it probably is not valid.

The interaction of individuals in our society, on every level, has undergone substantial change in the past few decades. Most of us will agree much of this change is for the worst. People do not seem to respond to each other in the same ways, nor is there the same degree of social interchange there once was. Fewer and fewer people are allowed to become a part of our daily lives. We seem to be able to count on, to depend on, one another for less and less. Even close neighbors do not seem to take a special interest in one another anymore.

Television has been blamed, perhaps rightly, for much of the decline in conversation and for a lessening of the social interactions between individuals. People do spend much of their time in front of a TV set. Average Americans do get most of their news from television, today. After all, in the average American household, the television is reported to be on for more than eight hours every day.[10]

We have become more isolated from others, yet we think of ourselves as being more in touch with what is going on around us. Both things are of themselves true. The fact is, we are becoming increasingly isolated from our communities. We are at the same time, also much more in touch. We may be more in touch, but only with what those corporations controlling the media wish us to be more in touch with.

Television is a very powerful medium. It is capable of both entertainment and of informing. Television and television advertising, along with advertising in general, has been blamed for creating an unwholesome demand and for stimulating an ever increasing consumption to replace what is missing in our lives. In reality, we are aware there is *something* missing in our lives. We are just not sure what that *something* is. It has been said we "want it all," yet we are willing to sacrifice some-thing more important, our relationships with others, to get it.

However, there is more to this phenomenon, this hollowing out of relationships, than just that which can be explained by television. People genuinely believe "others" will care for the needs of society. They expect someone else to do those things that need doing. They look to "others" to do it, rather than themselves becoming involved. Many look to whomever, the government, or to civic groups or charitable organizations to solve all of the problems of the community. We know this is not right. We all know it is the action of the individual which is important in our system of laws. Yet, we readily succumb to the notion we cannot make a difference by ourselves.

Many say we have "lost our sense of community," and that in general, today, "everyone puts themselves first." They note that we have lost sight of the American ideals, and have even lost those ideals that we at one time shared as Americans. They observe we neither trust, nor often depend on others, nor they on us. We may still greet one another politely enough, but will speak only when we cannot avoid speaking. People still "communicate" with each other. They may state their opinion, but there is little exchange of ideas. There is no longer a true dialogue on national issues even in the traditional enclaves of barber shops or lunch-counters. Talk radio has replaced the back fence for gossip. Few people know precisely how their neighbor feels about any subject. It seems no one talks with one another anymore. Therefore, few know the stand of their neighbor on any issue much less the issues of major importance.

The changes that have occurred in the last few decades have evidenced themselves in many and different ways, in all of the multiple social interactions we undertake daily. Things we used to be able to rely on are no longer true. Our contemporary society is full of uncertainties about jobs, relationships, the future. We feel powerless as individuals to accomplish almost anything significant. Many of us have begun to look out for ourselves and our own interests first. Americans have been increasingly pitted against other Americans. Few, today, feel the confidence to verbally express those deep concerns they may feel for what is happening to their country and to their fellow Americans. Yet many *do* know something is happening. Slowly, almost unnoticed, there have been truly fundamental changes occurring in the fabric of our society.

It is from this background in America that a new "Patriot" movement has arisen. The patriot movement has often been derided. They have been labeled paranoid and delusional. The Patriot Movement has been all but abandoned by the mainstream. But some of these are good Americans who are sincere in their feelings and beliefs. Most patriots are deeply concerned, but others are truly alarmed. They know something is changing in our America. They are not exactly sure what it is, but they do know, whatever it is, they and their friends have been hurt by it. They know things are not the way they used to be. They also realize it may be up to them to fix it, and they had best be prepared for whatever happens.

Many patriots seem extreme in their views and in their actions, but they see themselves as fighting for their country. Something in the free enterprise system of today is seriously wrong. The caring society they once enjoyed is now increasingly viewed as being seriously out of wack. In joining together, these individuals are preparing to fight for their very way of life. The free enterprise system *has* become seriously tilted against ordinary working people. The patriots may be wrong about many things. However, they are certainly right to feel things have changed, and in ways that help a few but seem to hurt them, their friends and, indeed, the entire middle class.

In the television tradition, responsibility for communication in the patriot movement is left up to the group's leaders. Like television, this dialog is one way only. The leadership speaks to the membership, and the membership listens. If the words of those leaders reflect the personal bias of the member, they will be repeated. However, the social pressure of group loyalty will often also keep individuals in line on issues with which they do not totally agree. We all tend to accept the explanations of the leadership, even if we do not fully understand them. This kind of a "tribal instinct" is responsible for much of the solidarity displayed within the patriot groups and even within interest groups in general.

As social animals, each of us feels the need to belong. We *all* feel this need. Each of us, too, will occasionally ally ourselves as part of an "interest group," be it as taxpayers, as gun owners, as stockholders, or as something else. Through alliance with these groups, we can feel we are a part of something. We all feel the need to be part of some group, as a part of something larger than ourselves. Our personal views may only be reflected in a portion of the agenda of the group as a whole. We may be passionately concerned with only the one issue, but through membership in the group we are tacitly supporting everything for which the group stands.

Trust and compromise would appear to have a poor reputation and track record today. People, in general, do not seem to put much trust in there being political solutions to problems. They do not seem to trust in compromise. Some are even fearful that politics and political compromise, the very trust in politics and the politicians themselves, may be what is ruining our county. We tend to respect those who will doggedly defend even a narrow or negative political position. We will indeed vote for, or perhaps even work for, or otherwise support those individuals who will staunchly and steadfastly stand for something we also happen to believe in, even if we agree with little else of the agenda.

Most individuals lack the individual courage to take any stand publicly. Since it is done so rarely by ordinary working people, public speaking is thought to require real bravery. People list fear of public speaking ahead of all other fears, even ahead of the common fear of going to the dentist. This single point may be the basis for the admiration of inflexibility in what would otherwise be unattractive politicians and political positions.
This may be the sole reason we will tolerate the abuses of fairness and of the rights of free speech that spring from the politics of division. Remarkably, many of us privately, as individuals, really do feel the need to be flexible, to compromise, to reach reasonable solutions. The success of the special interest group, itself, shows that people are willing to give up some things in order to accomplish the majority of their

wishes, or even just the one goal of a special interest that is personally important to them.

This political climate may, indeed, be ripe for a rapid change. The importance of the "Special Interest" in politics is at a crossroads. The people are angry. They want opposing interests to come together to work things out, to solve the many problems facing our country. Yet the special interests will continue to seek to defuse any compromise, to cloud and confuse the issues.

The various activities of selfish interests to influence legislation can only be expected to increase. The already bloated importance of money in politics and to the special interests may only escalate as the costs of lobbying for what becomes an ever more narrowly supported agenda can only go up. Those with extreme views and other interest groups will obviously have to continue to raise and spend great sums of money on advertising their viewpoints, just as the radical elements without money will have to escalate the level of violence to gain increased attention for themselves.

Those with extreme views and narrow interests are already using all of the tricks to divide us and to promote their own agendas. They are employing the tyrant's tools of scapegoating and of blame shifting. Special interests are hiding their true purpose behind deception and false pretenses. At first, all of the special interests wish to appear to be reasonable, to appeal to basic fairness and common sense. However, they may soon have to emerge from behind that curtain, to take the lead in arguing on their own behalf. Hopefully, this will expose them to the American people for what they are. This will expose them as being purely selfish and out only for themselves.

Many examples of what first appear to be offered as reasonable solutions abound today. Although the now infamous "Harry and Louise" commercials designed to scare Americans into opposing health care reform were obviously sponsored by the insurance industry, you can never be sure of the truth of the claims, or of even just who the true sponsors are. The sponsors of Harry and Louise were the hundreds of smaller health insurance companies who sell a very highly profitable type of pre-paid health insurance plan. These commercials stoked the fear people would not be able to choose their own doctor, or to even continue the relationship with their own physician, if the Clinton health care reforms were enacted.

That these smaller insurance companies were so very profitable meant they might not have survived under the President's proposed health care reform. The larger companies, with the major share of the health insurance business, were preparing to go along with some sort of health care reform. These larger insurers were actively involved in trying to cut costs and save money for their policyholders. As one such cost cutting method, these major insurers wanted their policyholders to see physicians who participated in their plan or group, or to at least see those who give discounts to their plan or group. These larger companies, with their related health care plans, were themselves the reason patients may not be able to continue to see their own physicians. So, while a majority of the insurance industry was preparing to go along with some kind of health care reform, the continuing pursuit of excessive profits by just a few individual health insurance companies helped to prevent any health care reform at all. Their opposition to any health care reform would, in fact, lead to a much higher cost of health care for everyone.

This illustrates a fundamental truth of buying into a special interest agenda. The very groups who cry out the loudest for something may ultimately be the only ones who would benefit. Indeed, some of the agenda called for in public affairs advertising and info-mercials can even be counted on to be counterproductive for the rest of us. What sounds like simple fair play may end up hurting the rest of us, both individually and as a civilization. What sometimes appears to be a real, common sense solution on the surface will very often turn out to be the complete opposite.

The true purpose of many such "grassroots" lobbying groups is, also, often hidden or disguised. Even the names of these groups are designed to be misleading as to who is really behind them. Many groups that appear to be for the benefit of one purpose are usually designed to benefit another. Some groups such as those designed to appeal to sportsmen interested in hunting and fishing were organized and funded by those who are interested in gaining access to public land for their own "other" uses.

One example is the Wildlife Legislative Fund of America. Just before the 1994 election, the WLFA accused the Clinton Administration of trying to "dismantle the hunting and fishing programs in the National Wildlife Refuge system." It fired off press releases that were picked up and printed verbatim by many members of the sporting press. These press releases were intended to make Clinton look bad and to drive sportsmen to the Republicans.

After the election, WLFA counsel, Washington lawyer Bill Horn, admitted that the Clinton administration was not trying to stop hunting and fishing but that the system had been aggressively acquiring habitat without having adequate monetary resources to manage it all. It further turns out that Horn had served under Secretary Watt at the Department of the Interior during Reagan's first term and was the man responsible for attempts to open the Arctic National Wildlife Refuge to oil drilling.

The Wise Use movement, a conglomerate of grass roots front groups funded and organized by the resource extraction industries, are using hunting and fishing as stalking horses for their real agenda: protecting the stranglehold that those industries have on rural America, particularly in the West. Wise Use is trying to peal off the environmental movement's traditional support by pitting hunters (who tend to be rural and conservative) against environmentalists (who tend to be urban and liberal).[11] The goals of environmentalists and sportsmen in preserving the environment are similar. Their mutual interests needed to be united, but instead, were divided. They were divided to increase the profits of those industries with the most to gain from the plunder and destruction of the environment.

Who Can We Trust?

When everyone is out only for themselves, they can be trusted to look out only for their own interests. Who can the people trust to tell them the truth? The search for unvarnished truth becomes harder every day. Just as not everyone can be out *only* for themselves, there must be someone who will tell only the truth. Who do Americans trust? Who do they turn to?

The Gallop organization has been polling the American public since 1976 for their views of professional standards of Honesty and Ethics. This poll asks Americans to rate professions on their overall Honesty and Ethics and the combined score of Very High and High is reported. For the past seven years the rankings have been consistent, with the exception of 1994 when medical doctors slipped, likely due to the health care debate.

Gallop poll: Honesty and Ethics

Trend: 1988-1995

Percentage reporting standards of Honesty and Ethics (High and Very High- combined)

	1988	1990	1991	1992	1993	1994	1995
1. Druggists, pharmacists	66%	62%	60%	66%	65%	62%	66%
2. Clergy	60	55	57	54	53	54	56
3. Dentists	51	52	50	50	50	51	54
4. Medical Doctors	53	52	54	52	51	47	54
5. Engineers	48	50	45	48	49	49	53
6. College teachers	54	51	45	50	52	50	52
7. Policemen	47	49	43	42	59	46	41
8. Funeral directors	24	35	35	35	34	30	35
9. Bankers	26	32	30	27	28	27	27
10. Public opinion pollsters	NA	NA	NA	NA	NA	27	25
11. Journalists	23	30	26	27	26	20	23
12. Building contractors	22	20	20	19	20	17	21
13. Local officeholders	14	21	19	15	19	18	21
14. TV Reporters/commentators	22	32	29	31	28	22	21
15. Newspaper reporters	22	24	24	25	22	17	20
16. Business executives	16	25	21	18	20	22	19
17. Stockbrokers	13	14	14	13	13	15	16
18. Lawyers	18	22	22	18	16	17	16
19. Real estate agents	13	16	17	14	15	14	15
20. State officeholders	11	17	14	11	14	12	15
21. Labor union leaders	14	15	13	14	14	14	14
22. Senators	19	24	19	13	18	12	12
23. Insurance salesmen	10	13	14	9	10	9	11
24. Advertising practitioners	7	12	12	10	8	12	10
25. Congressmen	16	20	19	11	14	9	10
26. Car salesmen	6	6	8	5	6	6	5

Nationwide, pharmacists lead the way for the seventh consecutive time; with 66% of Americans ranking them very high or high, pharmacists better their 1994 ratings by four percentage points, and equal their previous highs reached in 1988 and 1992. Car salesmen continue to occupy the ethical doghouse: with only 6 percent of Americans rating them highly (and 61% low or very low), they remain the only group in the nineteen-year history of the Honesty & Ethics Poll *never* to have received approval from at least one in ten Americans.

From the Gallop poll, we see that politicians are way down on the scale of trustworthiness. People obviously feel they cannot trust their political leaders. This feeling is likely made much worse because of three current political trends:

- Much of the art of contemporary politics has been to employ scapegoats and to develop wedge issues with the intent of dividing us, or to make us angry, or to keep targeted groups at home and not voting.

- Elections today depend heavily on raising special interest money that must be repaid, and is ultimately repaid by legislation favorable to those same special interests.

- Public cynicism is so rife, that negative and increasingly personal attacks on opponents are usually believed...

Negative Campaigning Works!!

It is little wonder many people and the press are cynical of everything that a politician says or does. It does not raise the level of the debate, if a politician has additional well funded opposition in the form of special interest groups. These special interest groups can legally use the "independent expenditure" of their own money to constantly remind the public of any alleged shortcomings of a targeted politician. Truth and fair play have been sacrificed on the altar of money and of winning at all costs.

For our society to progress, to even survive, the over reliance on special interest money and rules which allow the think tanks, party campaign committees, and others to make independent expenditures against political candidates cannot be allowed to continue. Our freedom cannot allow that a market be made in our laws, and that politics and politicians be "for sale" to the highest bidder.

Politics is the only venue from which to solve the problems of our nation. Politics is not a war to be won and the opponents vanquished. In our democracy, politics is the forum for free and fair debate and discussion of the issues which affect all Americans. The political arena is where problems are resolved in a free society. Hopefully, we can *all* win, from those solutions which are ultimately arrived at.

For a society to remain free, elections must be kept fair. Money has become so important to politics that elections are in danger of becoming like the courts, where the side with the most money almost always wins. Nothing less than our future as a free society is at stake. Therefore, the playing field of politics must be kept level. The opportunity for political debate must be kept open to all who wish to participate.

Our founding fathers envisioned the political process as the way for labor and for the common man to seek redress for inequities, as a counter balance to capital and to the rich, who could always take care of themselves. They never predicted the rise of the special interests. They never imagined that money would find legal ways to control both the votes and the behavior of the voters. The political process is now controlled in the same way that wealth can control commerce. Money, spent to advertise, to shape a message, and to control the press, controls the process. In the very least, the politicians need for money tips the balance in favor of those with more money, no matter how compelling the need for the country to take an opposite course.

Just as the level playing field of commerce is the essence of the free enterprise system, the same is true of politics. Our free market economy, on which we base our freedom as individuals, does not allow for the strong to take advantage of the weak. Our system encourages equal access to the marketplace as the glue that holds society together. For our system to work, everyone must have equal opportunity for the exchange of goods and services and most of all, for the interchange of ideas.

Labor, capital and ideas are all required in our free enterprise system. They are equally important for a society to grow and to prosper. Those individuals with one or more of the above will, of course, do better in the marketplace. This is as it should be. However, fairness and even the perception of fairness is also important. As important as it is to maintain a level playing field for commerce, it is just as important, if not more so, to maintain a level playing field for politics. Along with the importance of there being actual fairness, the perception of fairness and of a level playing field for politics is very important.

In order to assure the playing field will remain level in politics, we do not allow that votes be bought and sold. What is legal, and what is not, is already well defined under existing federal election rules. Those with the most money should not be allowed to bend or to change these rules. We must be vigilant about even the perception of fairness. Free elections legitimize government. Free elections legitimize the governmental transfer of resources. Therefore, if we want our citizens to stand behind the decisions made by our government, we must insure that they remain convinced of their legitimate origin.

As unappetizing as the thought may be to many, politics is how the pie is divided. Politics develops the laws of the land. Politics decides who pays taxes and who does not. Politics decides who will get special treatment or even who will get direct subsidy from the government. Politics can allow some to abuse our common resources for individual gain, and leave others to suffer or do without. Politics is how things get done in our society, be it for you or for your opponent. Therefore, the political process must be kept open and honest, and as the playing field for competing ideas, be kept as level as possible.

Governmental transfer of our pooled resources can be, of course, either for good or for ill. We must pay taxes not only to support the building of roads and other hard infrastructure but also to maintain our public and social infrastructure. The transfer of public resources takes many forms: from outright payments to tax breaks that no one else gets. We must therefore, endeavor to insure these transfers are always done for the higher purposes of good government. Whether we care to know all of the details, or not, we are each dependent on fairness in the political process to shape our individual futures. The people must always be able to trust their leaders and to trust their government.

Today, politics is increasingly used by a small minority to get their own way over the rest of us. Radical agendas are not the only guilty parties. Other selfish interests are also at work. Some in the leadership of America's two major political parties are, also, themselves guilty of trying to undermine trust. Money is raised on the extremes. Jesse Helms need only point at Ted Kennedy and Ted Kennedy at Jesse Helms to raise money from their respective supporters.

The party leadership, itself, often benefits by keeping us polarized on the extremes. It helps them to maintain their power. Sometimes, this concern with the maintenance of power is more important to the parties than winning elections, or even governing. However, moderation and compromise is where the solutions to the problems of our nation must come. Instead of being divided for the profit of some, we must be brought together for the profit of all.

We need to lessen the influence of money, lower the special interest rhetoric and find out what we have in common as Americans. We need to find a new higher ground. We need a new political center, one that embodies the viewpoints of all, yet excludes the illegal and the extreme radicals that often will dominate either the left and the right.

We need to set as policy, things which will benefit all of us, as a culture and civilization, and are not just things of benefit to those with a financial stake in how our laws are written. We need leaders who can deserve our trust. We need leaders we can trust to make decisions to benefit all of us, not just the special interests. We must rebuild trust in our system and its leaders. People need to know they are able to trust their leaders to truly act on their behalf and on the behalf of society as a whole.

What we need today is a new trust, a national conversation, a forum where we all can come together to shape the national debate. It is certainly true tyrants don't want the citizens to talk among themselves. They and the special interests would rather control the dialog from a central source to take full advantage of having more resources and much more money than do individuals. That special interests can raise and spend large sums of money is their sole advantage.

With money the narrow and special interests can buy access to, or even outright control of the airwaves. Those who control the airwaves control the talk, or at least can control what is being talked about. This is especially true in broadcasting today, now that the "equal time requirements" and the "fairness doctrines" have been repealed.[12] This problem may be even more severe in the future of a *Market Democracy* because of the rapid combination of media outlets which is allowed in the 1996 Telecommunications Act.

What justifies our Trust?

Americans, in general, do not expect to be able to trust anyone. However, Americans, as individuals, still can, and do, show trust in their everyday lives. They still trust and respect the professionals in society.

There are many reasons for this to be true and the Gallop poll confirms them. For the last seven years, pharmacists have scored the highest. One reason pharmacists are so well thought of is that service in a pharmacy is unfailingly democratic. It is an unwritten rule, no matter who you are, in the drugstore setting, all patrons are treated equally. In a pharmacy, no one is allowed to break line because of social status or importance, or get in front of a line due to the value of their purchase. All can reasonably expect to have health care questions honestly answered, even if they just yell them out in the general direction of the prescription department.

People highly value their relationship with professionals, especially their doctors, and fear being forced to change. The importance of this trust was illustrated in the effectiveness of the "Harry and Louise" commercials against health care reform. This degree of trust is further illustrated when people are quite willing to wait long periods of time for professional advice.

People will wait patiently in the reception area of professional offices, while it is quite obvious that others, who have come much later, are being seen ahead of them. People still trust, and are willing to give the benefit of doubt to professional judgement, even as to prioritize the urgency of cases.

There are other reasons for people to trust professionals in society. Professions by definition have a written creed or code of behavior that requires a higher standard of conduct. People do not ask about these standards in advance, nor insist on having everything spelled out in writing. People trust professionals because there is an implied contract with society. They can just "know" that professionals are trustworthy. The people feel assured they will be able to trust professionals due to the existence of this "unwritten contract."

This "unwritten contract" with society is also the reason people become so angry when they think they are being misled or mistreated by a professional. Even though the letter of the law, or the standard of practice may be complied with, they expect much more from one who is respected and trusted as a professional. This unique and extraordinary expectation is true whether they have a regular relationship with that individual practitioner or not. The perceived violation of this trust, the violation of the unwritten agreement, rather than the reasons usually cited, is perhaps the basis of most malpractice litigation.

Americans feel they have a special, personal relationship with the professionals they utilize. Their trust in the existence of an unwritten contract even extends to not checking the bills of professionals for accuracy. People who would examine a grocery bill item by item for an error in addition or for a wrong price, will blindly trust professionals. In a most blatant example of the abuse of this trust, some hospitals use it to guarantee their profit margins. We all trust that hospitals are "honest" and are there "to help." Yet, most of us are also aware that hospital bills are "padded a little" just to make sure that enough is collected from those who can pay, to cover those who cannot.

Trust is very important to the workings of our system. Today, however, this ever widening "gray area" of our system is rapidly approaching fraud.

In traditional health care, many costs were shifted from those who received services to those who were able to pay for services. This is a major shift in the perception of just what constitutes fairness in America. In practice, this "cost shifting" is an example of communism in its purest form. Communism, the uncorrupted ideology, allows that each individual should receive according to their need and contribute according to their abilities.

Having health insurance companies decide our needs for us, does not make communism any better. When this practice is tolerated in a free enterprise system, only the few ultimately profit from it, at the expense of all of the rest. It combines the worst aspects of either system, a lower standard of care, but for the profit motive, rather than as a method of caring for more individuals.

This practice of cost shifting has raised health insurance rates for everyone while, not coincidentally, increasing the profits of insurance companies. Hospitals routinely pass along unpaid cost by over-billing those who do have coverage. At one time, insurance companies simply paid those inflated bills and then passed the cost along to their policy holders. The higher costs are passed along, because the insurers earned a percentage of the premiums collected and paid. The larger the amounts that are collected and paid, the larger the commissions for the insurers. In the scheme of things, insurers would readily tolerate and even encourage cost increases, because the more health care costs, the more they made.

Insurance is ultimately based on trust. It works by placing, through mutual agreement, small amounts of money in the form of the premiums paid by many individuals into one large community pool of money. People then trust the insurer to hold and invest this pool of money until it is needed to pay the relatively larger expenses for those participants in the pool who do become ill. This system works, because not everyone will become ill at once, and the pool is always being replenished with new premium payments.

Everyone realizes they may be asked to pay more in premiums if the pool is depleted by having to pay out more money than was anticipated. These increases in premiums are assumed by the policyholders to be due to either an increased incidence of illness in the community or to increased cost of care. However, no one, generally, knows exactly what the additional expenses are or what they cover.

The insured also realize that the insurer will keep a portion of the money collected for administrative expenses and for profit. We do not have national health insurance today, or any other health care reform, because the status quo became so profitable for many insurers. In the pre-paid plans, insurance companies collect the money that they think they will need, in advance, to cover the projected costs, plus an industry-wide average 50% markup. Insurers have become increasingly able to project what their costs will be and how much additional money must be collected to replenish the community pool. The money is collected in advance, and the process repeats itself. What keeps insurance able to stay ahead of rising costs, and very profitable, is the ability to raise rates, in advance, to keep the pool at a certain level against likely expenditures.

Rising premium costs, of course, takes more money from our paychecks, either directly by deductions or if the insurance is an employment benefit, by depleting the amount of money that employers will have available to pay wages. People resent having to pay more and more for health insurance, but understand that rising costs must be paid. The people trust the insurance companies have a fiduciary relationship with them.

We expect that insurance companies are required to look out for the best interest of their policy holders. This is not, however, strictly true. Insurers are not regulated in the manner that banks are, on matters such as rates and truth in lending. Insurance companies, in fact, have gotten the Congress to exempt them from our nation's anti-trust laws. Insurance companies are first and foremost business ventures. As such, they are strictly out for themselves and for higher corporate profits. Yet most people are trusting that insurers will also have their best interest at heart.

In the last few decades, there are many more "unwritten contracts" and "gray-areas" of our trust that have been increasingly violated in the minds of many. These "unwritten contracts" are mainly expressed in things that people have thought they could always count on. Most of us feel hospitals are there to help us when we need them. This is no longer universally true. The list of things we feel we can always count on, has become shorter every year. As we continually discover we have been wrong about things, we only become more cynical as a society.

This cynicism and lack of trust is pervading all aspects of contemporary society, even our most interpersonal ones. Women should expect to be able to trust their husbands. However, many women who have acquired sexually transmitted diseases such as AIDS, have gotten it from their husbands or steady boyfriends, men whom they had reason to think cared for them. There has always before been that balance between behaviors thought of as being gullible and those thought of as being excessively distrustful. We do not need to become more cynical, but we do need to become more aware of the forces acting on our society and also of those which need to be corrected. In that same vein, we need new standards, a much higher standard, of national political trust, before it becomes too late for us to even to be able to expect that trust.

Our forefathers faced many of the same problems that we face as a nation today. In the less than one hundred generations since Christ was alive, history has repeated itself many times, from fatal sexually transmitted diseases to the general disdain for politics. History repeats itself, because human nature itself does not change. We, as human beings, and as a people, have tended to do the same things, in the same situations, over and over. Human behavior has been the one constant of history. By looking at history, and at how people have behaved in the past, we may readily predict how they may react in the future. In this way, we may prevent the impending onset of a national decline.

Until now, we have remained relatively free to make our own decisions and our mistakes. Now, however, we are on the verge of a complete and total breakdown of trust in our community, it's systems and in it's government. We face a crisis unlike any that has occurred in the recent past. We have less options in dealing with it than we have ever had before. This breakdown of trust, combined with the lack of options that we have, and a crushing debt, could very easily and very quickly, end our civilization as we now know it.

As Americans, we have diverse interests and on the surface appear to have little in common. However, our debt is the one thing that we all have in common. As of 1996, every man, woman, and child in the United States is in debt for at least eighteen thousand dollars.[13] This represents the individual share of just that portion of the federal debt that has already been incurred. This, in itself, may just be a small portion of what may eventually be owed. The growth of this debt is due both to gross irresponsibility in our system of politics, and to gross irresponsibility of the leadership of our government. We have this debt, ultimately, because some special interests benefitted from it, even though the vast majority of Americans did not.

Our leaders willfully and knowingly violated our trust. We spent the decade of the 1980s with the impression that a conservative administration was cutting the fat from government... when just the opposite was true.

Civilization

Many today are greedy. They want things now. They demand instant gratification. They don't seem to care about the interrelationship of everything in society or what the future will hold for their children or grandchildren. Many do not feel that they are a part of a community, or even connected with one another. They seem to think only of themselves. Many persons who are without children cannot understand why they must pay taxes to help educate other people's children. It is as if they do not realize the benefit that they get from living in a stable society, or that it is truly in their benefit, as well, to teach the rules to others.

Due to the complexity of our society today, many individuals don't even see how they fit into the overall scheme of things. They often tend to overestimate the importance of their own individual contributions. They think society owes them. They are not at all aware of just how interdependent we all are. Many do not realize that human beings may only survive as part of a group, that we need each other in order to survive. Many individuals continue to think of themselves as being totally independent of others, when they are not.

In the beginning of civilization, people gathered together first in groups of families, and then in tribes and groups of tribes, primarily for protection from mutual enemies. They also, very early, made the discovery that division of labor and the sharing of resources made things better for everyone. Each individual, by working together with other individuals, in addition to being much safer, was much better off than trying to live or work independently. By working cooperatively in a stable society, everyone gets more, with less work. This rule, although also "unwritten," will always apply to human society.

From the beginning, the growth of production through working together was very dramatic, and all shared in the increased bounty. Each individual, directly, and with their own eyes, could see where the increase had come from. Each individual knew what their efforts were, and worked hard to maintain their place in the joint productivity of the group. From the boy who gathered flint to make spear points, to the girl who helped her mother prepare animal skins for clothing, each individual had a part to play in the maintenance of the society. Each individual could point to his or her actual accomplishment and know just how much that singular deed had ultimately helped the group. Today our roles are much less clear.

With less work required to maintain survival, time became available to promote higher level activities. There was now time to allow for civilized pursuits, and to encourage the growth of culture. The time that became available to create art and music provided enjoyment to everyone involved. Common everyday activities served to build and increase the people's ties with one another and with the community. Everyone had a place in the group and understood their relationship with and within the group. Then, even small children could easily see and copy proper behavior. Everyone knew exactly what was expected of them and knew exactly what they could expect of the others. The cause and effect relationship of positive behaviors were plainly visible to everyone in the group.

The unwritten rules of conduct, the basic rules of manners and etiquette, were understood by each individual in that group and thereby smoothed group interactions. Today, we have the benefit of those who have gone before. It would seem that it is no longer necessary to relearn every rule of building a successful society, therefore these rules remained unwritten. Today, these hard won lessons have remained unwritten. They may also remain unheeded, however, until it is too late.

An important unwritten rule in successful societies was to care for its weaker members. In earlier times, farmers cooperated in barn raising and shared with one another in hard times. A spirit of community existed that could always be counted on. Everyone helped each other because they knew that if they needed help, the others would be there for them. There is a certain amount of "enlightened" self-interest in helping your neighbor. It is just like that today, only we do not now know the names of all our neighbors. When people are working together in a functioning society, it always improves conditions for all citizens. By working together, everyone gets what they need, and often much more. In working together, a larger pie is made available for all to share.

Individuals are more likely to be helpful to others when they have a history, a reputation to maintain in their communities. More than likely, if you live in a small town, you've lived there all of your life, and more than likely your family has a history in the community. Today, many people do not live in the community into which they were born. If they have a history, it is relatively brief and their community involvement is also likely to be somewhat superficial. In many places in America, small town life is still very much like it used to be. In a small town environment, you expect to again see those who you are dealing with. You are therefore, in the very least, much nicer than you would be in dealing with a total stranger, or in dealing with someone that you never expected to see again.

As is expected, the ties of many to their community are not as strong as they could be. Therefore, today, people are usually surprised to see someone go out of their way for another. Although they are not seen very much, anymore, Americans still appreciate small town ideals. They respect those who display those basic American ideals. As president, Ronald Reagan had much of that small town way about him. He was folksy, friendly, and extremely reassuring and patriotic. He often spoke optimistically of a simpler way of life and of those simpler times.

Sure, there were limousines and lavish celebrity parties and the attention to high society, but most people paid little attention to that aspect of his life. After all, Ronald Reagan had once been a Hollywood actor. He therefore, had plenty of friends among that elite. Indeed, he had friends everywhere he went. To most Americans, Ronald Reagan at least gave the impression of the caring for others which is embodied in small town and community values.

George Bush was less outgoing and populist, yet he, too, often talked of small town values and of community. Unlike Ronald Reagan, his was a more patrician background. Therefore, when he talked of helping others, it was often more in terms of *noblesse oblige*. George Bush had a long history of service to the community. He had served in the Congress, and was appointed by President Nixon to several important posts before becoming Vice-President under Reagan. As President, Bush promised "a kinder and gentler nation" and often spoke of the "thousand points of light," of volunteerism and philanthropy, but most often spoke of them as a substitute for government action.[14]

While both men claimed common values, what actually happened in the America which they led was quite different. *Noblesse oblige,* in practice (as more than just a noble concept) is more effective in helping the rich feel better about themselves than in actually helping the poor. We do have a common self-interest, but self-interest in the decade of the 1980s, too often, simply meant greed. The 1980s were a time of profound change for the middle class in America. Most of us ended the decade less well-off than when we started, but not so shockingly less well-off as to start a revolution. We had been reassured by our leaders that things would get better, and things had always gotten better before. The best description of the economic and social changes that occurred during this period is contained in the 1990 book by Kevin Phillips, *The Politics of Rich and Poor*. Perhaps, the best summary of the problem, may also be found in the liner notes of that same book:

> "The enormous concentration of wealth in the United States during the 1980s- most of it in the hands of the top 1 percent of Americans– will provoke what Kevin Phillips calls a watershed change in American Politics.. This Republican "heyday," as Phillips calls it, has increased the share of income to the top 1 percent of Americans by $100 billion to $150 billion a year, inflating markets in everything from stocks to Picassos to million-dollar homes, even as other Americans, from Minnesota farmers to fifty-five-year-old middle managers and nineteen-year-old ghetto youths, see the American dream fade before their eyes. Phillips combines this analysis with a provocative interpretation of American political history. He shows how the 1980s were the third era in which Republican policies managed to concentrate vast wealth in the hands of a favored few. The two previous Republican "heydays" were, of course, the 1920s and the Gilded Age of the late nineteenth century. In all three "heydays" Republicans presided over boom cycles marked by conservative ideologies and probusiness governments promoting less regulation, high interest rates and low taxes, periods in which the rich got richer on a crest of debt and speculation. In all three Republican "heydays"

the downside has also been similar: collapsing farmland values, the decay of older industries and even a recurrent increase in homelessness." [15]

In this book, Kevin Phillips predicted that the excesses which occurred in the 1980s would lead to a reversal of that trend. He predicted that the abuses would lead to a new politics. After all, the first two periods of Republican excess led to the Progressive Era at the turn of the twentieth century and to the New Deal of the 1930s.[16] This time, however, things really were different. This time the truth has truly become muddled. Most voters and, indeed, many experts do not even fully understand the complexity of the problems underlying our economy. When people say that "they just want the government to leave them alone," what many really mean is that they want the government to leave them alone, but also to leave the subsidies that they receive alone, as well. They may wish to cut government, but not the government programs which benefit them.

Many of the proposed solutions, such as across the board tax cuts, or a flat tax would make the federal deficit worse, while again helping mostly the top 1 percent of Americans. The excessive tax breaks and economic unfairness, that are the root causes of this inequity, have now become institutionalized. The elite one percent are allowed to use their money to buy politicians and politics. In this way they may maintain, and yet even build on, their advantage. It is much like the compounding of interest. Bank accounts that start out large can only become much larger. We know that even small changes, over time, can ultimately make a very big difference in the ultimate outcome. However, given more time and the ability to make larger changes, who can predict what could happen?

2. Orderly Society

As society becomes more complex, somewhat differing rules need to apply. The value systems that worked well in a largely agricultural, rural and small town societies do not seem to work as well in a highly mobile, urban and suburban environment. The generally accepted rules of responsible gun ownership is an example. What works well in an open, rural environment will not always work in a more crowded, urban situation. The underlying principles remain the same, however, they just require more structure in order to accomplish the same ends. Still the prime function of self-government is to maintain order in society. To continue to do so, should only require developing a more formal structure to what has always before been intuitive good behavior. To remove, or to radically change this underlying constitutional principles of self-government serves only to allow some who control the system to benefit only themselves.

In the beginnings of civilization, as division of labor became more specialized, trade became possible and desirable. There will always be someone, in a free society, who produces more than the rest and has a surplus to keep or to trade. Our system actively encourages trade. This is a key difference between all of the different forms of socialism and our free-enterprise system. This single important trait also differentiates our form of society from that of the lower colonial animals such as bees and ants. With bees or ants, all surplus is held in common. There is no need for barter or trade, nor is there any need for the social interaction and the growth of relationships that develop between individuals due to trade. Bees or ants do not count on the growth of relationships to hold their communities together, therefore, bees or ants have no need to strengthen social relations or to increase the interactions of the individuals.

The communities of the colonial animals are held together because each member is genetically identical. They all share the same parentage, or at least the same genetic complement. As human beings, we are each genetically different, most with different parents but all with differing levels of natural talent and abilities. Our situation shares with the bees and the ants only the need to be a part of a society to survive. Our differing individual abilities allow us to easily fill widely different and changing niches unlike the colonial animals. The interaction of individuals in society is the glue that holds us together. Barter and trade, the give and take of commerce, is the glue that holds us together in our free-enterprise system.

In our culture, the free-enterprise system leads to innovation, to competition, and ultimately to the advancement of society. Allowing individuals to set and to pursue their own goals generally promotes progress in a society. In the free marketplace, good ideas are rewarded and poor ones languish. Trial and error is encouraged in the free enterprise system, and all are invited to try their hand. An orderly exchange of goods and services ultimately benefits all in society. Higher standards of behavior are both welcome and desirable. Trustworthiness and competence too, are rewarded in the free marketplace.

The unwritten rules of fairness are almost intuitive, yet not everyone will always do the right thing in every circumstance. There seems to always be someone, strong or weak, who would take advantage of others or would have advantage taken of them. Therefore, codified rules for the conduct of trade became necessary, both to protect property and to encourage trade between the citizens. Rules which guarantee fairness and the equal access to markets are necessary in any orderly society. Standardized rules of conduct that apply to all participants are necessary to insure a level playing field for trade, commerce, and for the development of business relationships.

Historically, "Strong-Man" rule was the first put forward to promote order. In most cases, however, the price of protection was much worse than no protection at all. The strong man leader usually took more away from commerce than the order restored to it could provide. Fortunately, commerce by its very nature causes changes in the concentration of assets. After all, successful trading produces profits. Profits will allow for the accumulation of wealth. Out of this new growth in wealth, there arose a prosperous merchant class, that was then able to make sure that their interests were protected, without having to rely on a strong man form of governance.

The emerging merchant class was interested both in self-protection and in protection for their trading partners. By insuring a free and fair market, they thereby encouraged potential trading partners. A free and fair market therefore encourages more trading and thus the potential for more profit. A strong middle class made up of merchants and shopkeepers encourages order in society. They are not only much less likely to put up with the "Strong-Man" form of government; they are also less likely to allow excesses like those that spawned our own American Revolution. Only when strong men are allowed to dominate does our system become hopelessly rigged to favor the interest of the elite over the rest of us.

Moreover, the stores and shops of the merchants, themselves, also promote social stability. They promote stability by providing a central focus for public interaction on a daily basis. The daily physical and social interaction of citizens serve as a reinforcement for a sense of community. One of the reasons that pharmacists are well thought of today, is because of the many fond memories associated with early drugstore experiences. Memories of kindly Ol' Doc and of hours spent socializing at the soda fountain were powerful reinforcements of social interaction. It is sad times cannot once again be like that.

In those earlier days, individuals started their business careers in their communities. Most people started out by helping in neighborhood shops and stores. In those days, people had much more opportunity to trade their labor for goods. Virtually everyone could find something to do, for some one, at some price. Young people, of limited means, could improve themselves through work. They could advance both financially and socially by working for and associating with those who were better off. Apprenticeships and the opportunity to work in jobs along side community business leaders, as role models, was once very common. This avenue of social advance is almost totally absent today.

As a strong middle class continued to grow, elected officials were placed in charge. Popularly elected officials are sensitive to the unwritten obligations that are the basis of our form of society. They are much more attuned to the will of the people than are strong men or their appointed agents. Elected officials are more able to respond exactly to what is needed by a majority of the people. Therefore, they are allowed to make decisions for us, without everyone meeting to discuss every issue that arises. They are able to respond more efficiently to the changing needs of the citizens.

Elected officials may be corrupted from time to time. They may take money to influence the market in favor of one element of that market. In the earliest beginnings of commerce, the resulting unfairness in the marketplace would quickly raise alarm with those being unfairly treated. In earlier times, it was easier to see who was on the take. When things were simpler, it was much easier to tell to what degree the marketplace was being harmed. When discovered, the crooked official could then be quickly replaced before much harm could be done to the market.

The role of a federal government in establishing and maintaining an orderly society is to provide the framework, the level playing field for competition within our free enterprise system. The clearest analogy of the usefulness of the Federal Government to an orderly society is that of the traffic signal. We all understand that with a stoplight, everyone gives up a short wait in order to be able to gain clear access. This concept illustrates the "Win, Win" aspect of good government.

Today, in that stoplight analogy, the special interests and other wealthy elite are using the federal government as a tool to speed their own way, yet flash yellow or even remain red for most of the rest of us. That the signal is no longer fair, as in the case with the Congress where laws are made to favor wealthy contributors, is without question. It is no longer fair, when debate on the issues in the Congress is replaced by last minute votes and by voting after midnight. It is unfair when laws are secretly changed by the addition of special provisions to other unrelated bills. It is not fair when laws are changed without open debate or by simply deleting that program's funding from appropriations bills.

In essence, those with the most to gain are getting their own way by buying off those in charge of programming the signals. They can then blame the signal, the government, for all of the problems that are caused for the rest of us. Moreover, in today's infinitely more complex market, those elected officials who have been corrupted by one or more elements of the marketplace are much harder to spot. They may be only discovered after much damage has already been done to the market, to the community and to the future. They may, yet, never be discovered, or even their very existence uncovered, if the press is also controlled by the same elements that controls the crooked politicians.

With the media consolidations and the mergers that have been allowed to happen, today, the odds are improved that all of the newspapers and the television stations in a given community may be owned by the same company, or else be affiliated in some way. This is not just speculation, it has all happened before. Anti-trust laws were initiated for good reasons. Trusts and Monopolies also combined the ownership of various newspapers, business interests and public utilities before the turn of the last century, as well. Unfair monopolies and trusts had once before controlled what was said in public and what was written in the press. This rising unfairness has occurred before. We must study our history to know what could happen.

The Nixon and Agnew 1968 presidential campaign was the "hallmark" event in the trend which triggered the politics of the 1980s and 1990s. The success of that single political contest led directly to the most recent selling-out of America by it's elected officials. That 1968 campaign was a particularly expensive political campaign because Nixon did not wish to risk losing again in a presidential contest. In 1968, Nixon and Agnew sought to blame others for the nation's problems, and at the same time to gain credit for providing strong leadership. This feat took an incredible expenditure of campaign funds. Therefore, to pay for all of the broadcast air time, for the ad and speech writers, and for the public relations professionals, both candidates became literally "for sale" to the highest bidder.

Although only Agnew was caught and forced from office due to bribery charges, they both were heavily involved in influence peddling. Their success was a signal to a whole new generation of politicians that money could safely operate above the law. In the beginnings of this *Market Democracy*, a country distracted by the rhetoric of social issues and the yearning for an orderly society would not be paying attention to who was gaining and who was losing from the public treasury. Many political campaign "reforms" were instituted subsequent to that election. These included PACs or political action committees, which favored the rise of the strong special interests. Politicians did well from these political "reforms," and as can be expected the special interests, themselves, also did very well from their investments in politicians during this period.

The Nixon campaign led directly to the development of a new type of politics in America. Many new political "tools" were developed and refined to win elections. Among these were scapegoating of minorities and outsiders, the targeting of straw men "elites" to be knocked-down, and the cheap use of patriotism to gain votes. As used first by George Wallace, in the 1972 presidential campaign, standing for "Law and Order" had overt racial overtones, yet also appealed to the universal desire for an orderly society. Law and order appeals may yet be used, today. They trigger racial mistrust, but are also extremely effective at getting votes.

Because public safety is still a prime obligation of government, the government can be attacked for not doing enough to fight crime. Some have even scapegoated the government and social welfare programs as a cause of crime. Theoretically, however, crime is only encouraged by increasing unemployment and the perceived lack of hope for better opportunities. Therefore, crime most often affects the poor; however, the welfare of the poor is not of concern to those using fear of crime as a political tool. They wish only to use fear of "crime" and concern for public safety as a wedge to divide us, to distract us from their manipulation of the public treasury.

Orderly society is important to us all. Some, in using the fear of crime and the absence of orderly society, are only looking to promote their own, unmentioned, agendas. Since the first duty of a federal government is to provide for the national defense, now that the fear of attack from abroad is almost nil, has crime again become the hot political issue in federal races. Crime is a serious problem that needs our full national attention. Yet, even violent crime will not be the greatest problem facing our country, if we continue to let others divide us into opposing interest groups so they will win elections. This divisiveness caused by fear may cause us to think of our own self-interest above that of the long term best interest of the whole of society. Divisiveness can only lead to more violence and more crime as more individuals are excluded from the benefits of society and begin to loose their stake in maintaining an orderly society.

Therefore, we are hearing calls for a "Strong-Man" to be our president. The advocates of a Strong-Man presidency are still using "crime" as an excuse for advocating tough stands. Conservatives prize stability above all else, but some are especially enamored of the strong man form of government. Conservatives by definition wish to maintain the status quo, a status quo which favors mainly them. Early man also traded his independence for a strong man form of government. They too wished to live in an orderly society. However, today, just as then, the strong man will always take a larger share of the economic pie. This will always happen because a strong man form of government does not encourage the creation of opportunity. The strong man model of government does not encourage economic growth, nor the creation of a larger pie for all to share.

Democracy

Each of us in America is important to the big picture. All of us are important to the smooth functioning of society. The CEO and the worker on the shop floor all are all equally important to growth and to the ultimate success of any business venture. Society, itself, does better when all segments of society are working to advance the whole of society. We too, need to work together to create more resources, both with which to reduce the national debt and still to continue the progress of society. Just as any worker can hinder progress by throwing a monkey wrench into the works, we can all move forward by doing our best and by working within the group, to advance the group. If the action of an individual is important, then the actions of many individuals working together, in a democracy, will become <u>very</u> important.

Our government has always, before, been a true democracy. We are a Democratic Republic, where our directly elected officials make most of our important decisions for us. Democracy in the American form is best viewed as that approximate midway between not having any government at all, and having a socialist state that controls everything. American democracy therefore lies somewhere between the two extremes of "The Law of the Jungle" and "Survival of the Fittest" on the one hand and pure socialism on the other. It is not perfect, but as Winston Churchill once said, "Many forms of government have been tried, and will be tried in this world of sin and woe. No one pretends that democracy is perfect or all-wise. Indeed, it has been said that democracy is the worst form of government except all those other forms that have been tried from time to time."

Churchill was correct in his assessment. Democracy can be unwieldy in practice. But, after all, no one wants a dictatorship, which is arguably the most efficient form of government. Strong man governments, such as monarchy, do make decision making simple. Yet only a glance at the British Monarchy shows just how simple they can become. Decisions arrived at in a democratic process are not always reached in the most elegant way. However, when all citizens are involved, in a true democracy, it is unquestionably the fairest form of governing. The dynamic tension between opposing viewpoints sometimes leads to remarkable compromises and to creative "win-win" solutions to what seem to be intractable situations.

However, for democracy to work, citizens have the obligation to be informed. If citizens do not pay close attention to the balance of power between the two extremes, then democracy can be the worst for the majority rather than the best.

Democracy needs and encourages, it demands, that individuals become involved in decisions made by their government. Individuals may become involved on any level of that decision making process. They may become involved in choosing the decisions to be made, or involved in making the decisions. They may also leave the decision making up to their elected officials, and then vote them out office if they do not like those decisions. Some individuals in our country would prefer that the government make all the decisions for them, while others would be happy if there were no governmental decision making process at all. Majority Rule is the compromise that we make between these two extreme positions.

In applied democracy, there is simply a matter of degrees between having too much government and of not having enough. In keeping with the spirit of the Constitution, should the government intervene in a particular situation or should it not? Government interventions are often necessary to prevent or to cure the abuses that will always occur. Given the necessity for the sharing of authority, the question becomes: what kind and how much? Moreover, there is a fine line between what works and what doesn't and what is needed and what isn't. The law of diminishing returns applies, as well, in deciding what we can we afford. The ideal is to preserve as level a playing field as possible, so that each idea may compete in the political arena on it's own merit.

The idea of political parties is not mentioned, at all, in the Constitution. However, our two party system came into being almost before the ink was dry on the signing of that great document. No one really knows why we have just two major political parties, but we in America have always had only two major political parties. There is some speculation as to why a two party system tends to develop in a free market economy.

Since labor and capital are both equally important to the free enterprise system (along with good ideas), the two parties may each approximate the general interests of each of those two elements. Today, the Republican party would roughly represent the interests of capital and the Democratic party might well represent the interests of labor. There are no American parties that exactly represent the highly diverse interests of the elites verses the working classes, as do the Conservative and the Labour parties in England.

The interest of Americans in political parties is not all that sharply defined. Our interests in political parties has always been more in general direction rather than in achieving specific goals. We instead develop broad coalitions that will only generally represent the interests of the group. Mostly, as voters, we are interested in seeing that the dynamic tension of opposing ideas keeps us somewhere in that broad middle ground of our common interests. There are, however, highly ideological activists that can be found on the extremes of either party. These activists are usually not interested in compromise. They may, in fact, seek to prevent it. David Walls in his book, *The Activists Almanac*, states that this is one reason that third parties can't work:

> "The American constitutional system is stacked against minor parties. We don't have a parliamentary system with proportional representation and a prime minister chosen by the parliament– which is what it takes for a true multiparty system to flourish, as it does in Germany, Italy, and Israel, to take some interesting if not always encouraging examples. Our single-member district, winner-takes-all elections, with chief executive elected at-large (a system duplicated at the national and state levels), contains a logic of winning that leads to two-party system, in which each party seeks to build a broad majority coalition.
>
> As a result, the Republican and Democratic parties are loose electoral alliances, not the disciplined, ideological parties of Europe. American parties are permeable; they're open to anyone who registers with the party– and most primaries are open to any registered member who files, and choices are made through open primary elections. With parliamentary parties, you join only if you agree with a given ideology and program, candidates for public office are chosen only by party conventions, and party discipline is imposed on elected officials. The open American system presents space for issue-oriented organizations and movements, along with a

variety of special interest groups to influence public policy both from within and from outside official party structures.

Since the Goldwater presidential campaign in 1964, conservatives have captured much of the Republican party organization at the grassroots, often controlling the nominating process. In 1980 they finally nominated their candidate for president– Ronald Reagan. Their success meant that conservatives who start "third" parties quickly get marginalized– look at the experience of the Libertarian party or the American Independent party. Similarly, most progressive social movements are found in the Democratic party... When insurgent social movements have succeeded in the United States, it has been through one of the two major parties– the farmers' Non-Partisan League in North Dakota in the 1910's (largely as Republicans), the labor movement in the 1930s, and the civil rights movement in the 1960s (the latter two largely as Democrats)... Our only example of a minor party becoming a major party is the emergence of the Republican party after the collapse of the Whigs– and that was once, in the 1850s, over 140 years ago."[17]

As a general party philosophy, Democrats believe that the citizens will make good decisions for themselves. They believe that when every individual's viewpoint is debated and considered, the majority decision will be the correct one. Republicans tend to favor the selection of delegates from the masses to make the decisions for the group. However, both methods of self-government require the participation of many individuals to be truly representative of the will of the people.

The Democratic philosophy can only work well with an educated and involved citizenry. The Republican model doesn't require that everyone always be involved or educated on every issue. However, if too few are educated on the subject at hand, the electoral elite can take advantage of the possession of power to pass laws that favor themselves. There always seems to exist a healthy dynamic tension between these two political philosophies. When Republicans call for politically popular initiatives that the Democrats feel may be too complicated for most people to understand, Democrats turn to traditional Republican arguments while Republicans will offer those which have before been traditionally Democratic ones.

In reality, democracy does work best when there is a strong, moderate and educated middle class, with a vested interest somewhere in that broad expansive middle. The power to govern comes from this grassroots level. Yet, it is freely relinquished. The competition for control of this power, elections themselves, help to ensure the decentralization of power. The center of power, therefore, always will remain somewhere between the extremes of full and no government intervention in our daily lives. The dynamic tension between these two extremes further leads to our uniquely American outlook, where anything and everything is possible and that every child could grow up to be president.

In our representative form of democracy, members of the group should make decisions that they believe to be in the best interest, both long and short term, for the rest of the group. This differs from "mob rule," where each member of the mob is looking out for their own self interest or for the interests of the group as they are perceived to be at that particular moment. Some individuals are looking for an "instant democracy" through the modern technological improvements of computers and communications. Those who seek to increase democracy through the concept of "electronic town halls" are only seeking to improve on the concept of mob rule. There is no give or take in discussion, nor is dynamic tension possible, in mob rule. Perhaps those who are looking to institute mob rule are doing so because it easily develops into the "strong-man" form of government that they would really prefer. Once a "mob" loses interest, or is distracted by another issue, strong men will always rise to the occasion.

Because dynamic tension is so important to the smooth functioning of our society, those of moderate viewpoint are essential to the prevention of major polarizations. As long as we respect the worth of every individual, respect the religious practices of others, allow individuals the freedom of their own opinion and encourage decisions to be made on the level closest to the problem, our system will always work. We must work to insure that every voter has all of the available facts on which to base his or her decisions. We must endeavor to make sure that even the ideas that place our ideas in a bad light can receive exposure. If the price of freedom is eternal vigilance, then the cost of democracy is unbending moderation.

Moderate politicians elected to the 104th Congress were scarce. Most moderates of either party were either defeated or decided not to run again and retired. This is because today, money to run election campaigns comes mostly from special interest groups, and from those with extreme views. Few moderate candidates were elected in that Republican controlled 104th Congress, because the bulk of money was raised from those with a non-mainstream agenda and the wealthy elite. Control of the 104th Congress is, therefore, polarized on the extreme right-wing, because that is where most of the money for Republican campaigns comes from. Yet, there is genuine need for balance in the Congress. We must prevent the laws of our country, those which maintain a level playing field, from tilting to favor the endeavors of those with an extreme view, or from further favoring those who would make political contributions to gain a financial advantage.

Elsewhere in our country, with the sole exception of partisan politics, the trend to moderation is accelerating. Some of the divergent thinking that led to our nation's ills, such as the view that environment vs. industry is an either/or proposition, is now moderating. Responsible persons are beginning to see that everything on our small planet is interrelated. While most see the need for both industry and ecology, many now view them both as essential and equal in importance. As citizens, we want to preserve the environment and our industries. Politics will continue to remain radical as long as that is where the money to run campaigns comes from. However, we as voters, want simple solutions that are fair and "win, win" if possible.

In our personal lives, many of us now are revolting against the philosophy of greed and the pursuit of money and power at the expense of the dignity and worth of others. Industry is capable of producing goods and of not hurting people or the environment. Individuals may earn a living and at the same time help, not hurt others. We each know right from wrong. We know that every individual is important in a democracy and that all deserve a basic fairness. Some would treat politics as if it were war, and they would take no prisoners. Our leaders should be able to lead us without resorting to dividing us into opposing factions to make it easier to dispatch us one by one.

Starting in the 1970s, as jobs became increasingly scarce because of slowing growth in the economy, we started seeing political divisions. Hate rhetoric first escalated against the unemployed, mostly against black men and women. Gradually, the interests of black workers were pealed off from that of white workers in political rhetoric. By the 1980s, the interests of men and women in blue collar jobs became somehow different from those of other workers and were ignored. By the 1990s, those who stood up for the rights of women and minorities were the subject of ridicule. Those female political activists were demeaned. They were deemed "Feme-Nazis" in certain segments of the media. A new "political elite" soon emerged from within our division. This was not un-like the emergence of "elite" groups in high school. Unlike the "high school elites," however, this new elite group was interested in having more opportunity for themselves and in removing opportunity from *anyone* not like themselves.

American citizens should not be turned against one another in order to gain a political advantage. We should not wish to kill or to destroy our political opposition. Americans cannot be pitted against other Americans because they differ on some issue or in some detail. We are in this together, and can find reasonable accommodation of all. If the economy is good, we seem to all get along. If the economy is not good– blame, scapegoating, and finger-pointing becomes the order of the day. All political causes find ways to call attention to themselves, although some have done so by terrorism and violence.

The terrorist bombing of the Murdah Federal Building in Oklahoma City had at least one good result– in that it took the hate out of many American hearts. Early news reports had linked the Oklahoma City bombing to an individual of middle eastern decent. People were quick to show anger and many rushed to scapegoat that particular group. Eventually, when the real suspect was apprehended, many of us regretted our rush to judgement. Those who fanned the flames of hate were then exposed for what they were, and for what they were doing to our free, fair and democratic society. They were only doing the bidding of those who would divide us for advantage only to themselves.

The Republican party has expressed some good ideas and has advocated some important goals. Democrats too, have some good ideas and also an interest in reform. However, they both carry some equally negative baggage that goes with the responsibility for the representation of their opposing special interest groups. The emergence of moderates who can embrace the best ideas of the two parties, without that excess baggage could lead to creative and energetic solutions.

Moderates will fuel the dynamic tension that can develop between opposing viewpoints, and that leads to unexpected compromise and common ground. The rise of moderates, with their ability to work for the general welfare without having to favor the traditional right or left and associated special interests, promotes fairness and progressive policies. In the highly partisan political climate of today, it would seem that only a stalemate in the balance of power, only a virtual deadlock in control can lead to the rise of moderates.

America must always continue to function as the "melting pot" for persons of differing ideas. The interaction of differing viewpoints, each competing in the marketplace of ideas, keeps us always fresh. We must continue to renew and enlarge our shifting center. We must continue to find ways to include all of our citizens in the challenge of rebuilding our democracy, our country and it's culture. Our diversity of thought and the continuing struggle to obtain a balance can only make us stronger.

The American Dream has been the envy of the rest of the world. We can not again approach it by turning citizen against citizen. We can only do so, by encouraging innovative and fresh solutions, by restoring fair competition, and by rewarding hard work.

Liberty

If democracy is that perfect balance between anarchy and socialism, liberty is a perfect balance between freedom of the individual and protection of the public good. We, as a free nation, believe that when any one person is unfairly denied their freedom, liberty is ultimately denied to all of us. In some way, we always seek to balance that individual freedom with our common needs and with the needs of the state. Our unique American definition of freedom allows for great leeway in interpretation, and our systems allow the individual a great deal of freedom.

We only do not allow individual freedom to impinge on the rights of others. We do not depend on detailed listings of what is, and is not proper behavior. We place a special trust in individuals to know the difference between what will, and will not be tolerated. This trust in balance and fairness, although unwritten, is expected in our relationships. As a nation, we place honor in the golden rule and endeavor to honor it, even if it is not adopted officially as law.

The love of liberty, as much as the desire for freedom from tyranny, sparked our Declaration of Independence from Great Britain. One of the more odious transgressions by the king of England leading to the American Revolution was the Stamp Act. The Stamp Act placed a special tax on paper, and on the written word. It was, in essence, as much a tax against the freedom of expression, as it was a form of taxation without representation. Among other provisions, the Stamp Act levied a tax of four pence on each almanac that was printed in the colonies. Unfortunately for King George, Benjamin Franklin was a printer of almanacs and therefore had a strong self interest in opposition to this act. As could be expected, his was one of the first patriotic voices to speak out against the unfair tax.

Moreover, people joining together and doing something about that perceived injustice, rather than simply grousing about it, and then acquiescing, was at the time a truly revolutionary idea. Everyone knows that there is strength in numbers. This was not the first time that people found strength in the veracity of their beliefs. This was the first time that the people organized to do something positive about it. It had been simply unheard of to talk of a challenge to the most powerful force of that time. Yet the appeal of liberty was so great that the people knew that it was in their own best interest to force a showdown, and they were willing to act. Therefore, delegates from all of the colonies met to firm their resolve. After much long and sometimes acrimonious debate, action was unanimously arrived at. On July Fourth, 1776, the Congress approved the Declaration of Independence.

It is said that after the Declaration was signed, a deep solemnity rested upon all present, and profound silence pervaded the assembly. It was, at last, finally broken by Dr. Franklin, who turned to Thomas Jefferson and to the others and remarked that, "We must indeed all *hang together*, or, most assuredly, we shall all *hang separately*."[18] It is certain that the intention of Benjamin Franklin was, in a not so subtle way, to remind that August body of their mutual self-interest. Liberty cannot simply be achieved, unless *all* are committed to it. It is still in our own best self-interest to look out for one another. In doing so, we look out for ourselves, as well. The power of numbers works as well today, as it did then... and the force of a powerful idea can still be just as great.

It is in our best interest to look out for *all* of the people. In the forging of the great document, the interests of all individuals, free and slave, were considered. An early draft of the declaration, specifically condemned King George and slavery. This paragraph read:

> "He has waged civil war against human nature itself, violating its most sacred rights of life and liberty in the persons of a distant people, who never offended him, captivating and carrying them into slavery in another hemisphere, or to incur miserable death in their transportation thither. This piratical warfare, the opprobrium of infidel powers, is the warfare of the Christian King of Great Britain. Determined to keep open a market where men should be bought and sold, he has prostituted his negative for suppressing every legislative attempt to prohibit or to restrain this execrable commerce."[19]

This paragraph was left out of the final draft of the Declaration of Independence, not because it offended slave holders, but solely due to the high regard for truth and justice. All of the other charges leveled against King George, as an individual, could be shown to have been created by his personal sanction or by his delegated representatives. Such being the case, it was manifestly unjust, indeed not strictly true, to charge him with the evils concomitant to slavery and the slave trade. The slave trade was begun and carried on long before even the reign of the first King George; and it is not known that George the Third ever gave his assent to anything relating to slavery, except to abolish it and declare the trade a piracy.[20]

In slavery, our nation was to face its most divisive struggle over liberty. The Declaration of Independence clearly states "that all men are created equal." If these words really do matter, if we were to remain a free people, a resolution to the injustice of slavery was bound to occur. The question of slavery was forced to be resolved by a civil war, but other attempts to deny liberty continue to exist, and we must resolve that they too, not be allowed. Our liberty is in protecting our mutual self interest. Liberty can be assured for ourselves, only when we look out for, and are willing to fight for the rights of others. We, as a people, will survive these crises, just like we survived the Civil War, because we as Americans, truly believe in, are committed to, and struggle to insure liberty and justice for all.

Today there is a potentially more divisive crisis over "liberty and justice for all," when the courts allow criminals to go free on a technicality, or when a civil jury awards a large amount of money for seemingly trivial damages. We face turmoil when someone who is morally in the wrong, wins a case because he is legally in the right. Fortunately, these things happen rarely. However, when they do happen, they receive considerable publicity from those who would make changes to our American system of laws. Often, the odd example or the anecdote is used to inflame the rhetoric against the way we do things in America. The facts usually do not bear out such cries of alarm.

The American system of criminal justice is the most fair in the world, however, the balance has shifted recently in favor of the criminal. Today, our government spends more money on the defense of the accused than it does on their prosecution. Money spent on a defense that involves winning at any cost, using every legal trick or delay in order to win is neither right nor fair. We must be fair but we must continue to work to refine our system of justice. The shift in justice which appears to favor criminals is not simply a trade-off to preserve individual liberty. Fairness and balance is needed. The needs of society and the rights of the victim must continue to be of the greater importance. We must also remember that in carefully protecting the rights of others, we are also protecting our own. Those Germans who remained silent when the Nazis came for the Jews, had no one to speak-out on their behalf when the Nazis came for them.

The higher awards for punitive damages in our civil court system appears to be trending in the opposite direction, but that is not exactly true. This apparent trend is blamed for increasing jury awards which alarm business and industry CFO's. In actuality, many apparently high jury awards are decreased on appeal. The seemingly trivial injuries involved are often much more severe than the awards detractors will admit. Indeed, many industries and their lobbyists are scapegoating the civil court system in an attempt to gain unfair advantage over consumers. This may be yet another instance of using the appeal for increased justice, to increase injustice. The court is not a war to be won at any cost by one side or the other. It is a place for justice. American justice, like American democracy, looks to balance the need of individuals with the needs of a just society. When this does happen, we are all ultimately the winners.

The legal profession may be itself to blame for some of the shift in our system of justice away from the center. Lawyers may feel justified in encouraging their clients to sue, but only they will benefit whether their client wins or loses. Court decisions still too-often become a contest of which lawyer does the better job of decimating the other. Still, the largest share of blame for the shift from center is due to a shift of the public attitude away from the center. The "me first" attitude, the "everyone else is to blame" attitude, and "winning is everything" attitudes play a much greater part in the decline of liberty than legal theatrics. Working for the common self-interest has been replaced for the most part by those who are working only for selfish interests.

The shift in the civil court system towards excessive punitive damage awards is an attempt to protect the public by insuring that corporations take responsibility for their actions. The shift of justice to favor criminals is an example of just how much citizens will endure to insure a system of blind justice. It illustrates to what lengths we Americans are willing to go to balance individual rights with the complete absence of rights as seen in a dictatorship or a communist society. We must always very carefully balance individual freedoms with the needs of the state, but we must also further consider the rights of the victim. Equality of treatment under the law is not always popular nor is it always easy. Still we must honor our commitment to it and to all of the parties involved. To do otherwise would play into the hands of those who would use it against us.

3. *Liberty in Decline*

In our country today, a rich man has an excellent chance of getting away with murder.[21] A wealthy man who steals from widows and orphans can realistically hope to keep the greatest portion of his ill-gotten gains if only he spends a portion of it on the right public relations firms and/or the right lawyers.[22] Somehow, the shift in justice that tolerates marginally legal activities and which tolerates white collar crime doesn't seem to bother "conservative" pundits and the TV preachers as much as crimes which are acts of passion, although it still greatly offends the majority of us.

The Simpson murder trial illustrates our system's high regard for individual liberty. That a black man may have gotten away with the murder of a white woman illustrates that race has become less of a factor in our society than financial or social standing. This case illustrates the importance of money to the workings of the system. The basis of our system of laws, the Congress, operates in much the same way. The elected Members of Congress now act in the same fashion as lawyers or public relations experts. They will represent even the most narrow of special interests over the public interest, in return for the money that it takes to mount a campaign.

There is a difference between what is right and what is merely legal. The ability to tailor laws to suit wealthy individuals and corporations, or to negotiate right and wrong with a checkbook, after the fact, is a more serious threat to the concept of liberty and justice for all, than crime itself. Society cannot afford to, nor should it have to, put a policeman on every street corner.

Society needs to be able to trust that individuals, especially elected officials will want to do the right thing. Observing the spirit of the law should be just as important, if not more so, than observing the letter of the law.

If people are not going to be self-reliant, thrifty, honest, fair and just, truthful, generous, kind and considerate of one another, there is no hope of maintaining liberty and self-government. Unless we, as citizens, are restrained by loyalty to these noble concepts, there is nothing to prevent one from taking advantage of the others. Only the eternal commitment to the Constitution and to spiritual ideals can provide eternal liberty.[23] The checks and balances in the Constitution were designed to protect all of us. Each of us agrees to give up some of the things that we could do, some of our own potential rights, both to protect our own rights and the rights and freedom of others.

Today, many individuals avoid serving on a jury, a responsibility that is necessary to provide a system of justice for us all. People take majority rule for granted and neither register nor vote. Many of those who do vote, do not research the issues or the candidates, blindly believing the big public relations campaigns that are designed to influence their vote. Although these publicity campaigns obviously cost a lot of money, most do not question whose money it is or why they are spending it. To lose ones freedom through exercise of those same freedoms is a very real threat. Adolf Hitler was, himself, first *elected* to office.

Hitler was elected because he appealed to the baser instincts of the German people, telling them exactly what they wanted to hear. Today, we should question the motives of those who express our fears and who seem to agree with everything that we feel. Mario Cuomo put it best when he said "Politicians, today, take all the fears and bigotry of society...distill and repackage it.. selling it back to the public as some sort of miracle elixir and cure." Except, today, the term "Hollywood Elite" is now being used as the codeword for "Jew," and "immigrant" the codeword for "gypsy."

Scapegoating broad groups such as "Jews and Gypsies" gives the public a focus to the fears that we each hold inside. Hitler knew that, too. We then easily fall prey to the notion that in getting rid of those targeted groups, we would be rid of the problem. We know that this does not work, but by allowing ourselves to be divided into opposing special interest groups, we can no longer see others as individuals. We can no longer see ourselves as a part of the same society, where we all will sink or swim together.

Scapegoating is again fast becoming "the way" to gain a political edge. The think tanks run polls to find out what may be bothering the citizens. Politicians then use these fears to try to move the voters. Such is the current political rhetoric against the "Welfare State." There is genuine public fear of public policy developing into a welfare state. Yet, those who use the term "Welfare State" in a way to frighten citizens, are by dividing us, also acting to advance the formation of one.

Two-thirds of those on welfare are children. Just as children cannot help who their parents are, blaming everyone for the situation in which they find themselves is not always fair. Those who would divide us on the issue of whether or not to help our fellow man, only encourage the decline of liberty. The actions of these politicians only further increase the need for public assistance through their insistence on a government policy that produces less opportunity, increased poverty, and a shrinking middle class. This is exactly how is happens.

Instead of scapegoating broad groups for political advantage, we should instead seek that which we have in common. Instead of scapegoating those who are unemployed, we need to help those that can work, find work to do. There have been many changes in the job markets of the past few years. Low skill jobs have mostly gone to cheaper overseas labor. There is now less work available, especially for people with few job skills. Work, any meaningful work, is important to the dignity and to the well being of each of us. Americans particularly take much of their individual identity from their occupations.

The vigor given to quick federal deficit reduction will by most accounts increase unemployment to six to seven percent.[24] If at the same time, cutting funds for job training and requiring persons to find jobs in order to receive public assistance, could greatly increase the number of job applicants for every position. This will only further increase competition for the low skill, low wage jobs. An increased competition for work, in a free market, always lowers wages. This, in turn, will further increase pressure on all wage earners, indeed, lowering the standard of living for all working families.

In the last twenty years, excessively conservative economic policies have worked to put small American business owners at a disadvantage against large multinational companies. Heavy borrowing overseas to prevent raising taxes or to lower taxes on the wealthy has, quite logically, increased the amount of American debt in foreign hands. Much of this debt has been converted into equity ownership of what were once American businesses. The ownership of many American brand names is no longer American.

Large corporations have increasingly laid-off workers and shipped jobs overseas to take advantage of cheaper labor. Like it or not, these products are then imported, which hurt our local industrial job creation. Unfair competition from large mass retailers has put many small family-owned local retailers out of business. Lax enforcement of our nation's anti-trust laws has cut entrepreneurial job creation, because even the best of entrepreneurs cannot compete with unfair monopolies. Insisting that programs such as the EPA and OSHA pay their own way, through fines levied against industry, have discouraged industry. Tolerance of excessive speculation in the markets have led to quick profits for a few, but less security for the investments of the rest of us. Many changes which occurred in the 1980s by administration policies have slowly, and gradually, but ultimately led to the lower standard of living that the middle class experiences today.

When recessions occur, the automatic social stabilizers of unemployment insurance and temporary aid programs, and the social safety net programs of food stamps, and welfare, all help to keep families afloat. This largely prevents recessions from becoming deeper. So, today, by encouraging businesses to lay-off workers, while eviscerating the safety net programs, we further increase the risk of a social collapse and of a class war.

Some ideologues feel that we are indeed locked in a real war, much like the war of ethnic cleansing that was fought in Bosnia. Ideologues are treating those with simple political differences like they would treat their enemies in real war. Instead of the dynamic tension of political discourse that brings fresh solutions to mutual problems, they are simply trying to "kill their enemy." The trouble with this viewpoint is, that the perceived enemies are also American citizens, and also deserving of the protections of the Constitution.

For the American form of Democracy to work, there must be checks and balances. Anti-trust laws maintain a level playing field for commerce and prevent collusion. Securities laws help to stabilize markets and to prevent insider trading and fraud. Federal Election Laws prevent the shift in control of our government too far in any direction through unfair election practices and illegal monetary contributions. However, of all the checks and balances in our democracy, the most important of these is the regulation of voting and elections. Above all, for a democracy to work, voters need to be able to make informed choices.

Self-government requires the informed participation of citizens to be truly representative of the people. Voters must have the facts, and be able to see through the misrepresentations. The voters must still make good decisions in spite of the special interests spending large sums of money on what be false and misleading broadcasting to furthers their own positions. They must make good decisions with politicians using their office to mount endless investigations, and to stage daily press conferences to disparage their political enemies.

The repeal of the broadcast fairness rules in the 1980s gave rise to the emergence of unfairness and scapegoating in the 1990s. However, most people still believe that journalism standards are at the same high level that they used to be. People still think that reporting is required to be fair and impartial. The rise of sensational and cynical reporting has been attributed by the public as mostly differences of style rather than the fundamental change that it is. The public still thinks that their right to know is being protected under federal law when it is not.

The press, too, lost objectivity in these decades. Too often, what the public got was a reporter's opinion, when what we are expecting to get are the facts, and the facts that were confirmed from at least two different and impartial sources. The traditional tools used to maintain a level playing field for reporting, or for anything else, are not working. The Federal

Communication Commission, the FCC, which regulates the use of the public airwaves was in 1995 under threat of being de-funded by Congress and suffered up to 30% cutbacks.[25] The Justice Department had not prosecuted a major anti-trust case since 1983. Fair trade laws are of benefit, primarily, to small business. The complete lack of regulation enforcement worked against those small business and to the benefit only of the strong. Companies have been damaged or destroyed due to laws that were passed by the Congress to favor one industry or corporation over another. No newspaper reported this process, no television network covered what was going on. Why were there so few reports about those who used their office for personal gain or about those who write the laws accepting money from industries and corporations who benefitted?

Campaign contributions make things happen in Washington. The Federal Election Commission has been given little enforcement capacity to keep elections fair. They too, are under threat of being de-funded by the Congress and have no money to investigate illegal campaign practices. Individuals are limited to what they can contribute to political campaigns, but they do get around the limits. It is illegal for corporations to give money to Congressional campaigns, but they do. Campaign finance reform is stalled, but is still badly needed since money and the pursuit of money has now become the most important part of an election campaign.

Money buys access to the legislative process. Enough money can even afford lobbyists the ability to write the laws to suit themselves. To those who truly hate government, this is seen as an improvement. This elimination of the middleman results in the direct control of our government by the moneyed elite. Money has, itself, shifted the balance of political power into the hands of those with money. Political power has shifted on advertising, on hate and smear campaigns and on activities breeding mistrust, funded by those who would benefit. Questionable and illegal campaign contributions were used to elect a new majority in Congress. Many got themselves elected using the argument of "Government is bad, give us a chance to fix it, things can't get any worse." They were wrong. Things can get worse, in fact, they can get much worse.

Perhaps the saddest part of a democracy that follows demigods into decline, is that the individual citizens are so used to bending to the will of the majority. We are all used to giving up some of our own liberty for the greater good, to ensure the liberty of all. It is extremely rare for an American to refuse to bend to the will of what they think is a sizable majority. In a democracy, rival factions are reduced to making bad and then worse decisions which are ever more politically popular. The electing groups will themselves grow even more extreme. In this fashion demigods are replaced with worse demigods until majority rule no longer applies.

Only a broad understanding of how things work, only the education of our citizens, can stop the decline of liberty. It is hard to reinstitute a true democracy once it's decline has been started. The few informed Americans who do bother to vote are now the only ones standing against it's decline. Only when the others discover and act on the truth, can the anarchy that the patriot militia has anticipated be avoided. Unless we act quickly to level the playing field of politics, the patriot movement may prove to be justified in their fear of the federal government

The Principles of Our Government

The founding fathers based the great compromise that led to our Constitution on simple, yet sound concepts, such as that of the three-legged stool. Three legs are the fewest that will provide a firm foundation. A three-legged stool provides a very solid support, yet is also the least complex of all. The Constitution is also very simple in concept, and like a three-legged stool, it too will never wobble. The idea of having three pillars on which to support our government offers simplicity, yet effectiveness. The rules that are the easiest to understand are also the easiest to follow. A system which relies on intuitive fairness will also not tend to become unwieldy due to the over-complexity of it's laws. The best laws are those of human nature, those laws which enforce themselves.

Our founding fathers visualized three equal branches of government and envisioned three basic concepts on which our union would be founded. The three branches of government are the Executive, the Legislative and the Judicial. We all know that having three equal branches of government provides "checks and balances." The separate branches were designed to work in harmony and in opposition. They were designed so that in conjunction, in that dynamic tension, they would both insure the freedom of the individual and the survival and welfare of the whole, in the body of the state.

The three founding concepts are the simple, basic truths we all hold in common in order to join together as Americans. These were the ideals that guided the founding of our great nation. These are the beliefs that make our society unique from all of those that have gone before. The patriots were willing to die for these noble concepts, yet, they remained unwritten, largely because every American intuitively agrees with them. Their principles are found in every line of the Constitution. They are: respect for the worth of the individual, the desire for spiritual freedom and the need for the decentralization of power. These concepts were the basis of the Constitution and are, therefore, the basis for our society of today. They also can form the basis of a new dialog among the people.

Appreciation for the worth of the individual is proclaimed in the Declaration of Independence, the Preamble and in the entire Constitution. The Declaration of Independence declares "That all men are created equal; that they are endowed by their creator with inherent and inalienable rights; that among these are life, liberty and the pursuit of happiness." Worth of the individual was a truly radical concept over two hundred and fifty years ago. The needs of the state, and of the king, overrode all other considerations before that time. Our motto of E. Pluribus Unum, "Of many, One," may also literally be translated as "Many Individuals, United as One." This radical idea, that previously unrelated individuals can come together to form one great nation, further stresses the importance the Constitution places on *worth of the individual*.

Spiritual freedom, both freedom of thought and freedom of religion, is guaranteed in the first and ninth amendments to the Constitution. It is notable religion, itself, is not even mentioned in the body of the Constitution. This omission was indeed deliberate because many early colonists had come to America to escape religious persecution. They came to America seeking freedom of the spirit, "spiritual freedom," in America. The founding fathers had seen what the development of a state religion had done in Europe. Some had even been excommunicated from the Church of England for their rebellion against the king. The patriots were very careful to exclude any mention of a state religion, to insure it be kept separate from politics.

Spiritual freedom is a much larger concept than simply freedom of religion. The American spirit is, itself, broader and much more inclusive. It is the freedom to dream and to follow those dreams. America is viewed by the entire world as the "land of opportunity." Immigrants have come to America since it's beginnings to enjoy this spiritual freedom, yet, few can define exactly what it is. In an attempt to explain in more modern terms the concept of spiritual freedom, some have compared it to the franchise that American Express has established.

American Express offers a credit card with no pre-set limits. Spiritual freedom is like that credit card– in that it confers both rights and responsibilities. If we are willing to work at life, and to meet its terms, Americans have the freedom to advance as far as they can, without undue interference from the state. The sense that anything is possible is unique to the American spirit. Warren E. Buffett, perhaps America's most successful investor has stuck with his investment in American Express through all degrees of poor management because he sees the singular value of that franchise.

Our founding fathers had a very strong desire to insure the decentralization of power. This was very clear in their desire to prevent the rise of a "strong-man" form of government such as the system of royalty they had just overthrown. Checks and balances to prevent the accumulation of power were important then, and are still very important today. Division of the federal government into three separate but equal branches prevents any one from dominating the others. Division of power between the federal, state and local governments prevents the accumulation of absolute power which will *always* corrupt absolutely.

Political power in America comes from the individual and from the informed vote of that individual, just as the power of America's markets come from the decisions made by individual consumers. Since all power, indeed, comes from this "grassroots" level, it needs to remain as close to that grassroots level, as is possible. We need to continue to zealously defend the checks and balances in the Constitution, so the power will indeed remain with the people and not be given up to the special interests. Only in this way can we continue to insure none will dominate the other.

Our country is again in great need of true patriots. We need those who will speak out for the common good, as did those original patriots. We need strong local leadership for our country, not the centralized "strong-man" form of government for which many are calling. As a nation of individuals, we need the kind of leaders who will accomplish the difficult task of bringing us together to accomplish our own individual tasks. We need leaders who are visionary, yet those who can find merit in the opposing viewpoints. We need those who will work in their communities and, yet, see the larger picture and work for the good of the entire society.

We still need those national leaders who will bring us together to cooperate, to collaborate, and to find the common ground of our mutual interests. In our increasingly complex society, the market will often only highly reward those with extreme technical and professional specialization. There are even orthopedic surgeons who specialize in surgery *only to the right hand*. This work is very important, but we also need doctors trained to visualize the overall condition and to focus on the health of the total being. As interdisciplinary skills are important in health care, we also need all of the trades and all of the individual talents in order to form a fully functioning society.

HMO's and managed care plans are on the right track when they approach the care of individuals in this holistic manner. However, they move away from Constitutional principles when they deny individuals the best possible care by refusing to pay for medical specialists or for care by the leading practitioners in their respective fields. Appropriate care, provided early in the disease state, most often will save money.

No one benefits from prolonged medical treatment just as no one benefits from prolonged arguments. We need leaders who will encourage the separate branches of government to work together, not just to communicate *their* positions. We need the back and forth dialogue of a true conversation in order to find the common ground of true compromise. We need to identify and to resolve real problems, rather than the perceptions of problems raised by the propaganda machine of narrow and special interests. Our leaders truly need to lead, to do what needs to be done, resisting what may be popular at the moment.

We need patriotic citizens who would risk offending others by standing up for what is right, and who will put the good of the country above their individual self-interest. Political power must remain with the individual citizens, because even good choices can become counter-productive if someone else makes all of our decisions for us.

As Americans, we are all justly proud of the Constitution and of the ideals and the principles we stand for as a nation. That we, as unique and separate individuals can share these same American Ideals, despite having differing and often conflicting personal values, is what makes our country great. Many changes are occurring in our world of today. There are substantial changes occurring which have fermented turmoil within our nation, it's organization, and it's structures. We may have many and severe challenges ahead, but we are still a great and strong nation. Our shared culture and Constitution can provide a foundation upon which, together, we can rebuild our common interests and once again regain that common ground upon which our nation was founded.

Developing the Role of Government

Before the 1929 stock market crash, the depression and the era of the Franklin D. Roosevelt presidency, government was generally laissez-faire in its approach to markets. The free market controlled and policed itself, and the government stayed out of it. The worst abuses of the free market, the monopolies and trusts, had by that time been contained by the anti-trust provisions of the Sherman Anti-trust Act. This Legislation was, at the time, seen as the maximum that the government should do to intervene in providing a level playing field for trade and commerce. Capitalism was in the view of writer Kevin Phillips, "wild, free, and untamed."

The Stock Market Crash of 1929 and the Great Depression changed all of that. Unemployment hit one in four American workers. The people demanded that government do something to control the wide swings of a market that a strictly unregulated environment will allow. FDR responded with the Securities and Exchange Commission, The Federal Deposit Insurance Corporation, farmers loan programs and others. All of these were seen as necessary government interventions to protect companies and individuals and to prevent the recurrence of wild gyrations of the market.

The people approve of some government regulation and of limited intervention to maintain the level playing field that is the free market. Anti-trust legislation is needed to prevent the strong from "buying" the playing field and taking advantage of the weak. Regulatory bodies are in place to prevent misrepresentations and risky behavior from hurting investors. We all agree it is in our best interest to prevent farmers from going under due to one bad growing season and that some sort of farm loan program is in the national interest. The reforms under FDR were considered successful and led to the longest sustained period of growth in the history of our economy. The working class became the middle class as a result of these policies. Many of the most conservative capitalists begrudge what was done in the New Deal to raise the working and middle classes. They rail against public "meddling" and "interference" in economic matters. They forget that the institution that is Capitalism, itself, also teetered on the brink of destruction before the implementation of the New Deal reforms.

Logically, government must have become larger to accomplish those tasks newly undertaken by the federal government. However, at the start of this era only about ten in every one thousand Americans were employed by the federal government. Government employment on the state level at that same time was fifteen in every thousand. Currently the federal government is as small as it has been in the last three decades. The number of federal government employees is as small as it was when President Kennedy was in the White House. About ten in one thousand Americans still work for the federal government, a number that is declining, while almost sixty in one thousand are now employed on the state level.[26]

One vocal group, supposedly ideologically against all government regulation, say they wish to turn regulatory authority over to the states. They say the federal government is just "Too Big." They blast "Big Government" as the cause of all of our problems. That inflammatory argument, also originally from the 1972 George Wallace presidential campaign, just does not wash today. The fact is, special interests are much more likely to be successful in blunting regulations they don't like on the state level, than at the federal level. Government is much more bloated at the state level than at the federal level, at least judging by the numbers employed in each.

These same vocal individuals, true to their stated dislike of regulation, would allow pollution and exploitation of our environment to provide for a short term profit for some, at the long term expense of the rest of us. Those with any long term view, would have to be bribed, or insane to take such positions. Society, itself, could only develop when those first lower animals developed their physiological rectums– to prevent them from fowling the nest. Stable societies could not form as long as individuals had no control of where their waste products were deposited.

We truly do have a limited amount of clean air and clean water. As a basic, solely economic argument, if we allow some to pollute, it will increase costs for the rest of us by having to clean it up enough to make it usable again. The economic argument for pollution goes much further than just calling for a level playing field for the polluting endeavors. We are all being asked, in effect, to subsidize the profits of that polluting enterprise. We are each being asked to support polluters both financially and with increasingly higher costs to the health of the community and of the planet.

Roosevelt increased federal support for education. Seeing the health condition of many young persons reporting for military duty, Truman began federal programs to fund school nutrition. Some would now cut these funds for the education of future generations, in order to provide tax cuts to a few or to fund tax breaks for certain corporations and industries. This not only reverses the trends of government policy during the last sixty years, it amounts to political payoffs to special interest groups.

It is in the best interest of all of society to meet the needs of our children. They are our future. The political rhetoric of those who would change the role of government cannot provide adequate cover for the reality that they wish to use the system for their own goals, rather than revamp the system for the benefit of all. Education of the children, to insure they are given the opportunity to become the good and productive citizens of the future, and to care for us in our old age, is basic to all of society. Every civilization has education of the children as a goal. Without the education of the children, society, itself, has no future.

Many other worthy programs which were developed over the last thirty years are now also in jeopardy. Affirmative action and those taxes which go in any way for social welfare or social stability programs are now under a hard-edged conservative assault. Affirmative action gets the blame for those middle-class jobs which were lost, but were lost mainly due to conservative policies restricting growth and the policies which exported jobs overseas. The unemployment, welfare and Medicaid systems are under duress for many of these same reasons.

Social Security and Medicare taxes have gone up for the middle class largely because they are capped so that the wealthy does not have to pay their fair share. The working poor now pay a much larger share of their incomes in taxes than ever before. Taxes were cut for the wealthiest Americans and corporations during the 1980s. The end result is that the rest of us now must pay more, to make up that difference. The fundamental fairness that America was once known for, is now in danger of dissolving into disunity. The level playing field of commerce is now seriously slanted in favor of the few.

4. *Government's Proper Role*

In the unwritten agreement that first allowed the formation of civilization, each individual has an opportunity to be productive in society and to share in the proceeds of the increased production. The cooperation of individuals in an orderly, free-market society has historically been the best way to accomplish that goal, to get more for less. Even today, the basics are the same.

Our federal government is necessary to provide for the common defense and to ensure a level playing field for trade among the people. The pure function of the federal government in an orderly society is that of referee. It is not necessary for it to become involved in every decision. Government is not to be in the business of interfering in the private lives or in the market transactions of individuals. The free market has it's way of correcting and stabilizing itself. A free market generally needs only the presence of an interstate power, a federal authority, to keep the abuses of trade from getting out of hand.

The maintenance of a level playing field for the interaction of labor, capital and ideas is the most important governmental function in the free enterprise system. If a central government will provide for the common defense, a stable currency, and insure fair trade, then almost through a kind of decentralized control– commerce and the resulting social interaction take care of virtually everything else. This interaction, the "dynamic tension" of opposing ideas where one cannot totally dominate the other, is what makes America great. Even your competitor has a few good ideas. If the market forces you to incorporate his good ideas in with yours, then everyone benefits.

Today, many look to the government for a leg up, for an edge, for something that will only benefit them, or will benefit only their individual enterprise. This is, after all, the goal of the special interest group. All interest groups, left and right, are guilty of this, since it is their stated purpose to promote their own interests. Some interests, however, may also be in the national interest. We should support those things which are also in the interest of society. However, in choosing which of the opposing interests to support, and therefore who's ox gets gored, there is the potential for increasing the unfairness in society.

There are many in the Congress who will give their support to just about any cause, in return for a contribution or other financial consideration. Whether it is a just cause or not does not matter. This is wrong. Benefits to one group over another will be of only a short term duration, because ultimately we all will lose. Making the pie bigger is far better than fighting over the same pie. If we will work together, the economy will grow, and we will all do better. This will always be true of our society. Americans have a long history of overcoming any challenge by working together to solve problems.

The purpose of the federal government is not to micro-manage the economy, nor to dictate to individuals what they can and cannot do in the privacy of their own bedrooms, but to stay out of the business of individuals, as much as possible. Government policies which promote low growth and high interest rates favor an entirely different group than policies which promote higher growth and lower interest rates. To favor capital over labor or labor over capital is not the true purpose of government. The purpose of government is not to favor one group over all of the others, but to keep things fair, and to oversee the honest exchange of goods and trade among the people.

What we are in great need of today, are true patriots who will stand up for these noble concepts. We must stand against the power of special interests who wish to further concentrate power in the hands of an elite. We must stand for the decentralization of power. We need truly patriotic individuals who will stand up to those groups who wish to gain unfair advantage over all of the other groups. True patriots will stand against those who seek to impose their narrow view of morality on the rest of us. We must stand together for spiritual freedom. We must stand for the worth of every individual and for each individual receiving an opportunity to contribute to society. When we work together, the entire economy will grow, and we all will benefit from the resulting increase.

That no one wants to work is a complaint that is often heard today. That everyone feels that the world must owe them a living, is heard again and again. Yet many good Americans are working as hard and as many hours as they can– and are still just barely scraping by. Some individuals who are receiving aid from the federal safety net programs (AFDC, food stamps and Medicaid) are also working in part-time and pick-up jobs on the side. This may be wrong, yet, they too are just barely making it. It is hard enough for us in the middle class to make ends meet. What will happen to these "marginal" working class individuals and to their dependent children, much less those who are totally dependent on government social programs when all federal programs are cut?

The rise of homelessness and a permanent poverty in America may not be just the result of a lack of work ethic, either. It is due to many other things, such as a changing job market, a lack of demand for certain job skills, and to wages kept artificially low due to a complicated set of factors. Our laws should still help to keep the level playing field of the free market as level as possible. When laws are changed to favor the rapid turn-over of capital, the export of high-wage jobs, leveraged buy-outs and stock options over the labor of average Americans; we find ourselves in the situations that we have today. That "No one wants to work" may be because many have found even working very hard has gotten them nowhere. It is now the general feeling in America, that those who labor the least seem to acquire all of the benefits of the labor of others.

Americans have always before truly believed in the worth of labor. They have always believed by working hard, they would always get ahead. This may no longer be strictly true in today's America. The value of labor has declined, as have wages. In fairness, capital is not always doing much better either. In the last decades of the twentieth century, capital investments in such things as computers and machinery have sometimes been obsoleted very rapidly, often in only two years. As we evolve into a truely international market, many things we have always thought we could count on will not be there for us. Change will be the only constant. Who could have figured that such a solid company as IBM could, in just a few years, lose almost half of its value due to capital obsolescence?

Changing Institutions

IBM at one time was considered by many to be the best of all possible places to work. It had what many thought to be "lifetime" job security, a corporate culture that rewarded risk-taking, encouraged growth and provided great benefits. IBM employees worked together with a common vision and in the process created a larger pie for all to share. Yet, changes in the business climate forced even IBM to lay-off and retire close to half of its total work force. Being in the right place at the right time with the right team is the time honored recipe for success. Managers who are presiding over such success often begin to think it was their decisions which were responsible for it. This has been repeated in the history of corporate decision making, time and time again. The payment of a large salary to the CEO is no guarantee of good decision making, and IBM in the space of just a few years became almost half of the size it once was.

Intel corporation is another company which could dominate because it was in the right place at the right time. Their specialty is in the manufacture of computer processor chips. These processors are used in the personal computers that obsoleted the main frame computers of IBM. IBM literally gave the market in personal computers to Intel by basing the IBM personal computers on off-the-shelf Intel products. Yet, Intel too is at risk of a future obsolescence. Faced with it's first competition, Intel took to the courts to maintain their monopoly of the market. Losing there, management began to up-the-ante by raising the level of competition with technological advances. The technology of integrated circuits is, therefore, forced to progress rapidly for Intel to retain market dominance.

This strategy works for as long as the companies competitors do not quickly catch up. In the computer industry, the odds are very good technological advances can be quickly matched by competitors, so Intel sought to also use the "good will" of their brand name with the *Intel inside* campaign. Intel could later use this brand identification to compete with their own best customers, those computer manufacturers who had been using Intel chips. However, before Intel could market it's own line of "Intel brand" mother-boards and computers, management was caught covering-up the fact that they had knowingly shipped defective processor chips to these manufacturing customers. Instead of quickly coming clean and admitting their mistake, the court of public opinion, was ultimately the only thing that forced Intel management to offer to replace the sub-standard computer chips.

The profit mark-up on computer chips is measured in hundreds of dollars. Labor is just a small portion of the cost. Yet, Intel management has decided they will build overseas plants to produce their next generation of computer chips.[27] This will mean the shuttering of what will soon become obsolete domestic plants, and the further loss of American jobs. There were no good reasons to send these American jobs overseas. The fact is, as foreign builders learn how to build the plants and foreign workers are trained to operate them, there will be nothing to stop foreign companies from eventually opening up "across the street" from these plants. In the longer term, the overseas move can only hurt Intel and also the other American computer companies.

The American corporate system for rewarding short-term profit over long-term vision has time and time again betrayed our nations social stability. AT&T gave up it's lucrative monopoly on long distance service in order to get into the computer and information systems business. Ultimately, however, AT&T's

1989 purchase of NCR to gain this capability ended in it's 1996 bail-out of computer manufacturing and the lay-offs of 40,000 additional workers. What he country needs is better and higher paying jobs. Yet AT&T is outsourcing production and laying-off workers, while Intel is moving production overseas. What we really need is job growth, yet, much of big business is rapidly laying-off employees in the name of higher efficiency and of improving productivity. Some of these managers may think they have found the secret to success in copying those short-term methods that IBM was forced to turn to.

Today, ninety percent of jobs creation is in small businesses. However, small businesses are often handicapped in many areas such as competing for employees. Big business has more capital and the resources with which to compete with benefits and salaries. Large employers can get tremendous discounts on insurance and other benefits that smaller employers cannot obtain. Since benefits are such a large part of the total compensation package for today's employees, large employers can save even more by the early retirement of their older workers.

Especially if it is laying-off or firing its older and better paid workers, big business can afford to pay higher than average starting salaries to younger workers. In fairness, not every company is doing this, but big business gains and the rest of us lose when older and higher paid employees are let go. Newly hired, younger employees work for less money. They also do not care as much about retirement packages nor are they as expensive to cover under existing health insurance plans. "The system" in today's America can only give short-term benefit to those companies that get rid of older workers. Longer-term, they too will only lose.

Moreover, the country as a whole, loses as well. The country loses the skills of those 45-60 year old workers when they cannot find jobs that require the level of skills they have acquired. We all lose when they cannot afford health insurance and loose their homes and savings or may become wards of the state because of a serious illness. We all lose when formerly good and productive citizens become bitter at the prospects of a much lowered standard of living. Everyone loses when resentment spreads among qualified persons who are under or un-employed, worst of all, when they resolve that in the future they will look out only for themselves.

We need individuals to cooperate and work together to make our country grow again. The sad fact is, once everyone is out for themselves even the most optimistic of entrepreneurs won't take a chance on starting a new venture. Small businesspeople especially have trouble finding employees who will do an honest days work for what they can afford to pay. Many employees do not appreciate the risks that small businesspeople take or understand the thin margins on which they operate. Disgruntled employees will steal, slack-off, or hurt the business by alienating customers. They do not seem to understand that in the longer-term it will hurt them too, and it also hurts all of us.

People must work together with a common vision to make any enterprise successful. This is why the crooked politician and the shady operator do so well, at least initially. They share a common vision in taking advantage of others and so are aware of every angle and short cut. The rise of the unscrupulous, leads to a political and business atmosphere that does not encourage the building of lasting and trusting relationships. Small businesses especially are hurt in such an atmosphere. Small business do not have the political clout that can allow them to go to the Congress for relief or some special tax break. Because small businesses are usually very thinly capitalized, when suppliers or customers play hard ball with them, they can very easily be put out of business. This, in turn, reduces jobs and opportunity for everyone, including those who might have provoked it.

In the New Deal, the Democratic Party raised the middle class on economic fairness issues. In a free enterprise system, it is the equal access to markets and to the resulting profits that are of the greatest importance. Hard work and good ideas should be rewarded. They are just as important to success as capital and the access to capital. Small merchants and small businesspeople must be allowed to succeed for our society to advance. Working people must earn a living wage for their efforts. The level playing field for commerce, the free enterprise system, must remain level for all. The market must be fair for labor, for capital, and for ideas, for our society to progress.

Many workers feel they have been abused by industry. The productivity of American workers is one of the highest in the world, yet wages have not kept up with that productivity. In the small Southern mill-towns, workers worked for low wages but felt their interests were being taken care of by their bosses. Workers could live in the mill villages, go to the company doctor, have credit at the company store, and go on field trips sponsored by the mill on Sundays. Occasionally, workers would become so far in debt with the company they were powerless to leave. However, looking on the bright side of a very dark part of our labor history, such workers at least felt they had job security, since the company was loth to fire them.

Today, many workers feel they have no job security at all. Very often, workers will work hard, but are left feeling unrewarded for it. Those who feel that are not being paid what they should be, often cannot quit because of the amount of personal debt they may have. They may become depressed and less motivated to continue to work as hard as they once have. Those who feel they have been exploited in the past may not wish to work as hard as they used to in their current job. Many American workers, even highly skilled technical workers feel trapped in their jobs and feel powerless to do anything about it. Only a few large companies, such as Nucor Steel have done anything at all, on their own, about this increasing problem. Nucor has allowed their employees greater control over their own individual production and, therefore, some control over their own wages.

Nucor was one of the pioneers of paying their workers based on actual productivity. Few other large non-union companies have come close to matching work with reward for ordinary working people. Fewer still, have advanced any innovations in business with this fundamental fairness as has former CEO and current Chairman of Nucor Steel, F. Kenneth Iverson. Most other American corporations, by way of contrast, are slow to innovate and quick to copy, to copy even the worst of the short-term solutions for a fast buck or a quarterly gain.

What we need is everyone working together to make more for each of us. Instead, what we often get is management always trying to find ways to cut the share of the other components. Today, as most other American workers continue to get the same or less, their bosses generally get more and more. Executives in industry and commerce are reported to be receiving ever increasing salaries. Newspaper business pages are filled with news of corporate bonus and stock options granted for executives. As a result many American workers sense the uselessness in trying to get ahead. Many no longer dream of making a larger salary, or of one day owning their own small business.

In the 1994 election, only twenty-three percent of voters with annual family incomes of under $50,000 a year, typically working families, even voted. As disappointed as many middle class Americans say they are when asked about the economy, the very people that the Democrats say that they want to help didn't bother to vote. When they did vote, they were just as likely to have voted Republican because of issues such as school prayer, abortion, or gun control. Whereas, the more inflammatory social issues are likely to directly affect less than a few percentage of them, the economic issues affect virtually everyone. The issues of fairness will affect the future of their children, as well.

The Republican strategy of getting working people to vote against their own economic interest through emotional issues seems to be working. Since only 23% of this group did vote, it means that 77% did not vote. Clouding and confusing the issue with anti-government rhetoric that keeps working people and traditionally Democratic voters at home appears to be the most successful strategy of all.[28] Keeping your opponents from voting means you can win with less votes.

Theoretically, all political parties should be on the same side on economic issues. We should all be for progress, for economic growth and increasing employment. Approaching full employment lowers the cost of government by reducing the need for subsidies and the amount of tax revenues that are needed to fund them. Higher rates of growth, and accompanying reduction of un-employment, instead of being a burden on the government, raises the amount of tax revenues generated, which then can be used for deficit reduction, tax-cuts, or other purposes. However, the elites prefer the unequal distribution of wealth and power. It is in this inequality that they obtain their power. The elites will continue to do better as long as we are divided into separate communities of rich and poor.

In our communities, the old bustling neighborhood shops have given way to the malls and super stores. Highly structured retail operations with their minimum wage, cookie cutter, staffing positions could more efficiently compete in the atmosphere of today. However, there are other effects to the community that have not been considered. For example, people who knew their neighbors before, suddenly did not know even the people who lived next door. The caring and the community that existed before was now gone, replaced by a need only for robotic service from detached individuals. The clerk waiting on you, today, could care less about you. She's perhaps been on her feet for 8 hours working for the minimum wage. The end result is that people are less connected to their neighbors and communities than they had been in a true free enterprise system. In removing the ownership of enterprise from the community, it's owners become an elite class and the rest of us merely tenants.

Our institutions are changing, and people are looking for the solutions to those problems resulting from the changes in the marketplace. Some have turned to fundamentalist leaders and ideologies for answers. The attraction of fundamentalism is that it offers pat answers. However, in the real world there are no pat answers or even easy answers. The real world is much more complex than this. There are an infinite number of choices that can be made, some that are better and some that are worse.

Unless we can think "outside of the box," outside of the restrictions imposed by rigid ideology, no progress can be made as a society. The Spiritual freedom guarenteed by our Constitution entails more than just the freedom of religious expression. The very spirit of our people needs also to be free. Society must be free to develop new ideas and to refine new ways of doing things, rather than be repressed by narrow dogma, for any true progress to be made.

Many believers in narrow ideologies try to paint those that would attempt to involve all sides of an issue into the solution, as being wishy-washy or confused. However, all normal individuals are a mix of differing viewpoints and attitudes. In our colorful America, nothing is simply black or white. No one should be completely conservative or liberal, we are all conservative or liberal about different issues. Most of us are a mix of thinking that defies being easily classified as left or right.

Most of us in the middle are fiscally conservative and more socially tolerant. However, many too can be progressive and forward thinking on financial matters as well as conservative about certain social matters. Many will accept some risk on financial investments in order to receive higher returns. Others abhor any risk when it comes to financial decisions. Socially, some may wish to avoid those who are somehow different from themselves. Yet, most Americans will embrace just causes, such as civil rights, understanding that they do not also have to like Latino art or to enjoy rapp music in doing so. Most Americans are tolerant of the social practices of others while appreciating traditional social mores and insisting on the same basic standards for all.

The danger of fundamentalist thinking is this: if an action is often repeated, just because it is proscribed, if it is indeed wrong, then the mistake is multiplied again and again. Many examples are found in the history of civilization. Easter Island, an uninhabited, desolate, barren island in the Pacific is known for the stone monuments, giant carvings of heads, placed on the hillsides above the shore. It is unclear whether these stone carvings had religious significance or were simply expressions of the egos of the tribal chiefs. The early inhabitants and their tribes competed with the other tribes to build and place these monuments along the shoreline. At one time Easter Island was covered with large trees. The trees were increasingly cut down to roll the large stones from the quarry, roughly five miles from the shore. After a period of time, they discovered that they had no large trees from which to make canoes. Without canoes, they had no way to fish for the tuna and dolphin that had been their main source of protein. No one foresaw what would happen, or perhaps even knew such a thing could happen. As no one had thought ahead, they simply continued doing what had always been proscribed.[29] In what had once been an idyllic location, society went into decline and ultimately disappeared.

In America, there is a campaign by fundamentalists to dismantle the New Deal trade and labor reforms. They are attempting to do this for reasons of ideology and of greed. The organizers of this campaign are using the many persuasive arguments developed by some conservative "think tanks." Many small businesspeople are convinced that their interests are being looked out for, as well. However, the fact remains that an excessively conservative climate for business ultimately favors big business over small business.

Elimination of all governmental rules and regulation puts small business at increased risk to unfair competition by big business. Opening a market to competition does not by itself make the market fair. Big business has shown in the 104th Congress it has the resources to lobby the Congress for things that will favor only itself. Small businesses are easily left out of this monopoly and are, therefore, soon out of business.

We continue a long history as a free people, some of whom gave their lives for that which we have now. We must study that history and learn from it. We have heard what is past is prologue, that history repeats itself. If we do not now study this history and learn its lessons, our country, this noble experiment in democracy, is surely as doomed as was the society on Easter Island or the ancient Roman Empire.

The Decline and Fall of Civilizations

The brick Rome of Augustus was in decline even before the great public buildings were rebuilt in marble. It was in decline because the moral fiber of the people was also in decline. A nation that started with a great equal class had divided into two, the rich and the poor, the Plebeians and the Patricians. Bribes and tributes were routinely paid to the leadership and selling-out had long become the order of the day. Roman citizenship was once a duty, as well as an honor, but now many stood in line to sell their vote.

The Roman Senate was populated by those who would use their position to enrich themselves. Laws were passed to aid Senatorial friends to the exclusion of everyone else. The free Roman farms that had united to form a great civilization were replaced by great Senatorial estates. Grand circuses were staged to bond and unite the people as Romans, to let them relive their great and glorious history, a history that was, itself, now only history. Just as today, the speech writers and the public relations professionals became much more important to the daily workings of government than the actual formulation of the public policy.

Public corruption was the vehicle which weakened Rome to the point of societal breakdown. The excesses of the elite and the barbaric practices in the arenas would have doomed Rome eventually, as Christianity was rising to fill the void left by moral decay. However, what was worse for the Roman Empire in the immediate term, was that there were Barbarians who were also *outside* the gate.

The Spanish Empire flourished in the fifteen and sixteenth century. Spain's rise was based on exploration and also the exploitation of the new world. At one time Spain was the richest nation on earth and home to a powerful elite class. The elite were the military, members of the royal family and the church hierarchy. But because the wealth of Spain came so easily, it never developed a large craftsman or tradesmen class, purchasing virtually everything that it wanted from other countries. If persons were not of the elite class, they were likely to be poor and farmers.

Most other Spaniards were sailors and soldiers, barbarians really, who conquered and brutalized the American Indians in the name of Christ. The leaders of the church themselves were not that much better. Between 1481 and 1540 during the Spanish Inquisition, in the city of Seville alone, some 20,000 people were charged by religious leaders with being witches and burned at the stake. Many fear if religion is allowed to likewise infiltrate the politics of America, we too would start having such witch hunts.

Spain never developed a middle class that was able to moderate the extremist elements of Spanish government, the church, and it's financial institutions. The conservative leadership did not encourage innovation or advancement of their people. They neglected to build their manufacturing base at home by choosing to import most goods. Therefore, when the supply of gold from the New World ran out, Spain was left with virtually no economy. Spain became the world's first military superpower to decline and to fall, quite simply because of the over-reliance on imported goods.

The Dutch Empire was similar to the Spanish Empire only in the fact that it, too, was based on exploration. New York city was founded by the Dutch as New Amsterdam. We all remember how they bought Manhattan from the Indians for sixteen dollars in beads. The Dutch differed from the Spanish in the fact that they were good craftsmen, good traders and had a thriving merchant middle class. These were good, hard working, honest, and thrifty people. The term "Go Dutch" used today and meaning that you pay for your own meals and entertainment is indicative of that thrift.

The Dutch were famous for their Delftware dishes and tiles, for agriculture, for learning and science. They invented the microscope and mechanical pumps and devices that harnessed the wind. The Dutch economy was strong but its parliament went into heavy debt to finance speculation on behalf of the elites. The wealthy elites wanted the safety of government backed debt, so they loaned money to the government at high real interest rates.

The elites did not care that the money be invested wisely or even what that money would be used for, they just liked the investment safety of the government debt instruments. In retrospect, the heavy speculation in rare Tulip bulbs should have been a tip-off to an impending collapse, just as we should have noted in the very early stages of our own Savings & Loan Association crisis.

The decline of the Dutch Empire was ultimately due to the heavy national debt which strangled the once thriving middle class. Homelessness and poverty soon swept a country which had once been thriving and was almost fully employed. The economy continued to worsen as the government cut expenses and raised taxes to repay the heavy debt. The Dutch leaders were not bad people, they just did not know what effect the excessive debt would have on the workings of the economy.

The Dutch parliament had simply allowed the elites to control the government and, therefore, had permitted the greed of a few to come before the common interests. Although the Dutch did not collapse into total decline, the nationally owned Shell Oil and a former colony, the Dutch West Indies, are about all that is visible of a once great international empire.

The Netherlands of the 1790s had absolutely no social safety-net programs. Therefore, it took the Dutch hundreds of years to reacquire a thriving middle class and to once again occupy the center stage of international competition. If the Dutch could have had the basic safety net programs– education, food, clothing, and shelter for the children, their climb back would have been much less painful and certainly much quicker.

In the long run, looking out for all of the citizens will ultimately pay-off. In the very least, someone must be able to buy those goods and services that capitalism so efficently produces. Capitalism is by far the most efficient system for a society on the way up, but it also extremely efficent on the way down. In the final analysis, capitalism needs to be buffered from it's own excesses. Taxes paid for social stability, if not because it is the humane thing to do, are certainly a cheap insurance against it's complete and total decline.

In a March 31st 1995 editorial in the New Your Times entitled "What became of my Democrats," Felix G. Rohatyn, the New York investment banker, also called for this new kind of "Advanced Capitalism." He advocated a new middle-ground between the hard-edged conservatism of the Republican right and the European-type welfare state. Mr. Rohatyn visualizes Advanced Capitalism as the appropriate mix of fiscal conservatism and a strong private sector with an active and supporting government. Few can disagree with that.

5. *A Nation in Decline*

We too, may be a civilization in decline. Television minister, Pat Robertson points out that in a 1994 Times Mirror poll, 80% of Americans agree that moral decline is a serious problem in America today. Pat Robertson links the moral decline to the lack of prayer in schools. He also lays blame to powerful liberal groups in Washington DC and in New York City. While these are very interesting things to blame, and Mr. Robertson has gotten many to agree with his view, this is not the whole and total problem. Moreover, blaming others is, very often, just another way to deflect attention from oneself. There may be liberal groups in those two cities, or liberal groups in other cities for that matter. However, they cannot be as powerful as the very powerful, and very conservative religious group with its media and financial empire: Pat Robertson and his Christian Coalition.

The Pat Robertson Coalition has taken charge of the blame game and has scored some points with the average American in doing so. If society, as measured by our ability to get along with each other, is indeed failing, it is surely happening with his help. Rather than working to keep us together, he is certain to divide off some part of it, under his control. By pushing hot button and divisive issues such as abortion and school prayer, he may at least be able to have influence over an extreme segment, no matter what.

When the Constitution was adopted, many states had already adopted official religions. Under the Constitution, official state support for religion and religious practices were no longer allowed. Mr. Robertson may not think that this is fair, but it is the law, and it is the law for some very good reasons. In it's 1962 decision, the Supreme Court agreed with the plaintiff that this was indeed the case. The sole item at issue, official state sanction for religious practices, was overturned by the Supreme Court. In the Supreme Court decision, only "state led" or since teachers are employees of the state, "teacher led" school prayer was declared unconstitutional and ordered removed from schools.

Yet, in typical American fashion, we overreacted by punishing everyone equally, and by limiting the rights of all. School administrators stayed as far away as possible from any practice that would be remotely linked to religion. The Christmas Pageants became Winter Pageants where the children sang about Frosty the Snowman instead of singing Hanukkah songs and Christmas carols. The Supreme Court ruling had little other affect, other than chilling any obvious practices that would tend to favor one religion over the others.

There were many other events and trends that also occurred in the early 1960s that contributed to a change in the moral climate: the Civil Rights Movement, the protest over the Vietnam War, the development of birth control pills, the popularity of rock & roll, and the recreational use of drugs. Any of these had a more significant impact on individual conduct than school prayer. This is not to minimize the impact of religion on the character of individuals. Because religious training is very important in the development of good citizens.

However, if the Supreme Court ruling on government led prayer in schools indeed had a part in our decline, it must not have been much of one. In fact, compared to the slow economic twisting in the wind, which has affected the vast majority of Americans, it was indeed small stuff. In an increasing number of families, the mother having to work to help support the family because the father could not make enough on his own anymore, had much greater affect on their children.

The Civil Rights movement led to the reexamination of much of what we had been taught in our society about race relations. The Vietnam war had taught us that our leaders would lie to us. Both movements legitimized protest as an acceptable means of redress. Drug and alcohol abuse filled a void that was left by the lack of meaningful work and a changing social order. There were other forces at work as well. However, there were three major areas where changes were occurring that played significant roles in the decline of traditional values. They were in education, in the workplace and in the community.

Changes in schools and in the educational system, although not necessarily the omission of teacher led school prayer, played significant roles. Children had previously been taught morals and values through the tools of rhyme and verse. Some of these rhymes and verses were beginning to sound dated to more modern 1960s ears, although the societal message was still very valid. Very important teachings of the past were often rejected, not because they no longer applied, but simply because of the way they sounded.

That "Children should be seen and not heard" sounded too Victorian and unfair to some parents and teachers led many to reject it. Many rejected it, yet the kernel of wisdom remained true. If it were rephrased as "Children should not run around and be noisy and interrupt adults when they are talking"– virtually everyone would agree with it. However, since the easy rhymes were ignored, many children without strict parental upbringing were denied rote access to the basics of moral and societal behavior. They missed out on being drilled on the easily remembered rhymes that previously had taught proper behavior.[30]

Civics, the study of how the government works and how laws are made, became no longer even a required course of study during this period. In the beginning of civilization the rules of behavior were obvious to even the small children, who could easily copy that behavior. Things are much more complicated today. Children still need to be taught the mechanics of getting along in our ever more complex society.

Many entry level jobs where our teenagers traditionally learned the basics of free enterprise no longer exist. Lawn service companies have mostly taken over the summer grass mowing jobs. Parents no longer allow their teenage daughters to baby-sit the way they used to. The small neighborhood merchants which in the past could have been counted on for part time employment are often no longer even in business. Instead of there being apprenticeships, teens can only find work in fast food restaurants.

Children, today, receive little education of what normal interaction in society should be. There are fewer role models in their communities. There is very little opportunity for our young people to get valuable life experiences before college. Many college students now graduate with so much debt they cannot possibly do public service work in their communities. They immediately must seek work in what often can be the disassociated, non-real world environment of big business.

In the adult workplace, rapid changes were occurring. New and more complex production techniques have left many factory and office workers disconnected from the purpose of their work. In earlier times, farmers planted the seed and followed the production though harvest. The farmers experienced the rewards for hard work and could literally see the fruits of their labors. The farmer and the other workers of that age had a goal that could readily be kept in sight from the beginning to the end of the process.

Starting in the 1950s, with circuit boards and modular components, workers began to perform tasks which were essential-but repetitive, boring, and seemed unrelated to a finished product. People began to feel less attached to their jobs and to their workplace. This feeling was often carried over into the community. The net result was a general decline in job satisfaction and an increased desire to obtain satisfaction in alternative, less productive ways..

Meaningful work is very important to our self-esteem and to our feeling of place in society. People will undertake boring, repetitive work for the good of the team. They will put off reward to accomplish a greater good. However, there is little job satisfaction in the workplace of today. Money and greed, which are now being hailed as the replacement for meaningful work, cannot replace a sense of accomplishment.

We need only to watch TV or read a newspaper to confirm our suspicions of a change in the moral climate. Perhaps those events are just being increasingly reported, but there are signs all around us of a breakdown in our society. Many civilizations have preceded us in decline. However, by learning from them and from their and our mistakes, we have a unique opportunity to change the course of our own history. Our founding fathers, the original patriots, also took full advantage of the same opportunity. They had a clear vision of what was needed to insure a free society. We need to again study them and redirect our efforts to accomplish their noble goals.

Up until the last fifty years, the biographies of the signers of the Declaration of Independence were taught in every classroom. Children could read about them and emulate the paths they took to make a difference to our history. Today, politicians are not seen as role models, they are instead looked down upon.

Today, we don't even require courses in civics. There is no such thing as a citizen legislature, anymore. We need to again look at what the original patriots envisioned, and let their vision again serve as the guide for our future. The principles they set forth are as true today as they were at the founding of our great county. We can insure the future growth and the very survival of our county and our civilization by rediscovering what is really important to us as a people, and as Americans.

The Role of Religion

Religion and moral values have an important role to play in a free society. If people are not restrained by their allegiance to higher moral values from taking advantage of others, then there can be no truly free society. People cannot live together in an orderly society when their sole objective is to look out for themselves and their own selfish interest. We must truly care about one another and look out for the interest of society as a whole for it to exist as a fully functioning unit.

Before the birth of Christ, Rome controlled much of the known world. There were many reasons for the rise of Rome as a great civilization and for the Roman civilization to dominate all of the others. However, a primary reason was that Roman law provided a sound basis for the growth of higher civilization, a fundamental fairness that all could relate to. Rome relied on self-enforcing laws. As a prime example, the Roman army issued one loaf of bread a day for every two soldiers. In the Roman system, the first thing that was required was for one solder to cut the loaf in two and the other soldier to chose which half he wanted. The early Roman law, quite simply, enforced itself, and that fairness provided the foundation for the growth of civilization.

There is no doubt that Christianity was responsible for saving knowledge, learning, and even civilization, itself, in the dark days following the decline of the Roman Empire. As bad as the Roman Empire had become, at least, it had provided order. The sudden collapse of the Roman civilization and the authoritarian rule which had developed from it would have led to a total anarchy without the message of Jesus Christ. The rise of Christianity was surprisingly fast, but understandably so because it was so desperately needed to fill the gap left by the collapse of Roman rule. Theologian, Helmut Koester said that "One reason that Christianity succeeded, and quickly, was its alternative model for a functioning community. Very early, there's the obligation to care for the poor, for the sick. Love is nothing sentimental, it is a very practical thing– lending a helping hand, building peaceful circles. This was attractive to a great number of people." [31]

Christ's teachings took the place of Roman law. It was that simple. With the fall of the Roman Empire, there was no longer a Roman garrison stationed on every corner to insure law and order. Selfish and anti-social behaviors were unrestrained by outside forces. The teachings of Jesus replaced those external policemen with internalized ones. Those who had accepted Jesus Christ as their lord and savior had the blueprint for orderly society, the message of Jesus Christ, dwelling within them. This is why they very early became known as "Christians," or "Little Christs," because they behaved as he would have behaved.

Early Christians were able to police themselves and their community by policing their own behaviors. This unswerving faith, their good-behavior, and their self-control even inspired the behavior of those around them. As opposed to the many volumes of very specific laws of the Pharisees, which Jesus himself often ridiculed, they had only to ask themselves "What would Jesus want of me?" The correct solution does not require volumes of laws, when one already had the answer to every question within themselves. True Christians need only ask themselves "What would Jesus do?" when confronted with each new challenge.

The founding fathers understood this and wanted Spiritual Freedom for all of our citizens. They were mostly of Christian backgrounds and very much in favor of religion and of encouraging moral growth in our society. Understandably, with the history of religious persecution in Europe, they just did not want to encourage any one particular religion.

The founding fathers did, however, wish to encourage the growth of high moral character in our citizens. Moral law was very important to the development of our secular law. The Ten Commandments are just as much the basis of our economic relationships in the free enterprise system as they are of our religion. Coveting, stealing, lying, and murder are just as much violations of our economic law as they are of our moral law.[32]

Morals are important to success in any field. In fact, one who does not quickly establish a reputation for honesty and truthfulness rarely succeeds in business, religion or politics. Those that would take advantage of others may appear to win in the short run, but they will ultimately lose. The charade may be maintained for a short while, but the truth will eventually be revealed.

The same thing also applies to governments. No government can make greed, or stealing, or lying morally acceptable by passing a law that states differently. A vote in the Congress of the United States cannot make these things right any more than the moral law itself can be changed by a majority vote. Morality cannot be created, or changed, or legislated. Moral law is constant.

Moral law is at the very basis of the free-enterprise system. Observing the commandments against bearing false witness and against stealing are at the heart of every successful career. This is a question of morals, to be sure, but it is also a question of economics. In our free enterprise system it is good business as well as good morals to love one's neighbor as oneself. The enterprise that is conducted on the basis of serving others is much more likely to grow and prosper.[33] In fair elections, the politician who is honest and who genuinely cares about others is more likely to be the one who is elected.

In the history of civilization, there have been politicians who have used him, and wars have been fought in his name. However, today, a new group of religious opportunists have twisted the words of Jesus, turning the words of a man who talked of truthfulness and honesty and of helping the poor, into talk of hate and greed. The Reverend F. Forrester Church said "Today, Jesus' name is used to divide us, to make us intolerant, bigoted, hateful...Jesus is being betrayed by the people who claim to believe in him."[34]

Today, many are shocked to find their churches are unwittingly supporting and funding arson, intimidation and murder with their contributions to some of the "Pro-life" and other organizations. Some extremely right wing religious groups, such as the Veil of Christ, are using Christianity to justify their Aryian and Anti-semetic views. The Christian Coalition routinely spreads misinformation about the political positions of candidates whom they oppose. Just because these activities hide behind a higher moral purpose, it does not make them right. Today, too many are using religion as a vehicle to take unfair advantage of others.

Religious Opportunists

Some have gone too far in pursuing their religious versions of the free enterprise system. They may have turned their religion into a worship of money and of the golden calf. Pat Robertson labels his critics as "those who are against free enterprise and moral values." Is that because he is hiding his method of doing business behind religious freedom and the free enterprise system? Is it now considered religious to use one's ministry to enrich oneself?

Pat Robertson has made millions from the labor of religious supporters who have become involved in his many entrepreneurial ventures. Has Pat Robertson taken advantage of his followers? Perhaps, but while those same entrepreneurial ventures may be perfectly legal, are they morally correct? He has certainly taken advantage of the tax exemptions afforded to religion in separation of church and state, and has used both his ministry and his political arm, the Christian Coalition in his continuing attempts to control that state.

The basic appeal of KaloVita, Pat Robertson's multi-level marketing arm that sells everything from discount coupon books to vitamins, of Amway, and all the other religions of greed is they give one a sense of belonging, a sense of being a part of something larger than themselves. Although Amway may appear to be part of the free enterprise system, it may not be. Amway conventions are described as a cross between patriotic rally, tent revival, and the assembly of a cult. Is it not a religion? That Amway is not free enterprise is of concern, but who runs it?, and what do they want? is a much greater concern.

For the 1994 election, Amway made a 2.5 million dollar soft money contribution to the Republican National Committee. This was the largest single political contribution ever made. The billionaire owners of Amway also gave hundreds of thousands to Newt Gingrich through his GOPAC.[35] What gives? Both Pat Robertson and the owners of Amway are in that elite 1 percent of American wealth. Amway is a multi-level organization that has been promoted and marketed on the same lord, sublord, pecking order hierarchy that gives many Neo-Conservatives great comfort. Is it their ultimate goal to change American from democracy to empire, ruled by the elites?

Amway has made huge investments in the Republican party. What was their ultimate goal? Was it to control you, and your government for their own purposes? Do they promise a better life and, yet, urge individuals to ignore their critics? Do they ask individuals to work for little monetary reward? Like little Moonies selling roses for no pay, is it the unpaid labor of many individuals that has made the owners of Amway into rich men?

The religious theme, multi-level marketing schemes, at the very least, do better when times are hard for most Americans. They can only benefit from an economy where many individuals are looking for second incomes. They use religious motivation to urge people to work hard and to delay gratification. They feed upon, so are they also working to increase, the number of people who are desperate for work? For their own profits, do they wish to provide a "home" for those individuals isolated from the rest of society or for those who feel the need to belong?

The multi-level marketers would actually benefit from America being a two class society. Very few individuals actually advance to the top or even beyond the lowest rung in their organizations. However, promoters of multi-level marketing schemes keep holding up those who have made it as a goal for their recruits. The promoters appear to be looking for those persons who are motivated by fear of poverty or who are desperate to improve their lot in life. They are also after those trusting individuals who will work for an extended period of time on promises, but with no pay. The promoters cannot help but make money, because they have so many salespeople working for free in the present tense, and who are only looking to the future for their reward.

Selling the future to individuals, selling them on hope of a gain in the future, is very much like the business of selling them the hereafter. Some television preachers are in many ways like the rest of the television hucksters– they all seem to be pushing products. Defrocked evangelist Jim Bakker did not get into legal trouble for taking the people's money for an undelivered place in the hereafter, it was for taking money for undelivered time-shares in the world of today.

Most of us, in fact, are poor at sales. Once a multi-level marketing recruit sells to his or her family and friends, often it is hard for them to make any additional sales. This is when they very often will give up. Already a multimillionaire, one of the big Amway distributors invented a new twist. Since people often blame themselves for not being able to reach sales goals, he figured these people need inspiration, the kind of inspiration that comes from religious fervor. He saw an opportunity to sell training and motivational tapes. Today, he is one of the world's largest distributors of motivational tapes, earning as much from this "sideline" as he does from his Amway involvement.

For the 1994 election, his Amway organization went all out. One Republican candidate, an Amway distributor who had claimed that God had appeared, personally... to offer political advice– received hundreds of thousands of dollars from this Amway organization. These contributions were mainly in the form of one-thousand dollar checks, the maximum contribution that the law allows. They were in the names of the shipping clerks, secretaries, and loading-dock employees of many Amway distributors from all over the country.

Amway took some risky chances in order to win control of the Congress. A discharged employee revealed the distributors involved received credit on that companies books for these contributions, in illegal repayment for providing the money to their employees to make these contributions. FEC reports show one of the Amway corporations provided media and production time and many thousands of dollars worth of product, to this particular candidate. Corporate contributions, even of the non-monetary variety are also clearly illegal. The end result is that this candidate, now a Member of Congress, moved to Washington and into an Amway provided apartment.

Certainly, the twin appeals of God and Country have been very effective in recruiting souls in the service of Amway. However, why would Amway spend millions, and risk hefty FEC fines to elect a majority to Congress, when Amway would appear to gain little, other than PR, from controlling the way laws are written? The answer could be that there is much more to gain from just controlling how the economy operates. When times are tough for average working families, and even for doctors, do those targeted groups more easily fall for the empty promises of multi-level marketing?

Television Evangelist Pat Robertson, personally, has made millions both from the television ministry and by promoting the multi-level marketing schemes which were devised to make money from the labors of his followers.[36] When Jesus said that a rich man has as much chance of getting into heaven as a camel through the eye of a needle. He did not also instruct them to "Try and beat the odds." Jesus drove the money changers from the Temple. He did not then return to take their place. If our religious leaders cannot remain morally correct, we as a nation cannot be expected to either. If the moral laws fails, then the civilization will too. We need more and better examples of behavior for our children and young people to model themselves after, not less and poorer.

Pat Robertson's Christian Coalition has done many things in the name of Christ, more than a few of them designed to appeal to political constituencies. The Christian Coalition has weighing in against public support of the arts, because they do not approve of a small portion of it. Support for the arts is, itself, but a tiny portion of the federal budget. But why, other than to please a constituency, boycott Art? Art adds beauty and meaning to life and need not justify its existence.

We all need beauty in our lives. We are happier, and we work harder. It is good business as well as good for the human spirit to have the arts. Spiritual freedom is important, after all, churches have sermons *and* singing. Deposed evangelical leaders Jim and Tammy Bakker for all of their other faults, at least understood that. However, some in politics want to use religion as a tool to control the masses. They want to control what the people see, how they feel, and what they think. Unfortunately for America, there are also some in the religious community who are equally willing for this to happen.

In America, we go out of our way to protect spiritual freedom. We wish to preserve individual liberty and individual expression. We realize that our religion is based on faith, and politics should be based on fact. We understand the difference. Only a few religious fundamentalist societies in the world of today will try to stifle behavior they do not like, or to make use of religion for political ends.

Americans know that we cannot use the federal laws to regulate morality. No one wants the federal government meddling in their personal business, or especially in their most intimate personal decisions. Education and reason are the keys to changing unwanted behavior. If persons are aware and know the consequences of certain behaviors, they will avoid them. Taboo and superstition are not the best ways to regulate behavior, education is. However, there are always some who would control us in any way that they can.

6. Conservatism

Conservatism, as discussed here, is the ideology of maintaining the status quo. In theory, it favors stability and keeping things as they are. The concept of cultural stability certainly sounds attractive, especially in troubled times. However, the truth is that civilizations may only advance or decline. They cannot simply stay the same.

The rise of conservatism is precisely the mechanism which leads to the decline of civilization. A conservative element in society, however, is a good thing. It is too much conservatism that is harmful to a civilization, just as can be too much of anything. It becomes attractive, to some, to stop the forward progress of society, just because it appears safer to do nothing.

Logically, it always appears much safer to stay the same, than to change. To change is to take a chance. However, if roadblocks to forward progress are erected, societal momentum will be slowed, and eventually all progress will stop. By their very dynamic nature, civilizations cannot simply stand still. They must change when the conditions change, or they will die.

Historically, the rise of conservatism has reversed the forward progress of civilizations and started their decline by three methods. Conservative elites have tied the masses to the land by reducing mobility. They have reduced the opportunity for educational and social advancement. Finally, they insure that all mental activity expended is used to provide subsistence. Rising conservatism makes it harder for people to advance their standard of living, and in some cases, even to make a living.

Past conservative administrations and now, conservatives in the Congress say they are seeking to balance the budget, but by precisely the methods above. We should be wary of any programs that will create or encourage the above conditions. Are they trying to remove the basic public amenities that every other industrialized democracy enjoys? Is this done to insure America's poor and middle classes will not gain on the conservative elites? Could they be seeking to end programs which ensure equality because they do not believe that worth of the individual is a fundamental Constitutional concept?

By removing subsidies for public transportation, many municipalities must subsidize it themselves, or sharply reduce, or even end it. The buses, subways and trains many would use to travel to jobs outside their own neighborhood might not then be able to operate. The poor would then be stuck in subsistence employment locally or just be out of work. There is no other reason to discourage the fuel efficient and ecologically sound mode of travel that is mass transit.

Every other western civilization shows its recognition of education as a national priority. It is important to teach our children skills and to give them the tools necessary to compete in an increasingly international economy. The 104th Congress sought not only to kill the U.S. Department of Education but also federal support for education. The cost for education must either be shifted back to the individual states, raising taxes there, or be reduced to a level which can be easily afforded. The result is the denial of a good education and a bright future to many of America's children. Educational standards will vary dramatically from state to state according to the conditions of the local economies. Some states can afford to give children a good education, while others may not be able to. Those who do not get an education in today's highly technological environment will anchor a new American underclass.

Creating a nation of the very rich and of the very poor is not the goal of most Americans. Yet, we have been made aware of the possibility. "A new study says the U.S. has the largest gap between rich and poor of any major industrial country" was the headline of a Time article dated November 6, 1995.[37] A week before, in an article "A Tilt Toward the Rich?" in the October 30, 1995 issue of Time, the debate was "whether the Republican budget cuts will needlessly hurt the poor and the working class and thereby deepen divisions in an already polarized economy." Clinton chief economic policy adviser, Laura Tyson was quoted in this article that "These proposals are going to exacerbate the major problems affecting the country right now- the stagnation and decline in the earnings ability for at least 40% of the population."[38]

There is little hope in a conservative Congress of increasing the minimum wage for working people. People in the middle and lower economic strata are having to work harder and longer to make ends meet. Meanwhile, profits for the rich, the rewards of capital are increasing at record levels.[39] The conservative Congress is working to remove support for the arts and for public parks, both for ideological reasons and to provide tax cuts for the rich. They are attempting to remove the social infrastructure that provides relaxation and recreation and gives enjoyment to many who cannot easily afford it otherwise. As in a feudal system, there will be nothing to distract the people from working for a subsistence living.

By removing support for the arts, they not only remove enjoyment, but destroy our artistic and cultural heritage and prevent our children from ever learning about it. Removing public support for the arts will insure working people are not distracted, but will also isolate those people from anything other than what the elite want them to see or hear. It further prevents the emergence of artists and art forms that are not patronized or sanctioned by the elite. Even with great talent, the poor will be prevented from advancing, unless their art is approved by the elites.

Conservatives in the Congress have voted in favor of clear-cutting national forests, selling the rights to drill for oil in protected wildlife sanctuaries and to privatize public parks. As a nation, we have a lot invested in our system of public parks. They provide recreational and educational benefit to all of our children and to their families. To waste this investment, or to sell it to private industry would do irreparable harm to our American way of life. We need to continue to preserve our system of public parks for our children and for their children. Our parks system is one thing left to us by the foresight of an earlier generation. We must be sure to leave it to our children in the same condition in which we received it.

Our long history of support for public parks is only a small portion of the freedom of the spirit we all should enjoy under the Constitutional concept of spiritual freedom. Because native Americans believe there is a spirit present, that our environment has religious significance, it may be further protected against the conservative assault on it, by the Constitution's guarantee of religious freedom.

Conservatives say they wish to preserve order in society. Many, however, favor "preserving order" through the use of force. The idea of a strong man government has an increasingly popular appeal among conservatives. President Clinton, a conciliator, has been depicted as weak in the conservative press since the day of his election. Conservatives like Jesse Helms even feel free to physically threaten the president.[40] A portion of the electorate in voting for Ross Perot was, in fact, turning to strong men for leadership. There is a tendency to look to the powerful for protection in uncertain times. However, it is, by far, better to get individuals to cooperate as a working society by convincing them it is in their own best interest to do so.

As is used today, even the name "Conservative" has become a misnomer. Many new style conservatives do not want to conserve what we have now, but would change it to something else. They even call themselves revolutionaries. That there could be a conservative "Revolution" is an oxymoron. Instead of conserving what we now have, these individuals would seek a return to the dark ages where the majority were serfs and peasants living and working on land owned by a privileged minority. These revolutionaries are not merely conservative, but instead appear to be almost anti-democratic in their goals. These individuals are not Conservatives, they are something different.

Conservatives claim to favor poor people making it on their own, working for what they get, with no government handouts. Conservative think tanks have found that the term "Personal Responsibility" polls well with Americans as a conservative substitute for the Constitutional concept of worth of the individual. Truly, personal responsibility is a part of the worth of the individual, yet, it is not the whole plot and parcel that conservatives make it out to be. We do not only have a personal responsibility, but we also have a responsibility to the others as well. Society does not function to place blame nor for the strong to take advantage of the weak. Society functions because of our mutual self-interest in it doing so.

In America we've always before tried to keep people from slipping into a permanent poverty using federal programs for education and nutrition. It is only lately there has been increasing pressure to end these programs, to end the federal "give-away's." In practice, these conservative remedies work against the middle class and prevent the poor from making it on their own. While opposing government aid to anyone else, the conservatives support government policies allowing the rich to become richer and the concentration of power into fewer and fewer hands. This is in direct opposition to the Constitutional concept of decentralization of power.

Traditionally, special interests must ask the Congress for special favors. That the wealthy do not even ask that they be granted special tax breaks and government largess simply shows the new agenda to be, indeed, "something else." Government, under this new conservatism simply means cutting those "give-away's" to the poor and instead giving them to the already wealthy.

Every Conservative initiative: The 1981 Reagan "Trickle-down" tax cut, the 1984 Gramm-Rutman debt reduction plan, the 1985 Social Security Deal, the 1990 "Read-My-Lips" and the 1995 Conservative Balanced Budget Plans– all have painted rosy scenarios of increased economic growth to justify tax cuts, yet only the rich have ultimately benefitted. Even as far back as the conservative inspired Nixon inflation controls, each change, ultimately, benefitted only the already wealthy. This is little more than a "give-away" of the country to the rich. This is little more than a resurgence of Social Darwinism. Conservative ideologues have quit hiding it, and now espouse that such "give-aways" to the rich are actually a good thing.[41]

Neo-Conservatism

The Neo-Conservatives, or *Social Darwinists*, say they are "conservative," when they are not. Social Darwinism seeks only to advance an elite. That Social Darwinism advances an American conservative elite, or in the case of the former USSR, a communist elite, it does not matter. Old style conservatism was considered to be relatively benign. Rich right-wing old men recruited and backed candidates such as Barry Goldwater. They were merely seeking to prevent change, to maintain the status quo. Today, the neo-conservative politicians are *actively* trying to roll back progress, rather than merely keeping things as they are. It is *they* who are recruiting wealthy backers by offering them legislation and tax breaks in return for cash. In doing so, they crossed the line from maintaining the status quo, as conservatives traditionally do, to becoming something else.

When the Speaker of the House is offered a $4.5 million dollar bribe, out in the open, and nothing gets done about it, the sovereignty of our nation is in serious trouble.[42] When Billionaire Rupert Murdoch gets a two hundred million dollar tax break and billions more in regulatory relief, and no one else gets anything, our laws have been fundamentally changed to favor an elite over ordinary Americans. Corporate lobbyists and financial entrepreneurs now appear to be our unelected representatives in this *Market Democracy*.

The only plank of the 1994 Republican Contract with America to pass both houses of Congress and be signed into law was that to limit "unfunded federal mandates." Unfunded federal mandates are laws which are passed by the federal government, but which must be paid for by someone else, either by state and local governments, or by consumers. The first test of this law was when the milk producers lobby sought a law requiring that all milk sold in this country be fortified with powdered milk. This law would add 40 cents per gallon to the cost of milk for consumers. However, offsetting the cost to consumers, the milk lobby was willing to contribute handsomely to the Republican leadership.

The much vaunted unfunded federal mandate law proved to be toothless– as it was revealed to provide no penalty for the unfunded mandates. The "consumer protection" of the unfunded mandate law was satisfied by just their acknowledgment that these mandates were to be unfunded. However, cutting school lunch programs and raising the price of milk illustrates the real priorities of the Neo-Conservatives.

American government, and it's institutions are now for sale to the highest bidder. Rather than being truly conservative, rather than maintaining the status quo and trying to prevent change, the Congress will now entertain all offers. The Neo-Conservative agenda is truly different in it's lust for "Free-Market" reforms. Any narrow interest, with enough money, can now buy whatever changes they desire in our nations laws.

Traditional Republican conservatism went on the assumption that what is good for GM is good for America. General Motors (GM) was a euphemism for Corporate America. This is no longer the case. General Motors (GM) is still the largest American corporation, but no longer the symbol of American industrial might. Today's conservatism serves a similar role, but instead promotes the interests only of the elite. It assumes what is good for the elite is what should be set as policy. We would now be controlled by a conservative elite, not unlike the communist elite of the former Soviet Union. They, too, would tell us how to think and what to believe in and are more than willing to sacrifice the interests of the individual for the corporate good. Their goals are similar, as we have simply been sold-out to different masters.

The Neo-Conservative revolutionaries are advocating positions that history has shown to be helpful only to an elite. If we want to maintain a middle class, to maintain equal opportunity on economic matters and a level playing field for commerce, we, as citizens had better act. Too many are confused by the divisive social arguments and ignore the economic basis of strong man rule, that is *Social Darwinism*.

Neo-Conservatives have been greatly helped in their quest for political popularity by the word "Conservative" being confused in the public mind with conservative, as in, "the conservative and careful management of money." Putting the country in an ever larger and larger debt is not what most would call fiscal conservatism. The debt does, however, serve as a lever to reduce social spending and reverse gains that the Democrats have made in elevating the working class.

Many wealthy conservatives have benefited first from the subsidies and tax relief that created the debt, and then from holding the debt as a safe and sure investment. The stated goals of the Federal Reserve in raising interest rates and in pursuing slower growth has always been to prevent inflation, to preserve existing wealth. Many individuals think that the Federal Reserve is another government agency and therefore also looking out for their interests. That is not always true. The only provable result of an increase in the federal debt, in higher interest rates, and a slowing of growth in the economy has been to promote Social Darwinism and to help the already wealthy become more so.

The term "Conservative" has grown as a self-identification. In many places it has snob appeal. Many of the new conservatives conveniently forget the government programs which allowed them an education or kept their families afloat during the great depression, or insures their mortgage, or which helps grandma live independently. They want to climb the ladder to the top and pull it up behind them so no one else can follow. They have lost their connectedness with the rest of society. In a free country, we are free to live in walled neighborhoods and isolate ourselves from the poor. However, according to the unwritten agreements that first forged our society, stability requires interaction among all of its citizens.

These new conservatives (and those who think of themselves as conservative), may be closer to getting what they think they want, than they think. America may yet be on the brink of a rapid breakdown of our traditional democracy and the rise of a two class system. Events unravel fast in the world today. This is well illustrated by the brief amount of time that it took for communism to fall in Russia and Eastern Europe.

Conservatism, at one time, had gained credence by becoming confused in the minds of many with the highly regarded recycling and conservation movement. The vast majority of Americans believe in conservation and in being good stewards of our natural resources. They overwhelmingly believe in the concept of environmental protection. Neo-Conservatives differ from old style Conservatives in the fact that they now want the government to reimburse them for NOT polluting our common environment or to pay them "takings" for not polluting their own. Otherwise they do not even pretend to care for the environment we all must share and live in.

In the 104th Congress, a major pork producer was given the oversight of regulations concerning the environment. His home state of North Carolina lost more that one million acres of protected wetlands in his first year in office. In his home state, more hog waste is being generated each year than human waste. Although of almost exactly the same composition, only human waste must first be treated before being discharged into the environment. In 1995, when a twenty-five million gallon hog waste lagoon ruptured and ruined the shellfish and fishing industries along much of the North Carolina coast, his associates were not responsible for the resulting damage, either.[43]

The fact is, Neo-Conservatives want the government to pay pork producers *not* to build hog waste lagoons in sensitive wetland areas. These wealthy Neo-Conservatives can be easily spotted because they, unlike true Conservatives, want it both ways. They want the government to stay out of their business, unless the government can offer a subsidy or tax break, or be of benefit to them alone.

That a new conservatism appears to be growing in the former Soviet Union shows the Neo-Conservative trend to be universal. Change, even positive change, scares many people. They even bring up all the same old conservative arguments to try to stop it. They also wish to reverse the normal progress that society must make, and will go to any extremes. These people are not just being conservative, they are instead something else.

Many in Russia want their old communist government back. They know that the former communist strong men were tyrants, but as the argument goes, "at least the people knew where they stood." Some of the Russian people are so fearful of change, that they would happily give up their newly found freedom for the stability of a strong man form of government. Fear and insecurity combined with the lack of self-confidence or self-esteem only promotes Social Darwinism. Fearful people more easily give up their freedoms in exchange for security.

The arrogant fat cats, the Rush Limbaughs and the Jerry Falwells in America have justified to themselves that any lie or half truth is acceptable in the furtherance of their agendas. They survive on the insecurities of the public. They deal in creating a crisis of confidence with those who lack the ablility to see things for themselves. They have attempted to link the leadership of the country, our president, and even the president's wife to any number of serious crimes, including murder.[44]

Marxist philosophy also advocated dishonesty, and boasted of its cunning and used untruthfulness as an instrument of policy to gain its ends. The Soviet Union is gone now, and what used to be a rich and diverse political discussion in America has been silenced. There was actually legislation introduced in the conservative Congress that would impede the citizen redress of grievances before the Congress. It was fine for them to say "government is bad, elect us." But when it is *they* who are in power, they would stifle any opposition. The citizens are allowed to blame the stoplights, but not the parties who would run them.

Divided Americans

In the free-enterprise system, economic power cannot easily be separated from political power. Each ultimately depends on the other. We, as Americas, are all in this together and we had better soon wake-up to that fact. Just as there can be no mistaking a blow to the head– seeing stars and ringing in the ears is a dead giveaway. American society has been hit across the forehead with the "Big Ol'Stick" of government shutdowns and a wide division between our political parties. We have experienced a figurative wooden "2x4" wake-up call.

It is true that our eyes will only interpret the blow as flashing light or "Stars." Our ears can only interpret a blow to them as sound. The shining of a light into an ear will go undetected, as do sounds directed to an eye. As with our bodies, however, society needs the individual senses working together to interpret a true picture of our situation. We do not, however, need anyone else to tell us that something is seriously wrong in Washington.

Because we live in a free-enterprise system, we are used to the appeals made by marketers interested in selling us a product, good, or service. As we base our system on the profit motive, we know there are those who would take advantage of us. We are all aware that there are individuals who are solely interested in the separation of us from our money. We are even somewhat used to being lied to by those with non-mainstream agendas trying to convince us that it also is in our best interest to be supportive of their interests.

Some schemes to defraud us, financially, are quite clear to the average American. Others are much harder to detect as frauds. Therefore, in America there exist a network of federal, state, and local consumer protection agencies. However, there is nowhere near that same network in place to prevent us from being separated from our political power. Even the Federal Communication Commission rules regarding fairness and equal time for opposing viewpoints have been overturned. We are truly on our own in detecting the lie, or in identifying the truth, in political matters.

There is a limit to what each sense, or each individual American, may discover on its own. Each sense may only detect what it is capable of detecting or perceive what it is designed to perceive. Eyes only see, and ears can only hear. The citizens, therefore, must communicate with one another. Each sense is important, as is each American, however, only when working together, can the story of the whole become clear.

As individuals, we see things only through the grid of our own individual experiences. We see things the way that we expect them to be. As in the story of the blind men describing an elephant, each describes it according to the part of the animal that he is holding. Each can only report what they are able to and, that, only in relation to what they have experience in the past. In the discussion of elephants, it is the whole that is important.

In some quarters, individuals are even criticized for studying and interpreting the Bible for themselves. They say that we should already "KNOW" what the Bible says. However, when we read it, as if for the first time, ignoring that which we may have been taught to expect, many may see it in a whole new light. It is still the same Bible, and remains the best guide for living, because human behavior, itself, has not changed over thousands of years. We must study our Bible as well as study our history, because that history will often repeat itself.

It is far better to learn from the mistakes of others, than to be doomed to repeat them ourselves. We must study the much larger picture of our total history to avoid making the same errors again and again. The Bible is still the Bible. It is not diminished in any way by being studied in historical terms, nor can it be diminished by study in ways that may yield new insights into its teachings.

Very often as individuals, when we take the time to change our own viewpoints, we can see things from the viewpoint of others. That we all benefit from a more complete understanding is why we must treasure the diversity in America. Diversity of social and educational backgrounds insures that no detail will be missed or overlooked. Someone will have the view, or the education that would detect the sham or the lie.

In American society, all individuals are important, everyone has an input, and all viewpoints should be represented. Within the democracy of America, within debate and freedom of speech, the correct assessment of our situation will always be presented. Focus groups held on topics such as Affirmative Action give further insight into this phenomenon. At the start of the discussion, the debate is polarized at the extremes. The white participants say that they resent less qualified black applicants receiving preference over more qualified white applicants. The black participants resent the prior existence of discrimination that prevented qualified black people from even being considered.

At the end of the discussions there is broad agreement between everyone that their sole interest is in selecting the most qualified individual. Both groups are united in showing their dislike of societal preference. They each focus on the qualifications of the prospective applicants. By the finish, they each point to slow economic growth and to the lack of good jobs as the ultimate reasons for their being pitted against one another.[45]

The same thing occurs when the different generations are brought together to discuss Medicare reform. What starts out as an apparent deep division soon finds compromise and common ground. There are further examples from American politics, many of them directly applying today. By using a larger sample size when taking a poll, the results become much more accurate. As in conducting opinion polls, when the size of the sample becomes greater so does the accuracy of the representation of what a majority are thinking.

In 1948, the New York Times conducted a telephone poll that had Dewey beating Truman by a wide margin. However, what the pollsters forgot to account for in designing their poll was many Truman supporters did not have telephones. Therefore, their conclusions ended up being highly inaccurate. As it is with free and fair elections, the more and different viewpoints that can be represented, from more individuals, the more democratic and representative the results will be.

The dynamic tension between differing or even opposing viewpoints is the basis of our form of democracy. We work out our differences. When everyone participates in making the decision, a useful solution is usually arrived at. The solution reached by any group may not be perfect, but it will be close enough for that solution, to work for that group. Everyone having the opportunity for input makes the decision making process in democracy somewhat messy, but one that works.

The wishes of a majority must always be honored. Liberals fear conservatives, and conservatives distrust liberals. However, together the debate makes ours a great country. I would rather work to get enough people to say "Yeah, I agree with that." than to put an outright ban on even the partial and the half truths that are so much a part of politics today. When the people are told the whole truth, and have the information needed to make a decision, they will make the correct choice. Our democratic system works.

Social Darwinism would end even the pretense of democracy, in favor of a "Strong-Man" form of government. The Social Darwinists hold in common this wish to see the rise of an elite, although they exist in all income and social strata. In America, the Social Darwinists hold in common the belief that those who *already* have made it, are the only ones who actually deserve to make it. By using wedge issues to peal off the 51% of the electorate that is needed for victory, they have divided us on many issues.

Social Darwinism has attempted to divide our civilization along religious, racial, sexual, and economic lines. Indeed, scapegoating and the setting of blame were the tools that carved out a new Republican majority. Many Congressional candidates were elected because they, and the extended political machine of their party, scapegoated Jews, Blacks, Gays, Welfare mothers, and others for the problems of our country.[46]

The voters know they cannot individually observe each sell-out by an elected official. It is each of these, when taken together, which ultimately caused all of the financial problems for the country. However, they know what they do see. Those who scapegoat others for living off of the public treasury, are the very ones who benefitted the most from it's plunder. If we allow some to divide us for their own monetary and political gain, then we will most assuredly fall as a nation.

Darwinist theory, or "the survival of the fittest," predicts that the best will advance to the top by a "natural selection." Social Darwinist, feel justified in lying and cheating to accomplish their goals, to get what they think they want. Their's is an assault on meritocracy, pretending to be for meritocracy. Individuals may no longer get ahead simply because they have worked hard and deserve to. The American dream is over for most, because the few have used our American democracy and its systems to favor themselves.

Affirmative action gets the blame for lack of opportunity when the lack of opportunity is due to the low growth, and economic policies that favor jobs leaving the country. Moral decline is the reason given for the breakup of American homes and for the pressures on the American family. However, the reasons for the decline of American families are increasingly economic pressures– where once one salary could support a family, it now takes two. Both parents must work outside the home, leaving their children, alone, to fall through the cracks.

In turning American against American, our togetherness, our bonds to one another, and to our society have become strained. Fear and paranoia have been fueled by the inflammatory rhetoric. Those already "on the edge" were reinforced in their seemingly outrageous beliefs by the very tone of the anti-government propaganda. Many became increasingly suspicious of each other and of their government. Many have armed themselves in protection.

In the months preceding the elections of 1994, as our divisions as Americans increased, the "militia" movement grew. The militia movement was made up of patriots who were energized both by all of the incendiary talk and by their own increasing feelings of anger and despair. The Patriot Militias were a homogeneous group, mostly working-class, white and male. Certainly, the older men remembered America as it was.

It was they who had the honor and the privilege of serving their country in an earlier time. It was they who were now the victims of much of the unwelcome change that is occurring in America today. It is they who must work harder and harder to support their families. They are the ones who first knew that something must be done about the situation that is developing in their America. They also knew that it would be up to them to do something about it.

The militia members are almost all alike in job, religious, social and educational backgrounds. They shared many similar life experiences and outlooks on life. Most approach problems and arrive at solutions from what their military service has taught them. They are accustomed to conformity and to following orders. Unfortunately, this lack of diversity of thought will tend to put the same slant on every story, be it rumor or truth.

The militia members typically filter all challenges and problems through the grid of their own experience. Much of the information that they had gotten, from a Neo-Conservative element, was based on half truth and slanted interpretation. The "truth" became more twisted and convoluted with each telling, yet an element of the true need for action was still there. The half-truths fed on themselves and became the bizarre conspiracy theories that were developed to make sense of that which is observable.

Worst of all, in such an homogeneous environment as is the all-white militia movement, Social Darwinism encourages the development of an "us against them" mentality. The situation them becomes ripe for a more "radical" element to take control of the agenda of the group. Racism very early surfaces as a focus of the fear and the anger of the group. Minorities become the scapegoats for the much larger problems of society and of the economy that are not at all as obvious to them.

The "White Supremeist" and "Neo-Nazi" elements rise to the forefront in such organizations. Their heated rhetoric moves the members to action, and to things which make the situation much worse for a stable society rather than more stable for society, which was the initial goal. The end results are more fear and insecurity, not just within the militia groups, but for the entire population.

The gun manufacturing lobby had a vested interest in the panic. Worried persons will buy guns and the truly afraid will stockpile weapons. Fear and paranoia is good for the gun business. Rumor and crisis are the tools by which they can continue to build their business. As a result of the money poured into it by manufacturing interests, the National Rifle Association is now in danger of becoming more of a spokesman for the gun and weapons industry than for sportsmen.

We do not live in the same America that we used to. Today, average Americans seldom feel any kinship with one another. Our bonds of brotherhood have been strained. America is becoming more radical at its extremes. The spreading fear on these extremes, with the right stimulus, may spread to and involve the rest of us. Unfortunately, the profit motive is stimulus enough for some to continue to encourage it's spread.

7. *The Influence of Money*

As some wish to encourage gun sales, because they profit from them. That some would use the political process for their own gain, is nothing new. Voters have always been promised various things in return for their votes. Politicians have taken money from wealthy citizens to do their bidding since time immemorial. Richard Nixon was not the only politician to ever sell us out for the money to finance a campaign. However, the root causes of our present economic situation did begin during that Nixon era.

Lyndon Johnson was the last president to submit a balanced budget. In 1967, President Johnson was able to fight the Vietnam War, fund Medicare and Medicaid, fight a war on poverty and still have a balanced budget. He was able to do so because he also pursued an economic policy that encouraged business investment, capital formation and economic growth. Lyndon Johnson was hated by Conservatives, and not solely because he lopsidedly defeated conservative Barry Goldwater in 1964 either. Johnson was hated because he worked hard to improve the lot of the common man.

Conservatives prize financial conservatism and the stability of capital over everything else. President Nixon went out of his way to provide the kind of financial conditions that conservative capital markets (and wealthy contributors) wanted to have. Slow growth and low inflation favors capital and old money. Economic growth and inflationary expectations favor working and younger people. Always before, our economy policy had sought to favor growth and the formation of new capital. Our society had always before favored a growth economy and, therefore, the creation of more pie for all to share.

Nixon sought to slow economic growth. He became the first president of the modern era to establish price controls to slow growth, supposedly to prevent inflation. This low growth policy was allowed to be instituted due to an inflation rate that would hardly be alarming to us today. True, first class postal rates had doubled from five cents to ten cents in the period of 1967 to 1973. This became a major scapegoat of the Nixon administration.

However, these rates were then under the control of the Cabinet and of the Congress. While postal cost, indeed, exploded, a general inflation in the economy was not the real reason. Costs were up, but for two other and very different reasons: special bulk rates had been given to preferred businesses and organizations and the general level of service had been greatly improved.

The franking [free mailing] privileges of Members of Congress has always extended only to the normal service of first class postage. At the beginning of the Nixon era, if they wished the faster air mail service, Congressmen had to buy and affix an airmail stamp. Members of Congress from the western states, mostly conservative, felt that they were, therefore, at a disadvantage in communicating with their constituents. An experimental Congressional airmail service was begun to win favor with the Congress. This new service provided what was to become, essentially, next-day service to Congressional mail. Congressional Airmail was collected on Capitol Hill, bypassing the postal facility, and sent directly to the airport.

However, the Member of Congress was charged the standard airmail rate for this service. As could be predicted, Congress soon wearied of paying, and passed a law requiring that all first class mail be delivered by the fastest available means, including airmail, if applicable. While not as fast as the Experimental Congressional Airmail service had been, service by airmail was now free under the traditional Congressional franking privilege.

The cost of airmail was now, however, also included in the price of all "first-class" postage. This change was appreciated by the airline and aircraft manufacturers lobby, and not only because it increased airline business and, therefore, aircraft orders. It also ended the railroad postal contracts, effectively halting subsidies of transcontinental and inter-city passenger rail. Amtrak was put in place to wind down the passenger rail operations of the railroads. This was to become the first step to a virtual monopoly of interstate passenger transportation by the aircraft industry.

The new law directly raised the costs associated with delivering the mail and, ultimately, the cost of postage for everyone. It provided subsidies to mostly conservative western interests and took money from the mostly democratic inter-city areas. More importantly, it provided yet another excuse the conservatives needed to argue for the control of inflation– prices were going up.

President Nixon made many major changes in the direction of our economic policy. Since Republicans were traditionally seen as being fiscally conservative, Nixon was allowed by the Congress to run a "temporary" budget deficit, as later was Reagan. In 1972, Nixon appointed George Schultz as his Secretary of the Treasury. Schultz, a respected Professor of Economics from the University of Chicago, was an economic ultra-conservative whose academic credentials were unimpeachable, as were his conservative ones.

For his role in establishing an economy where only the elites would benefit, he was later elevated to Secretary of State under Reagan. The reputation of Secretary Schultz was essential to the conservative take-over of the Federal Reserve Board. Under Schultz, the direction of monetary policy was reversed, and any remaining pro-growth policy was put away.

Richard Nixon was a very astute politician. He did many things that appeared to help one group, but which actually benefited another. His very conservative appointments to the Federal Reserve Board were supposedly to insure that the growth of the nation's monetary supply would not trigger inflationary expectations. This might not have been the primary reason.

Could Richard Nixon have knowingly set in motion a Federal Reserve policy that resulted in an economy where only the wealthy could benefit? Did Nixon even plan the rise of Social Darwinism? While this is interesting, it is not very likely. The likely motive for the Nixon economic policy was to aid, and perhaps to add to, the traditional Republican base: those who already had money, those who sought to keep things as they are, and the large corporations.

Just as the conventional wisdom held that only Republicans were fiscally responsible enough to tinker with monetary policy and be allowed to run budget deficits, the red-baiting Richard Nixon was the only politician that would be allowed to open up China. However, the ultimate question that is raised by this is, Why did Nixon go to China? What were the real reasons for his abrupt change of heart? Could Nixon have simply been doing a favor for those few wealthy industrialists who were seeking to open-up new sources of cheap labor? Could the true purpose have been to lower wages in this country by making our workers compete with lower paid workers elsewhere?

Most wealthy individuals did not ask for these changes, or for any of the other changes that mainly benefited them. Yet they still enjoyed the short-term financial benefit that Social Darwinism yields to some. Longer term, Social Darwinism hurts us all. Yet, we can always be sure the politicians will usually try to court those who could help them. Their logic is irrefutable and has a long history of common usage. When bank robber Willy Sutton was asked why he robbed banks? His reply, too, was "Because that's where the money is."

More than likely, from it's 1968 beginnings, the trend to a conservative government in the latter half of the twentieth century began innocently enough. The politicians did not start out thinking that they would be bribed. They did not visualize that they would be founding a *Market Democracy*. However, when things are going the way that you would like them to, it is hard, especially for politicians, to resist pushing for more.

Jeffrey Madrick, in his 1995 book *The End of Affluence: The Causes and Consequences of America's Economic Dilemma*, makes a good case that the slow economic growth of the 1973-1993 period was the primary reason for the difficulty that government and our other institutions are in today. In the 1870-1973 period, the growth rate of the American economy averaged 3.4 percent after inflation compared with 2.3 percent during the 1973-1993 period. While a difference of growth of only 1.1 percent does not sound like much, quoting economist Herbert Stein, "The difference between 2 percent and 3 percent is not 1 percent, it is 50 percent." We had in this era, in reality, a 50 percent reduction in the growth of our economy.[47]

According to Madrick, "...the impact of slow growth, like the compound interest in a savings account, accumulates rapidly over time, and eventually makes a huge difference. During the mid-1970s, the loss of a percent a year in the rate of growth was on average a relatively small $100 billion a year... By 1993, however, the damage had grown enormously. In that year alone the gap between what the U.S. economy might have produced had we grown since 1973 at about our historical rate and what we actually did produce amounted to $1.2 trillion after inflation... Over the twenty years since 1973 the accumulated losses in goods and services due to slow growth have come to nearly $12 trillion."[48]

This historically higher growth in the economy is what had allowed us to fund the social programs of the New Deal. Madrick goes on to say "..had we grown about 1 percent a year faster since 1973 than we did, which would still have left us slightly below our historical rate of 3.4 percent a year, all other things being equal we could have easily afforded the rising cost of government and reduced taxes as well."[49] The excessively conservative fiscal policy that Nixon pursued, was ultimately only of benefit to the politicians who benefitted when wealthy contributors benefitted.

The Nixon sell-out of the average American, his embrace of the slow growth policy played a big part in the loss of Ford to Carter in 1976. Reagan did not beat Carter in 1980, Federal Reserve chairman Paul Volker did. Ronald Reagan was right in suggesting that we could grow our way out of a recession. However, he was wrong to say that, "Trickle-down economics," was the key. Real growth, instead, works much better.

According to Madrick, "Time and again, we have been told by experts and politicians that we are back on track, especially when the Republicans were in power during the economic expansion of the 1980's. That temporary prosperity was fueled by an unparalleled growth in federal debt from about $1 trillion to more than $4 trillion. The underlying economy, in fact, remained weak during the Republican decade. Productivity grew at only 1 percent a year, and wages fell for many workers."[50]

As to "prevent" inflation, the Federal Reserve established a policy of raising interest rates at the first sign of job growth. A decline in the unemployment rate would soon envoke a rise in the interest rate to bring employment rates down again. Is it fair to take jobs away from working people to primarily benefit those with capital? Less jobs always means lower wages. However, the link between inflation and job growth only exists in theory. In the last 25 years the only time wages have put pressure on prices was during the Nixon administration, and that was under price controls.

Today, profitable corporations idle workers in the name of greater profits, but they are also less able to respond to changes in the market or to competition. These same corporations would then ask the Congress to change the tax laws to favor their individual enterprises, so that they can better compete. Many of the business interests who contribute to Members of Congress, only do so because they want tax subsidies in return.

This easy acceptance of a slow growth ideology also works against growth. Instead of working to make the pie larger, there is now intense competition to see who can get a larger share of the same pie. These industries count on their lobbyists, on government largess, or on government bail-outs rather than engaging in true competition and innovation. The cutting of job growth to increase profits, cuts all growth, which in the end, leads to further rounds of job cuts.

Reducing expenses does increase short-term profit, however too much reliance on job cuts also reduces the potential for increasing profits through growth. Jobs and expenses must be further cut, to recover these lost profits. If business does increase, opportunity is lost and profits suffer due to the lack of enough personnel to take full advantage of the situation and because of the expenses associated with retraining.

Jobs are lost, yet capital freed up by corporate tax subsidies and tax cuts is not used to build for future profits either. It is primarily wasted. As long as excessive corporate perks, such as skyboxes at sporting events, are fully deductible for federal income tax purposes, there can never be a level playing field or a balanced budget. As long as excessive executive salaries and stock options are just as tax deductible as research and development, plus do not require the employer matching of social security that the salaries of regular workers do, they will only get larger.

Big business lobbyists and their backers want a capital gains tax cut. Many voters have been told that one would be good for business, and they believe it. What a capital gains tax cut would do, is to further encourage speculation and profit taking. It would encourage those with money invested in stocks to sell them to realize their paper profits.

To reduce the tax on paper profits would only encourage volatility in, and perhaps a major sell-off of, the stock and bond markets. This could only hurt the small investors and those with their retirement funds invested in stocks. It would trigger falling stock prices. A capital gain tax cut could help only the sellers because their gains will be taxed at a lower rate. It would hurt the market and virtually everyone else.

Brokers earn their commissions from dividing up existing wealth rather than building new wealth. Speculators have turned inside investors against investors on the outside. The Social Darwinist movement succeeded in turning the middle class against the lower class. Many white working class men are now convinced that their interests are somehow different from those of other working and middle class people. The average white male is now convinced that the rich white men will also better look out for their interest.

In America, everyone theoretically has the opportunity to advance so there is no history of "bashing the rich." However, with an economic policy of low or no growth, the odds are increasingly against the average working individual ever advancing, much less becoming rich themselves. The disparity of incomes between the richest and the poorest is now greater in America than in any other western country.[51] Yet an ongoing campaign has distracted the middle class from what they should be paying attention to: WHO BENEFITS, both from the debt and the continuing raid on the public treasury to provide tax cuts?

Indeed, many wealthy individuals and powerful corporations took part in draining the public treasury. Six hundred billion of our national debt came from FDIC payments to cover losses for S&L investors alone. The rest was for tax cuts that primarily benefitted the richest ten percent of individuals in our nation and for increases in spending on defense and other favored industries and on tax cuts for corporations.

Twenty years ago corporate income taxes amounted to 40% of total federal revenue. Today corporate income taxes amounts to only about 11% of federal revenue because of the 1981 tax cut, and other deductions, subsidies, and loopholes. The total annual revenue lost to the federal government because of all of these adjustments to corporate income taxes is $435 billion[52] Some of these "tax expenditures" are for good purposes. However, they too should be considered for cuts when middle class "entitlements" are to be cut.

Unchecked, our debt burden will still continue to be shifted into the future, to our children and grandchildren, through more middle class subsidies of the corporations and of the rich. The Neo-Conservatives say that they want liberal tax cuts for the rich and still reduce the debt. To do it, they wish to cut welfare and social programs to the poor, and programs for the children and the elderly.

However, they do not also want to cut welfare to the corporations and the speculators. If debt reduction is the true goal, something might be done to reduce the $85 billion in blatant "corporate welfare" that even the conservative Cato Institute estimated was in the fiscal 1995 budget. The elimination of just this unnecessary spending alone would cut the annual deficit in half.

We must continue to make progress on reducing our national debt. To do otherwise would be irresponsible to both ourselves and to the future. The problems of debt, if ultimately not resolved, could weaken the economy and hurt our position in international trade. If nothing were done, the tax burden, to service the interest on the debt alone, would be projected to take nearly all federal revenue by the year 2010.[53]

We must repay what we owe. However, we must not allow that debt, $3 trillion of which was acquired during conservative administrations, to be used as an excuse for conservatives to now dissolve the New Deal. Deficit reduction cannot be used as an excuse for the elimination of social programs. Many voters are convinced, wrongly, that cutting programs for the poor will offset tax breaks for the wealthy, balance the budget and pay off the debt.

On the contrary, even totally eliminating the 4% of the budget that goes for all safety net and welfare programs will not even come close to equaling the 34% of non-discretionary spending that goes to pay the interest on the debt.[54] In the 1995 Congressional budget, Social Darwinists wanted a new $300 billion in tax cuts over seven years for that same group who has always benefitted before. The $200 spent annually by that average family in taxes to pay for social programs is positively cheap compared to what it gives up for tax breaks to the rich and just to pay the interest on the debt from that earlier tax subsidy of the already wealthy.[55]

We need to encourage small business and those who will invest in enterprises which build wealth. We need the investment that will grow our economy, not the speculations that our tax laws currently favor. Buying companies and breaking them up and selling the assets only make money for those doing the deals. The resulting companies employ less workers and put less money back into their communities.

Corporate profits are larger than ever, mostly due to the efficiencies of downsizing and the laying-off of workers. Small business accounts for virtually all increases in employment. Small businesses deserve our support but are instead hurt by policies that encourage high real interest rates and give tax deductions for eliminating or exporting jobs, policies that favor only the wealthy and large multi-national corporations.

These financial policies favor the largest companies and investors, and those who make their money through the redistribution of existing wealth. They favor middlemen over those who actually do the work and over those who actually produce the goods and services. These policies hurt those who try to make more pie for all to share and help those who wish to fight and scrap over the existing pie.

Wall Street is enjoying record profits, quarter after quarter, yet only an average of 37.5% of 1995 corporate profits were paid-out to the stockholders. This is the lowest portion of profits paid to stockholders since records were kept beginning in 1928. The CEOs are apparently keeping most of it for themselves.[56]

Huge corporate salaries, stock options, special dividends and excessive bonuses are all completely deductible expenses to the paying corporation, for federal corporate income tax purposes. As long as the largest salaries are paid for providing quarterly profits and increasing the share prices, over providing long term vision, then there can be no real growth for all to share.

Social Darwinism promotes the rise of an elite and actively works against social stability. Social Darwinists are completely against paying for social programs, and are even against having to pay their fair share. They are against anything that is to the benefit of social stability. By their actions and the tone of their rhetoric, they are also against even those mechanisms of social stability which are free: things such as manners, politeness, civility and the respect for one another.

This continuing irresponsibility, this Neo-Conservative trend, reminds one of a giant game of *Monopoly*, the copywrited Parker Brothers game, where the object is to control an ever larger pile of money at the expense of all of the other players. At the conclusion, someone will win. But then, the game is over for them, as well. This game will be over for them, and will also be over for all of the rest of us.

Think Tanks

Think-tanks are organizations which raise money to promote an agenda. They occur in both left-leaning and right-leaning varieties, however, there are few in the middle. The more right-leaning ones have been the most financially successful of late. Wealthy conservatives and multi-national corporations can contribute unlimited funds to the many conservative foundations and "think-tanks." There is no federal regulation of non-profit and "educational" institutions. Therefore, they do not even have to report their contributions or to name their contributors.

The loop-hole was intended to aid non-partisan and educational policy research. However, the think tanks are much more than educational. What they really do is constant polling and the development and testing of wedge-issues and of scapegoats. When they find an issue that will move a majority, they have the resources to very quickly get a plan of attack into motion.

In the last several years, some big money has been funneled into these "think-tanks-attacks," money which does not have to be reported as contributions and is not subject to Federal Election Commission rules. Much of this money has been used by the conservatives to do incredibly detailed research of Democratic opponents and staff, and especially Clinton appointees. With every detail uncovered, this raw research is then submitted to polling to find out which issue will move a majority.

A proper spin is then applied– to stress a conservative message, and it is then faxed or delivered overnight to the network of conservative columnists and commentators who will rebroadcast it to the general public by the next day. These think tanks do not have to be fair about issues or in their attacks, either, because the FCC no longer has the power to insure fairness in broadcasting.

Paul Peirson in his new book, *Dismantling the Welfare State?*, points out the role the conservative think-tanks played in evolving the Neo-Conservative strategy to dismantle the New Deal. Their major contribution involved instructions on how to dismantle the New Deal without actually seeming to. According to Peirson, there were three ways recommended to accomplish this: "Make one really big cut or make tiny, almost imperceptible, cuts frequently," "Make someone else make the cuts," or to "Off-load the costs on to future generations."

In the first instance, the trickle-down tax cut of 1981 took away the money that had been paying for New Deal programs. One of the reasons voters so distrust political compromise, is that rather than allow any cuts in social programs, Democratic House Speaker, Tip O'Neill allowed Reagan to finance the increases in military spending with borrowed money. He gave Reagan his tax cut– but kept all of the other programs in place. The resulting budget deficit is what made the above third option possible.

Civilizations sometimes fall through major blows, such as wars, however, most decline through degrees. The changes that Nixon accomplished with the Federal Reserve Board's slow growth policy is an example of these many small cuts which truly added up over time as in the second option. Small imperceptible, almost daily cuts in the growth of the economy over twenty years adds up, over time, compounded in interest, to a very real loss of jobs, of income, and of the wealth in the middle class.

An example of the second strategy occurred when the Congress cut the amount of Medicare funds available to health service providers. To make up this difference, the providers simply increased the bills that they sent to their patients. Therefore, the providers, and not the politicians, got the blame. Another example was when the Reagan administration tried to make the states accept the responsibility for capping or cutting Aid to Families with Dependent Children payments. Today, all of the Republican welfare reform proposals include that same goal of shifting responsibility to the states. Block grants to the states are solely a way of shifting responsibility to the states.

Once the responsibility is theirs, federal funds can be cut and then totally eliminated. Giving responsibility to the states is not due to "states rights" arguments or because the states are more efficient, it is solely a way to off-load responsibility, so that someone else will have to make the cuts. This time the "spin" recommended by the think tanks is solely– " to encourage the innovation of the fifty different states in finding solutions." [57] Fifty different bureaucracies can in no way be more efficient or more fair than the one can be.

The final method developed to dismantle the new deal was to "Off-load the costs on to future generations." One option under this heading is to run large budget deficits. This had the additional advantage of making it almost impossible to finance spending increases on social programs in the future. This strategy was, in itself, the supreme triumph of the conservative think tank. The Reagan tax cuts and increasing the defense spending were politically very popular and their temporary positive effect could be felt in every Congressional district.

Writing worthless checks is indeed politically popular, at least until those bad checks become due. The lobbyists for this were giving money to both sides of aisle. It was much easier to go along with what was eventually going to pass than to risk a confrontation. Besides, those interest groups had vowed to work against any Member of Congress who did not go along. Therefore at that time, a majority in Congress was almost forced to vote in favor of the conservative plan, or to risk re-election.

Of the three strategies that were developed to dismantle the New Deal and it's reforms, that Peirson lists– obfuscation, compensation and "divide and rule"– he clearly regards obfuscation, or disguising your motives, as the most likely to succeed. Never tackle the problem head on. Conceal what you are doing. Shift the blame on to others. Always cover your tracks. Successful obfuscation, according to Peirson, explains at least 90% of Reagan's and in Britain, Thatcher's success. In Britain, Thatcher's Conservative party is opposed by the Labour party. Labour was able to make great gains after exposing the handiwork of the Conservative party.[58]

Unfortunately, in America, the conservatives have much more money to spend on dis-information and to spend on getting their message out. The upstart nonprofit Progress & Freedom Foundation, with it's cozy relationship with House Speaker Gingrich, spent during its first 20 months, roughly 43% of its $1.4 million budget, on funding Gingrich's televised college lecture series.[59] In America there is no strong single voice speaking up for working people and the middle class. This lack of an organized opposition helps the message generated by the think tanks to be more successful in confusing and dividing us.

Newt Gingrich raised uncounted funds (both legally and illegally) to help elect 68 new Republican members of Congress in 1994. The Conservative politicians who were elected in 1994 are indebted to the think tanks, to political action committees such as Newt Gingrich's GOPAC, and to those who planned and paid for their campaigns. In fact, they owe a tremendous debt to those who helped to elect them. There are no innocents in this group: they all know where the money came from and what they are supposed to do for it in return.

GOPAC raised tens of millions of dollars. Hundreds of thousands of dollars were raised from each of several individual wealthy conservatives and corporate interests. Federal campaign laws limit individual contributions to $1,000 per campaign with a $25,000 a year total limit on giving per individual. These limits were greatly exceeded by GOPAC. Federal law also prohibits corporate giving, however, GOPAC took large contributions from corporate givers and from those with a stake in how the nation's laws are written. The public should expect tax breaks and special legislation as repayment to the big business lobbyists and to the other backers who contributed to the 1994 conservative revolution. Gingrich told potential corporate contributors in early 1994 that "The train was leaving the station and if they were not on board, it would be a cold two years." These days, politicians and their handlers do not even bother to hide their shabby character, or even to nod at hypocrisy.[60]

There is plenty of talk about balancing budgets by cutting funds for the poor. There is almost no talk of balancing the budget by eliminating tax subsidies for the rich. While there is ample rhetoric in Congress attacking the existence of the debt, there is no mention of where the debt came from, that much of it came from granting tax subsidies to the rich and from the subsidy of favored industry. Indeed, the Social Darwinist contingent insists that instead of eliminating tax subsidy for the rich, we need *more* tax cuts for the rich.

The wealthy always seem to get their way with Congress. The saying "Money is power" has never been more true. Tax laws were changed in the 1980s to lower taxes for the benefit of the wealthy almost exclusively, while our national debt has exploded. Middle class taxes, cut at the same time, have crept back up to where they were— mostly through social security tax increases, which are a smaller percentage of income for the rich, and by the shifting of the tax burden to local governments, who then must raise taxes. Those special interests who benefit, use the Congress as a way to advance their interests.

Under this kind of control, it is impossible to raise taxes on the rich to the level paid by the middle class. The House of Representatives voted in 1995 to require a three/fifths majority rather than a simple majority to raise corporate or other income taxes. This will block any real redress of the inequities of the debt until a whole new Congress can be elected. A 40% minority of the Congress can now block any and all tax changes. This will prevent selectively raising taxes on the wealthy and on those who benefitted from the economic policies of the 1980s. Draconian cuts in the social safety net will now be the only way to balance the budget. The resulting pain will not at all be shared by the elite.

A return to a more progressive tax structure is indicated, but instead on the agenda are capital gains tax cuts and specialty tax breaks for corporations that have contributed to conservative causes and conservative candidates. Every conservative tax restructuring plan, flat tax, value added tax, or national sales tax proposes to continue the inequities– or even further reduces taxes for these groups. The difference in revenue must either be made up by raising taxes on the rest of us or on cutting government services. These types of subsidies to the rich can only make the deficit worse and further explode our debt. The sad part is, that if even the current level of individual and corporate tax breaks for those that do not need them were cut back, there would be no budget deficit at all.[61]

In the past, America used high inheritance taxes to prevent the intra-generational transfer of wealth. There was fear that multi-generational wealth would lead to the formation of financial dynasties. The Carnegie and Ford Foundations were one result of tax laws intended to diffuse great wealth. The end result of the establishment of these foundations has been overwhelmingly positive for the country. Something has overcome our traditional bias against inherited wealth and the political influence that it can buy.

Sam Walton knew he was dying, but Sam Walton also knew how to work the system. Before his death there was a great public relations campaign to improve his image. The Walmart Corporation lowered prices way below cost on many items, did charity work, spent extra money on advertising.. all tax deductible expenses. Sam Walton wrote a book, which would become a best seller, about Walmart and the American Dream. The Walton family spent hundreds of thousands of dollars on political contributions. Consequently a special federal inheritance tax exemption was passed by the Congress. Walton's was only one of many such special exemptions granted by the Congress that are estimated to cost the treasury $5 billion annually.[62] The end result was that the billion dollar Walton estate was transferred to his heirs, almost completely intact.

Financial dynasties are one thing, but political dynasties are another. We are currently in danger of forming a political dynasty that will forever end majority rule. We are on the verge of a pure *Market Democracy*, where those with the cash call all of the shots. Money has now become the most important part of political campaigns. This political trend of the last quarter century now will become the law of the land. Within this *Market Democracy*, it is the goal of many to have a "Strong Man" rule in America on a permanent basis. This consolidation of power will be accomplished quite simply through the institution of the politically popular "Line Item Veto."

The power of Presidential veto in the Constitution was meant to be used sparingly, and it was up until the Bush presidency. The veto was intended by the framers of the Constitution to be one of the rarely used checks and balances that prevent truly harmful legislation from becoming law. A veto power enhanced over that which is currently allowed would require an ammendment to the Constitution. Such powers are limited because they could be used against the will of the people. In the wrong hands, this more powerful line-item veto could become not just a weapon, but instead a gun held to the head of the American public and to the head of each one of their elected Congressional representatives.

The "Line Item Veto" in the Republican "Contract with America" is promoted as a "common sense" approach to trimming the fat from government. If the President does not like a portion of a spending bill (tax bills were not included, of course) he can veto it, line by line. The common sense portion of the idea is that good programs are not held hostage by having wasteful pork-barrel amendments tacked on to them. The worst part, however, the part that a tyrant would find useful, is that in the conservative backed bill, a 2/3 majority vote in Congress is required to override that presidential veto. The "Line Item Veto" indeed sounds like a good idea. However, in reality it means that the President and a minority of the Congress (only one-third of the congress, plus one vote) would be enough to control which legislation would become law.

With a President having a line item veto, any dissenting Member of Congress could face the very real possibility that all appropriations to their district might be lined out, or removed from consideration. As long as the President had at least a one-third plus one minority backing him in the Congress, he could effectively enforce discipline in that Congress. A "Line Item Veto" would allow virtually any President to have full control over the Congress, as long as he also had a small minority in the Congress that would back him.

Conservatives were confident that they could beat President Clinton in 1996, and reestablish the lock that they had previously held on the Presidency. Therefore they pushed hard for the line item veto. A line item veto has the potential to be "minority rule" at its finest. With it, conservatives will only need the presidency and a small minority of the Congress to achieve what amounts to a Strong Man form of government. "Line Item Veto" legislation passed both houses in the Republican controlled Congress. A final bill only needed to be "agreed to" in the conference committee before going to the President to be signed into law.

As the conservative think tank's coordinated campaign against the President began running out of steam and his popularity improved, it stayed in conference for over a year and a half. President Clinton had pledged to sign this legislation. However, the poll numbers for the Republican Congress fell farther in 1995 than did those for President Clinton in 1994 under full conservative attack. The Republican majority was forced to do something, because, after all, the "Line Item Veto" was one of the major items in their "Contract with America."

The "Line Item Veto" bill that ultimately did emerge from the conference committee was not really a line item veto at all. It was instead just a temporarily enhancement to recision powers for the President. A sharp legislator could put the spending authority in one section of their bill and the delegation into another and, thereby, get around the veto powers allowed in this bill. These powers themselves are limited. They are slated to expire in eight years after taking effect on January 1, 1997.

The bill that eventually did emerge probably will have little affect on the deficit. It only applies to that one-third of the budget that it relatively under control– discressionary spending, and will not, at all, affect that out-of-control portion of the federal budget– entitlement spending. This Line Item Veto bill will most likely remove the desire for, or the need for fiscal restraint from the Congress, and simply serve as a tool to shift the blame, politically.

Another "blow" for minority rule was successfully struck in the Senate. Seats in the Senate are fewer, but are also much more expensive to get and to maintain. This gives those with wealthy backing a better than even chance with which to gain them. Moreover, the Senate has power equal with the House to block legislation. Those forces which can afford to spend the money could likely control at least 41 seats in the Senate. These 41 seats are powerful enough to block legislation. Instead of a simple majority needed to pass legislation, they can effectively require a three-fifths majority in order to proceed with legislation by always invoking the little used cloture rule. By requiring that this rule be used, even in the most trivial of cases, a minority of the Senate can set and control the agenda.

The nomination of Henry Foster as Surgeon General was an example of this. Dr. Foster's nomination was blocked by a less than fifty percent vote because a sixty percent majority vote was required by the Republican leadership to bring the nomination to the floor. Having forty-one votes in the Senate was enough to prevent a vote by the rest of Senate. This is minority rule at its finest. Hundreds of appointments require approval in the Senate. For anything to be voted on, it must first get to the floor. If such anti-democratic measures are allowed to continue they could bring government to it's knees.

Overpopulation and Growth of Elites

There are many things on the horizon that will be challenging to American society. We are a great and diverse country, which is significant, because if we were all "just alike," we would all be producing or competing for exactly the same goods and services. However, this diversity allows us to be divided up by a special interest and our interests to be pitted against the interest of others. Special interests are for the betterment of that particular interest, over our common interests– the good of the entire society. The special interests have as a goal to end those unwritten contracts with one another which first allowed the formation of society.

Foremost among these challenges to our unity will be the stress of overcrowding due to overpopulation. In a stagnant, non-democratic, non-socially mobile society, these problems will become much worse. Too many people creates less opportunity for each, even with a level playing field for the competition for resources, and even with a growing economy. The pressure of overcrowding can potentially turn neighbor against neighbor, even without the added pressures of class envy.

California is one of the fastest growing areas in the world. Traffic congestion on the freeways, overpopulation by automobiles, is getting much worse and is a visible outward sign of the area's diminishing quality of life. Traffic in Southern California is moving, on average, ten percent slower with each passing year.[63] Automobiles and the attendant air pollution problems are largely the result of a lack of planning for growth.

The public and private infrastructure was designed for much less population density than now exists.

In the more crowded areas of California, competition for existing housing resources is intense, driving up housing prices so that many, especially younger, home buyers can no longer afford to own them. The ownership of the housing stocks are therefore transferred to those who can afford them. Only the elites are able to afford to purchase them. Therefore, only the elite will own those dwelling units, with the rest of us becoming merely tenants.

Further increases in housing scarcity can only result in increases in rent, and therefore increasing financial pressures on renters and ultimately an increasing poverty in the community. Immigrants are usually blamed for the problems of growth, however, they may not be the problem that we ourselves are. The birth rate in the state of California, in 1995, was twice that of India.[64]

Always coupled with the neglect of our unwritten social contract with one another, and the increases in overcrowding and poverty is the rise of the elite class. The two groups will also have no real contact with each other, as is required to maintain a stable society. The well off in America were permitted to isolate themselves from the poor. Initially, to be allowed to do so, they tacitly agreed to contribute to the maintenance of society through tax-subsidized programs and charities. Now that they have been spared contact with the poor, now that they have no bonds to the less fortunate, many wish to end the unwritten agreement.

California Governor Pete Wilson was a master at diverting attention from himself by scapegoating others. As the junior Senator from California, he very early became adept at taking credit for successes and avoiding blame for failures. He is the model of a new style of politician who is able to sound reasonable by directing our fears to fault others. His highly politically popular scapegoating of illegal immigrants began to ring less true when it was exposed for what it is, by the revelation that he has employed "between one and five illegal immigrants" as housekeepers.

Social conservatives in California, without understanding the societal forces at work, sought to promote a social policy that made things worse, potentially much worse. The elites in California preferred hiring illegal immigrants as housekeepers or gardeners instead of the many citizens who had become unemployed due to defense cut-backs and other economic reasons. Employing illegal immigrants only takes jobs away from legal immigrants and citizens. It lowers wages for all workers. Providing jobs for illegal immigrants only encourages more illegal immigration.

Scapegoating to solve a problem only works in the short run, and then only briefly. Over the long term, we all will lose. Laws intended to exclude others, to keep people out except when you want them will, too, only work briefly. Once order breaks down in society, primarily due to the reluctance of those who contributed to the problem to fund the huge tax increases necessary for enforcement, the existing social infrastructure will collapse.

In all of America, there is a true Elite Class of only about 1% of the population. They are able to decide their own destiny, as well as, that of others. There is perhaps another 10% of the total population who are favored, through position, or education, or some skill. With stockholder approval, or with acquiescence of the masses, they too, are mostly able to do what they want. Another 10% of the population is helpless, almost totally at the whim of the elites. The rest of us are somewhere in that broad middle. We were once the backbone of America. We have become what is now the shrinking middle class.

The latest definition of "middle class" is those families that can miss one paycheck and not be in immediate, serious, financial trouble. Today, there are even less of us in that category than ever. At the same time, there is more wealth concentrated in fewer hands. There is also more poverty than at any time since the 1930s. There are truly world wide dislocations of labor and capital that are responsible for this trend. However, we must do something quickly to reverse the damage that it can do to our social infrastructure. Indeed, our choices, any potential plan of action or change of direction that we may take, are further limited, due to our debt. However, doing nothing is not the answer.

There is no animal model of overcrowding, such as those developed with rats, that can be used to accurately predict what the outcome of this increasing conflict will be on humans. While animal behavior may be simple cause and effect, human behavior is much more complex. Humans in society are affected by much more than just the heredity that is responsible for pre-programming instinctive animal behaviors. Humans may readily learn and assimilate new behaviors and strategies for survival if they are allowed to do so.

Analogy also is very dangerous to use when trying to describe or explain laws of human behavior. We must have examples taken directly from the human experience to explain the uniquely human condition. Therefore, we are limited to looking at the historical record to find similar examples to study. Studying the history of civilization, even those civilizations that have been dead for a long time, is the best and most accurate way to study human behavior and it's consequences. Learning from history is the best way to prevent us from making the same mistakes which have always been made before in the human experience.

Linda Schele was the first to translate, to unlock, the highly advanced language of the Mayans. We, as Americans, can learn many lessons from her work. The Mayan Indians had a highly advanced civilization that lasted over 2000 years. It ended sometime shortly before the arrival of the Spanish in the early 1500s. European diseases and cruelty only served to finish them off. No one knows for sure what actually pushed the Mayan civilization over the edge– whether it was a major war, a series of droughts, or disease. However, several sources point to fact that the growth of the noble class had a lot to do with it.[65]

In her studies of the Mayans, art historian, Mary Miller calculates that if you start in the year 600 with a single noble husband and wife with four children, and they had four children that survived, and so on, by the year 800 there would be 700 people who had the right to claim noble status. So the percentage of people with high status grew rapidly along with the demand to access the kind of goods and privileges that marked them as noble.

This resulted in more kingdoms competing for fewer resources, with less no-man's land between them. The rise in warfare, coupled with overpopulation put a tremendous strain on the agricultural system. There are indications of massive deforestation in the final years. The end was pretty gruesome. There comes a point when there's so much stress in a society, that, as put by Schele's collegue, David Freidel, it just becomes pathological. We saw that with the former Soviet Union. It wasn't a slow gentle deceleration. It was boom.[66]

Overpopulation and pyramid building goes hand in hand. The rise of elites in Egypt called for monuments to the egos of the kings and the waste of valuable resources to achieve them. Elites have a need to feel elite. They universally love the thought of people toiling away under them. Elites will always find a way to fill the lives of those working under them with mindless toil.

Conservative elites think of themselves as being better than everyone else. They will often say hard work is what justifies their success. Hard work is important in wealth building; however, success is just as much a matter of timing and luck. There is no way to account for those factors in how well one individual does compared to another. There are even conservative studies that claim to prove one race is inherently superior to another. This cannot be true, because on average, all humans start out basically the same, with very little racial variation.

More than likely, this study is an attempt to justify to wealthy conservatives that they should not have to pay the taxes which go to provide for a stable society, or to pay the taxes that go, in any way, to help others. These conservative ideologies will always develop, as a means of justifying not having to pay taxes. Wealthy conservatives do not like to pay taxes, even taxes for a society that has benefitted mostly them.

Humans have the capacity for a wide range of different behaviors. However, they generally can be expected to endeavor to fit in with those around them. Individuals who are raised by savages and are always around savages, become like savages, even though their genetic parents may have been very cultured and refined persons. The general level of education as well as the environment in which they are raised, ultimately, has the most to do with human behavior.

Twins separated at birth and placed in widely differing situations, will take on the characteristics of those same situations. This always happens, mainly, due to the extreme adaptibility of human behavior. If one is raised in very rough working class conditions and the other one is raised into a very privileged situation, after fifty years, the differences between them should be quite evident.

The options for the human adaptation to their environment are almost limitless. Darwin was quite right that individuals will adapt to those positions available, or into those niches that have been opened-up unto them. However, unlike animal behavior, human behavior is also directly related to the degree of expectation that is placed upon that individual. Humans respond according to the expectations that they have, or to those that society has placed upon them.

Siblings may take spouses headed in different directions on the social ladder. The one who marries way below their former social position will soon settle into a lowered expectation. They will very soon not dress as well, take less care of their appearance, require medical or dental care, and generally meet the standards of the new social position rather than those of the former social position. The reverse is also true. Those finding themselves in elevated positions will quickly establish ways to cope with their newly elevated situation, until they do genuinely fit into them.

We are not as slaves to either our genes or to our environment. Individuals can and do overcome genetic dispositions and handicaps. Individuals, can and do, rise from humble origins to the very top of society. Other than a very slight effect of genetics, human behavior is pretty much shaped by their environment and the expectations placed upon them. Given education and a good environment, expect good things from most people.

Education is very important to the formation of good citizens. Will and Ariel Durant, in their book *The Story of Civilization* state that "What we are up against is the simple fact that man is still an animal. That the deepest thing in his nature is still the survival instinct and the hunting instinct. Those were necessary at one time when self-preservation was the rule rather than the pressure of society. So morality has an uphill battle against these two inheritances. You have to recognize the enormous difficulty in making an animal and hunter into a citizen, a civilized man." In their work, *The Lessons of History*, they note that "Civilization is not inherited; it has to be learned and earned by each generation anew. If the transmission of civilization though education should be interrupted for one century, civilization would die, and we would be savages again."

It is also true that if some feel that they are unfairly excluded from the benefits of society, from our unwritten agreements, expect them to revert to these basic instincts. Expect them to try to correct or make up for inequities, at least eventually. Short term, some individuals do benefit from holding others down or by not paying their fair share. Long term, we will all lose.

For our society to progress– or even to work at all, we must remember that we are all created equal. We owe our citizens, all of our citizens, a level playing field for growth and advancement. We must always have this level playing field, both for individuals or for the society as a whole, to be able to progress.

8. *The Constitution and Fairness*

Unwritten agreements are one thing, but the Constitution is a *written* document. Our Constitution is a soundly crafted and finely-tuned *written* work that reflects the interests of ALL individuals. The founding fathers had very definite thoughts on fairness. They had lived under the autocratic rule of King George and fought in the Revolutionary war against him. They had studied the rise and fall of civilizations and looked at the strengths and weaknesses of all of the previous forms of government. They were well founded in the Bible and the classics. They had all the benefit of the vast experiences of the past, and strived to create a document that was strong and flexible at the same time. They succeeded in producing a Constitution that has met all of those requirements and more. It was widely admired in its day, and it has withstood the test of time.

As formulated by those original patriots, our Constitution established universal agreement in three very important areas: It for the first time, guaranteed the rights of, and acknowledged the *worth of the individual* in society. In all previous forms of government, only the elites were of consequence. The sole purpose of everyone else was to serve those elites or, otherwise, to advance the goals of the state.

The Constitution codifies our belief in majority rule. It sets forth the principle that the actions of individuals are important to a stable society. The individual accommodation of others is required for the stablility of the whole of the society. Each individual, thereby, realizes that they must give up some of our own personal liberties in order to secure the liberty of all. Under the Constitution the will of the majority of the individual citizens establishes the rules for the body of the citizens. We all understand it is the Constitution which sets the rules for all of us.

Our Constitution was first to support the concept of *spiritual freedom*. This is freedom both of religious practice and the freedom of the human spirit. The freedom for individuals to be able to strive to get ahead is an important part of this. Individuals were encouraged, for the first time, not only to dream, but also to follow their dreams. Under the protections of the Constitution, individual citizens would be free to advance themselves, and also to advance their ideas.

To further amplify and to protect this freedom of the individual, the Constitution went to great lengths to provide for the *decentralization of power*. This was both to insure that the individual had a role to play in self-government and that none would acquire all of the power, or could find ways to dominate all of the others. Under the Constitution, our government reflects the collective will of the people. Our system works only through compromise, through evenly and fairly counter-balancing the individual interests of all– to protect the interests of the whole.

There is great talk today of amending the Constitution, of ending this need to compromise, as the answer to all of our problems. Those who think that constitutional amendments are going to force consensus are wrong. For proof, we need to look no further than to the 18th amendment to the Constitution, Prohibition. Prohibition was intended to stop the moral decline in America by prohibiting the sale and consumption of alcohol. Alcohol became the scapegoat for all of our problems. This law was passed in 1917 by a Republican controlled Congress in another high-minded attempt to enforce morality.

Instead of morality, what Prohibition ended up creating was corruption. What seemed like a noble idea led to the rise of some very ignoble things. Prohibition added a great many new words to American speech. It gave us words to describe what narrow vision can do to a great country, words such as speakeasies, bootleggers, and the mob.[67] With organized crime continuing in control of much of our daily commerce, we continue to pay the price for that earlier mistake.

Some have pushed for a balanced budget amendment to the Constitution as a method of solving the problem of the national debt. The Constitution currently allows great flexibility in our government, especially in budgeting. The balanced budget amendment says that the budget must always be in balance. In hard times or recession, government revenues go down, but government expenses continue.

To furlough workers in order to balance a budget would serve to make the recession worse. In fact, the government may wish to counter spend, to spend more in tough times on programs just to keep families afloat, until times improve. An amendment requiring the budget to always be balanced, like prohibition, could even be counterproductive.

In 200 years, there have been 22 amendments to the Constitution out of ten thousand that were proposed. Amending the Constitution is not to be taken lightly. The Constitution is a document to be respected and not to be used to favor some ideology or to settle trifling arguments.[68]

To satisfy public opinion with a long constitutional amendment process will only delay any real budgetary action. We don't need gimmickry like a balanced budget amendment. What we need are leaders who will make hard choices and hard decisions. We must encourage our political leaders to make decisions that will insure fiscal responsibility and level the playing field for fair competition and a true free market. We have already, many times in the last twenty years, been the victims of financial con-games. We have already been tricked into a Social Darwinism with "rosy scenarios" and "trickle-down" economics. We must now elect honest people, those who will be honest with the people, who will tell the truth and do the right thing, no matter what the political consequences.

A forced solution, a measure to limit our options in settling our debt, may sound like a good idea. Although just having to pay the annual two hundred and eighty billion dollar interest on the debt, in itself, takes away most options. We must still keep at least one option open, that of deciding whose interest get helped and whose will get hurt. A balanced budget amendment takes even that option away. It will be the children who will suffer the most. Although, we must insure the education of the children, so they become the future producers of tomorrow. Cuts would have to be made to education.

The job creation abilities of small independent business should not be sacrificed to create political contributions from big business, but would be. The long term interest of the country in its health and the environment should not be denied for the short term political gain of the politicians. However, we are, now, again being asked to pay more in taxes, to give up health care, job security, a clean environment, a secure old age, and our children's future– so that the taxes of the wealthy may be cut.

Our system does need real reforms. The first step to a true fix is a comprehensive package of legislative "do-overs" to the financial problems caused by prior legislation. Many problems were created by the attempts to cure other problems. Some of them were enacted due to simple misjudgement. However, most of this legislation was either unfairly lobbied for, or bought, or passed to promote a position no longer advantageous for the country. Many of these laws only benefit one group at the expense of another. Usually the interest of some will gain, but the rest of the taxpayers just end up paying more. All true patriots are willing to sacrifice in some way for the good of the country. A few politicians would use this patriotism as just another tool to get their own way on issues.

A Constitutional amendment to make flag burning a federal crime would be used as such a tool by some. They would use new restrictions on free speech to silence their critics. Some politicians do believe in sacrifice, however, they would use it to punish their enemies. They would, however, continue to preserve and to protect the benefits of the government for their friends and supporters. What we need are leaders who will remember all individuals are important, that we are equal under the law, and that none deserves more or better than all the rest.

Certain Christian religious groups also advocate constitutional amendments. They wish their interests be further protected under the Constitution. Some want a constitutional amendment to mandate school prayer. If so, they may also wish to mandate to which god this prayer would be directed. Student led prayer is allowed under the Constitution. If individual teachers are to be mandated to lead prayer, what if the teacher were to be a Moslem or a Buddhist, or a member of a religious organization that the parent is opposed to?

Prayer is important, but would you want your children praying to someone else's god? There is not even a complete listing of all of the different sects of just the Christian religions in

America, much less all the others. How can we know what beliefs must be accommodated? The vast majority of Americans want to allow prayer in public schools, but strongly oppose a forced prayer. The issue is indeed complicated, and yet, it too is protected by spiritual freedom. However, the Constitution, itself, protects only a freedom of religion for individuals. It in no way protects a freedom from religion. We must, therefore, find a way to put the teaching of morals and religious values back into our schools. Our children need to know that God loves them, and expects them to police their own behaviors.

Conservative Barry Goldwater, the 1964 Republican presidential candidate, is convinced that the religious right threatens to betray an essential principle of conservatism— the notion that government should stay out of peoples lives. "Mixing religion with politics," he argues, "doesn't work." Goldwater favors "using solutions that have worked in the past and applying them to solve the problems of the present."[69] However, not all early solutions were good ones. Certainly, we do not want a return to the poor houses, orphanages, sweatshops and debtor's prisons that some have favored.

We must, instead, attempt to end those conditions that are leading to the new economic and social poverty in America rather than resorting to those draconian measures proposed as solutions. It is the Neo-Conservative policies, themselves, that have worsened the social situation in America. Solutions which would further worsen conditions for the average citizen have even been proposed as cures for that original problem. If the Neo-Conservative revolution has accomplished anything; it has been to make Senator Barry Goldwater, America's foremost conservative, sound more and more moderate.

The More Things Change

A gradual phase-out could have been agreed to, under the rule of law. A timetable could have been approved by everyone in the Congress. Instead, the Republican Majority insisted on using extreme examples to incite emotions. They were confident they held the high moral ground and would be able to take advantage of it. The debate on the House Floor became increasingly bitter and personal in tone.

Many more members, mostly Democratic, were retiring, or resigning the Congress– abandoning that chamber like rats deserting a sinking ship. The Republicans knew they were going to win. They had a huge majority, which they considered a mandate, and knew that they would eventually easily prevail. Yet, they still sought to hold accountable all that were involved, including the poor, the elderly, and children, simply because they possessed the votes to do so.

Federal Debt reduction? Welfare Reform? No, the issues were slavery and the treatment of the post-Civil War South. Sometimes in politics, the more things change, the more they stay the same. There will always be ideological purists and extremists. Still, moderation and the respect for the ideas and the dignity of others is important. The ideal is to be sensitive to the feelings of others, while at the same time remaining thick-skinned when it comes to yourself.

In the early 1860's, to prevent war, moderates in both parties had sought to compromise. They sought to phase out slavery, gradually, on a time table that all would agree on. Our country, after all, had a history of indentured servitude. People had before worked in servitude for a period of time to pay-off their passage to the new world, then after a period of time, they would become completely free. The moderates argued to protect both the property rights of slave holders and at the same time to enhance the rights of slaves, ultimately leading to the freedom for all slaves.

Sensing that they held the high moral ground and had the votes to back it up, the Republicans in Congress simply ignored the moderates. Like in the 1995 debate over balancing the budget, the Republican Majority was less interested in the issue of slavery as a wrong that needed righting, but as an issue that could allow the advancement of their agenda. They held up what were the worst examples of abuse as the de facto standard of treatment for all of the slaves. The concerns of others were ignored.

The Republican majority used inflammatory rhetoric to beat the drums of war. They succeeded in driving-off even those many Southerners who were against slavery. In fairness, those interests supporting slavery were no angels, either. However, they were in a minority that might have readily accepted a deal. Since moderation was out of the question, the Civil War, a conflict that pitted brother against brother, was ultimately forced to erupt.

After that civil war, the South was devastated. The loss of life left no family untouched. Enormous property damage was evident everywhere. Since the Congress was not in session at the end of the war, President Andrew Johnson alone was obliged to determine how the Southern States would be returned to the Union. As the Constitution did not provide for such an action, the president did what he thought was proper. His plan, the one that Lincoln had tentatively designed, was to accept the states back into full fellowship, with only the most essential restrictions, as quickly as possible.

The Union had maintained all along that the right to secede did not exist, and that it was impossible for a state to withdraw from the United States. Logically, therefore, it should have only been necessary for the recently estranged states to take such steps as repealing the ordinance of succession and formally freeing the slaves- to demonstrate their change of heart- before resuming their former role in the nation. This was the simple policy of reconciliation.[70]

However, the Republicans sought to further punish the South. Once in session, the Republican Congress did everything that it could to continue and prolong the suffering of the citizens of the Southern states. President Johnson, who tried to restore moderation and civility, was impeached by the House of Representatives for his trouble.

As late as March 2, 1867 a bill entitled "An Act to Provide for the More Efficient Government of the Rebel States" became law over the president's veto. This law completely reversed all efforts by President Johnson to restore an equal union, and was shortly joined by three other acts that drastically altered the status of the Southern States.[71]

The slaves had been freed in 1863 and the 13th Amendment was passed by the Congress and ratified by the states, becoming official on December 18, 1865. Therefore, slavery was, by this time, no longer the issue. Hurting helpless individuals and making people pay for the actions of a rival elite was the real issue. For many years after the war, Southerners continued to suffer excessive and unfair punishment under the radical Republican Congress and were unable to elect their own representatives or to do anything else about it.

Because of the radical, activist element that often dominates the Republican nomination process, those candidates with radical, inflexible, and out of the mainstream beliefs are very often the ones who are nominated. Majority Republican Congresses, therefore, have the tendency to favor rigid rules that could punish innocent people and have a readiness to blame individuals for the situations that they may find themselves in, even though these conditions may have been out of their individual control. This hard-liner tendency is well illustrated in the Republican dominated 104th Congress. In their haste to cut the fat in federal regulation, they were willing to cut deeply into the flesh and bone, as well. *Time Magazine* columnist, Margaret Carlson described it in a contemporary article:

"Anyone pondering their sunset years will remember the expose' of the shocking conditions in nursing homes circa 1970. Woefully undertrained workers strapped patents to hard-backed chairs, fed them cheap diets and kept them in a whimpering state of sedation....
But in the blink of an eye these days, a carefully built construct of regulations can be blown away without so much as a formal hearing. As part of a crusade to curb federal authority, and with only a simple assertion that the regulations are burdensome, two congressional committees have sent it to the floor for a vote this week legislation that would repeal federal standards. There would be no protection against patients' being restrained, no standards on staffing or when someone could be discharged after using up all his or her money. Niceties like nurses would be optional, since there is no requirements in the new legislation that a licensed nurse be present. Instead there would be so-called patient rights– to receive mail, keep personal belongings and be free from abuse and forced labor– rights that may duplicate, but do not exceed, the Geneva Conventions for prisoners of war."

"Republicans justify the changes by saying the states know best how to run nursing homes. Of course, it is unlikely that with $182 billion less in federal Medicaid money over seven years the states will embrace high-quality care. The market solution would be to replace that nurse's aide at $10 an hour with an unskilled worker at $5 and to substitute thin soup and macaroni for meat and vegetables. In fact, it turns out that being humane actually saves money. Catherine Hawes of the nonprofit Research Triangle Institute estimated that after the 1987 reform legislation was passed, $2 billion was saved by 269 nursing homes from fewer emergency hospitalizations, less malnutrition, a 30% decrease in [infections from] the use of catheters and a 25% reduction in [injuries due to] the use of restraints. Says Sarah Burger of the National Citizens Coalition for Nursing Home Reform: "operators didn't know until they were forced to stop doing it that the main cause of incontinence and bedsores is being restrained and not being able to get to the bathroom."

But wholesale budget slashing will no doubt pressure some facilities to cut corners. Senator William Cohen of Maine, one of the few Republicans to oppose the rollback, warns, "If we weaken federal enforcement, we will be sent back to the dark days of substandard nursing homes, with millions of elderly at risk."[72]

Governments are known by how they use, or abuse, their power. Civilizations are known by how they treat the weakest of their citizens. If the citizens feel that they will likely be abused in their old age, they will be less inclined to sacrifice and work hard for good of that society. Fairness and equal treatment of all of its citizens is the hallmark of a great society, and it is one that will pay off in the long term. It was not until Franklin Roosevelt's New Deal did the South start to fully recover from the many unnecessary abuses of power that occurred during the post-Civil War era. Roosevelt's programs to rebuild infrastructure and put people back on their feet ultimately paid off with an economic boom in the South. Fairness and even-handed dealings by the government, too, will ultimately pay off, just as money spent on educating the children, money spent on giving them the skills to compete, ultimately repays society with their much higher productivity .

The Social Security Program, begun under Roosevelt, was a good and fair program. It is a prime example of fair and even handed treatment of individuals by their government. Originally it was visualized as a safety net and social stabilizer, to raise seniors over the poverty level, and to prevent large numbers of them from becoming destitute.

However, over the years its purpose has been changed. Money collected to pay for its programs have not always made it into the Social Security trust fund. This lack of dedication in funding does not affect the importance of the original goal of Social Security. It is important that the ideals, the core values, of Social Security be preserved, that is, Social Security is to help our seniors in their later years. Seniors should not now be punished because they tend to vote Democratic. Social Security taxes should not be excessively raised on working people, to punish the Democrats for what the system has become.

The Social Security System began as good public policy, both as a mechanism to insure social stability and as a system of enforced savings for the rest of us. Since the Nixon years, however, the Administration and the Congress have been using money collected for the Social Security Trust Fund to make the deficit look smaller, or for other uses. It is not being invested, nor is it being set aside for future retirees. Revenues intended for the Social Security Trust Fund, today, are being spent on payments to current retirees and towards paying the interest on the Federal Debt.

In 1965 the average life expectancy for a typical American was not much more than 65 years. Traditional insurance companies would not cover the elderly for hospital insurance, at any price. Because they could not get coverage, it was not uncommon to find seniors who were destitute because of prolonged or acute illness. President Lyndon Johnson wanted a way to offer hospital insurance for seniors and proposed Medicare as an extension to the Social Security program.

He was confident that his proposal for a health insurance addition to Social Security would have little net effect on the budget since it did not cover persons until they reached the age of sixty-five. His, was not so much a health care program, as it too was a social safety net. It was intended to prevent the bankruptcy of seniors and their families that had by then become commonplace due to the lack of availability of affordable health insurance coverage.

President Johnson's vision worked better than anyone expected. Having insurance that would pay for their care encouraged the free enterprise system to find new ways to care for seniors. Today, the average life expectancy for seniors is 75.7 years.[73] The 1965 projections of cost, based on the predicted usage were way too low. No one had predicted that increased care would help the elderly live longer and fuller lives.

The early projections, on which the amount of premiums collected was determined, soon had to be adjusted. Medicare was designed as a "pay as you go" system as a safeguard against providers raising rates or beneficiaries wanting more services in order to use up any surplus. Since that time, Medicare premiums have often been raised to cover increased expenses.

This was by design, since no traditional trust fund had been established.

In the 1970s, Congressional conservatives in coordination with the "Think Tanks" and other interest groups organized those in Congress who were unwilling to vote to raise premiums or to appropriate more money. Together they passed a funding bill where instead of raising Medicare premiums, the providers of health care were simply paid at a lower rate. The providers in response to lower reimbursement simply raised their rates, thereby shifting those uncollected costs of the care of Medicare patients over to their other patients.

These costs were then shifted by the health care and insurance industry to the payers of private insurance through increased premiums, and on and on. This initial under-funding of Medicare ultimately resulted in higher cost for everyone else in the entire health care system. The resulting cycle of "Cost Shifting," is largely responsible for escalation of prices in the entire health care industry. The inflation of health care costs far above the general level of inflation was a product of conservative think tank fiscal policy. The ultimate goal of the opponents of Medicare was to discredit the program, and ultimately to dismantle the entire New Deal.

In underpaying the public debt for health care, this fiscal policy did allow for taxes to be cut. However, this also did more than simply postpone the debt that we owed. It raised the rate at which we would be billed in the future- beginning what was to become an inflationary spiral in the cost of health care.

Because the under-funding of Medicare caused prices to go up to them, insurance companies acted to protect themselves. The private insurance plans, private sector health plans, and HMOs began asking for and receiving discounts from providers and hospitals. Therefore, to maintain profitability, hospitals began raising prices to everyone and shifting their unrecovered costs over to the government health care plans. Providers were forced to raise prices and shift the increasingly unrecovered cost of maintaining their practices over to the government, through billings made to Medicare and Medicaid.

Social Security and Medicare are important as social stabilizers. They are more than just a retirement program and a health insurance program. Everyone benefits when the weakest members of a society are protected. It makes the whole of society more stable. Yet there are many proposals are out there to scrap Social Security and replace it with some "other" unnamed program.

Others want to make Social Security voluntary and have a system of private retirement funds instead. The causes for a good program coming to this end are many. Social Security became a political football because Wilbur Mills, Chairman of the House Ways and Means Committee in the early 1970s, and then President Richard Nixon started a minor war over who would receive credit with elderly voters for the escalation of their Social Security benefits.

At the time, Mills was considering a run for the presidency and wanted to be sure that the seniors were behind him. The rivalry between Nixon and Mills was fierce. Each tried to "out do" the other in raising the level of entitlement and to provide automatic raises for beneficiaries. They were so successful that the problems of the unrestrained growth of entitlement spending can be directly traced to their actions.

Something can be done about the rate of these automatic cost of living increases. However, the major drain on the Social Security system is increasingly the rising cost of health care.

That earlier cost shifting done by the government, while increasing the health care cost for everyone, is now going the other way, and continues to increase the costs for everyone. Per-capita spending on Medicare has increased 70 fold in the period from 1966 to 1994. This was during a period when the general medical inflation rose 8-fold.[74] Much of the increased cost of private health care was being shifted onto the federal government through the higher prices that providers now charge to the federal programs. This is the primary reason that Medicare costs are now rising at twice the level of inflation.

The federal government, directly or indirectly, now pays for almost half of the nation's health care. Today the federal government spends $800 billion a year on health care, according to former Republican Senator and independent Governor Lowell Weiker, 90% of which is spent during the last four weeks of life. If this 90% figure is near to accurate, it provides additional incentives for hospice and the right-to-die debate.

This health care crisis will affect all of us, whether we are covered by Medicare insurance, or not. The federal government must now deal with the damage caused by the combination of anti-trust exemptions to the insurance industry and by conservative attempts to undo the New Deal. Today, the average worker already pays 16% of their salary in Social Security and Medicare tax, however, the maximum salary that these taxes are collected upon is $63 thousand. Therefore, those who earn the least– pay more of their incomes on this tax.

Those who earn the most– but pay the least, because the wealthy pay little or no Social Security and Medicare taxes, also benefit from a stable society. If we do not do something about it, Medicare and Social Security taxes are predicted to account for 25% of the salary of an average worker. If something is not done about health care inflation, at the current excessive health care inflation rate, the average couple retiring in 1995 can be expected to run up medical bills of $126,700 more than they will pay in premiums during their remaining lifetime.[75]

Not enough money is currently being collected from Medicare beneficiaries to fund the payments being made to the providers. However, just raising the rates, is not the answer. Medicare premiums are a much larger percentage of the pensions of the poorer recipients. Something must be done to encourage real reform of the system, because the co-pay and premium burden increasingly falls on those of average and lower incomes. There are eleven million seniors on Medicare, mostly women, who are just-getting-by on pensions and incomes of less than $8500 a year.

The Republican controlled 104th Congress, early on, showed their priorities when the House passed a $87 billion premium cut for the richest two million people on Medicare. Those who had their premiums cut were those with retirement incomes of over $75,000 a year and, therefore, also the most likely to vote Republican. Only after removing those individuals who can afford to pay more (and who indeed do have other options) from their obligation to pay for this plan, did that Congress begin cutting the funding for Medicare.

Medicare may be in a short term difficulty due to premium breaks for some– which raise the cost for the rest. We are all in serious trouble, in the long term, because of the effects of the shifting of the costs of private health care onto the federal government. This may have been done intentionally, or just have been allowed in repayment to the special interests for the earlier rounds of cost shifting which went the other way.

Either way, the initial under-funding of Medicare caused prices to go up in all segments of health care and resulted in the spiraling escalation of health care costs that plague us today. In essence, both the increases in the cost of Medicare and the resulting federal debt, is actually a result of earlier action of the Congress. Real health care financing reform is the only solution to both problems, both to control costs for the Social Security system and to reduce the federal deficit.

The problems in the Social Security system illustrate the worst aspect of what often happens in a democracy. Elected officials use government programs to win votes and placate special interests. The problems of Medicare and health care financing illustrate what can happen when the rules are changed to win campaign contributions from big money contributors and the special interests.

The effect that slowed growth has had on our economy and on the funding of social programs has been known for years. It is only getting worse. When asked what the best *single* thing that could be done to extend the life of the so-called "Medicare Trust Fund," Bush appointee, Deborah Steelman replied, "a four-percent growth economy every year through the year 2010."

The best part of a free society and freedom of the press, is the public can eventually find out what is going on. That is, unless the big corporations which own the media and the news organizations wish to keep it secret. Theoretically, in our democracy, politicians who have been bought-off by special interests can be replaced in the next election. However, campaign contributions from those same interests, and a cooperative press can keep them in office, seemingly forever.

Anti-Trust Laws

We had a situation– similar to that which we have today, in the final years of the 19th century. Then too, the rich and the powerful were engaged in forming monopolies and trusts to exploit the economy for their own benefit. After the Civil War, what was to become known as "The Gilded Age" began. Not unlike the tax cuts of 1981, in 1872 instead of merely reducing taxes for the wealthy, all federal income taxes were abolished. The wealthy were allowed to have just about everything their own way.

The most successful and greedy individuals, the Astors, Rockefellers, Carnegies, and Morgans, were held up in schools, the press, and the pulpits as examples of what had made America great. The rich and powerful controlled the economy, the Congress of that time and literally everything else in America, as well. *Laissez-faire*- literally, "Leave us Alone" became the catchphrase of the day.[76]

Using highhanded tactics, and liberal campaign "contributions," the robber barons ruled the roost in the Congress and the rest of the country for nearly twenty years. They were much more than just rich. They truly visualized themselves as role models and the prototype of a new American. They saw themselves as the product of a natural selection, much like Darwin had predicted in his 1859 theory of biological evolution. They genuinely thought that they had become millionaires due to Darwin's theory of "survival of the fittest." They were viewed by many and also viewed themselves as better than everyone else. They were, after all, rightfully America's new "elite."

Today, just as then, there is another side to this coin. When some gain, others generally lose. The unfair monopolies added great costs to all of commerce in return for the extra profit that the few enjoyed. The free ride soon came to an end with the complete collapse of the markets in 1889. The Sherman Anti-Trust Act was enacted by the Congress by the following year. This 1890 anti-trust law went a long way toward correcting the abuses of power of that earlier conservative heyday.

In such cases, federal action may be the only way to correct and to prevent the abuse of the market. Our federal government, at that time, established the adoption of antitrust laws as the best method to level the playing field, and to stop the abuse of ordinary working people by the elite. Federal Anti-trust laws are still, today, the best method to control the abuses of the market. America, in the 1890s, succeeded in solving these problems within the flexibility of the Constitution. In the 1990s, we must again stop the abuse of regular and working people by an elite. We must, again, enforce our anti-trust laws.

There are those, in the 1990s, who wish to revive the "Social Darwinism" of the 1890s. There are, today, groups that are favored by our laws over all of the others. The level playing field of commerce needs to be level for them as well. These special laws, tax breaks and exemptions that favor these elite groups cost all of us, both financially as individuals, and collectively as a society. John D. Rockefeller and the Standard Oil Trusts became so powerful during the 1880s that they could demand a rebate for every tank car carried by the railroads, even for those which were carried for *other* oil companies.

Today, our health insurance companies are exempted from those anti-trust laws which were designed to prevent such abuses. They routinely negotiate to receive extra discounts and rebates from health care providers, and therefore to shift their costs over to the other payers. They act as monopolies and set "take it or leave it" terms for providers. Insurers are allowed to negotiate terms that are highly favorable to themselves. There is no free market involved in these negotiations, either. Doctors, hospitals and pharmacies have no other choice. They must either give in, or not be allowed to participate in programs sponsored by insurance companies, which now dominate the market in health care.

It is interesting to note that inflation in health care costs has more than doubled that of the rest of the economy. The cost of Medicaid provided health care has doubled in the last 5 years. It has quadripuled in the last ten.[77] Private health insurance rates have gone up at an even higher rate. Insurance company stocks have increasingly set record highs and record yields. Insurance company profits have skyrocketed.

There may indeed be a cause and effect relationship between many seemingly unrelated events. Rebates to insurers are only one aspect of the problem.. Every individual pays more for insurance and gets less coverage and less financial security because anti-trust exemptions that were made to the insurance industry by a Republican Congress. Because of this anti-trust exemption, insurance companies cannot be sued for violations of the anti-trust laws. They may do what they will.

Because of the anti-trust exemptions, insurers can "cherry pick" clients that are not as likely to become sick, and refuse or deny coverage to anyone. They can legally charge any rate, or without notice raise rates to any level, or refuse to pay any claim. Society must either pay the increased costs for those who cannot afford to pay, or bear the loss of productivity and of useful lives.

This anti-trust law exemption to the insurance industry is the reason that Americans must spend over 13 percent of the GDP, or gross domestic product, on health care vs the 9 percent of GDP that other advanced western nations spend on their health care.[78] Insurance industry profit is the difference. Since the GDP is the total amount of money produced by the entire American economy, four percent of the GDP is indeed a lot of money. It is many times as much as would be needed to finance health care for *all* of the uninsured Americans.

The 1994 Clinton health care plan intended a portion of these excess profits be used for the health care expenses of the poor and the uninsured. Since there was so much money at stake, the industry used these excessive profits for their own purpose, to influence politicians. They used it in the battle to prevent there being any reform at all. However, in the less than two years since the Clinton health care plan was defeated, an additional two million Americans have found themselves without any health care coverage.

House Speaker Gingrich proposed privatizing the federal health insurance programs of Medicare and Medicaid. He wanted to enroll seniors and the poor into managed care and other private health insurance plans. He stated there will be a savings to the government if this were to happen. That this is not precisely true has been documented and his interest may not exactly be in trying to help the people. He may, instead, be trying to further the agenda of dismantling the New Deal, while also helping his supporters in the insurance and managed care industries.

Rather than forcing senior citizens into managed care plans; to really save money, we should repeal the anti-trust law exemption for the insurance industry. Real reform is necessary, but it will be all but impossible due to the special interest lobbyists and their hold over the Congress. Several Senators rush to claim credit for blocking all attempts at health care reform, perhaps, to receive increased contributions from those lobbyists who benefit from the status quo.

Toward the end of the 19th century, after many complaints of abuse and unfair pricing, Congress established the Interstate Commerce Commission. The commission was established to regulate the tariffs that the railroads charged. The railroads had been charging much higher tariffs where they had monopolies, to subsidize the traffic in areas where they had to be more competitive. The people were instead demanding fairness in the setting of rates.

The establishment of the ICC ultimately ended up being more to the advantage of the regulated than to the advantage of the traveling public. Rather than simply requiring the railroads to publish their tariffs, and to charge everyone at the same rate, the railroad lobbyists got special exemptions which raised the overall rates for all classes of traffic. Rather than allowing true and fair competition to set the tariffs, an anti-competitive, artificial price support system was ultimately set in place.

The insurance industry has fared even better. The last Republican controlled Congress enacted legislation giving the insurance industry total exemption from our nations anti-trust laws. The industry is now using it's federal anti-trust exemption to shift it's share of health care costs onto the government, employers, hospitals and providers. Yet, at the same time, it too, is raising prices to everyone else. Providers and the government get the blame for lower standards of care and for the higher prices. Insurers get the profits.

Less of us can afford health insurance because of the increasing profits that insurers demand. Few small businesses can afford to hire additional workers because of the high cost of health insurance and employee benefits. High health care cost work against the advancement of the individual, and also the entire economy by holding down employment and wages. The time is right to do something about this increasing problem.

The Interstate Commerce Commission was allowed to expire in 1996. It is also time for the anti-trust exemption to the insurance industry to expire as well. Exemptions to our nations anti-trust laws are always expensive for the ultimate consumers. In this case, we as a nation are paying at least thirty percent more for our health care than we need to.

9. Profiting from Trust

Federal "anti-trust laws" were originally instituted because some industries had used their position of trust to make huge profits for themselves. That the insurance industry was exempted from anti-trust laws does not mean that it, too, does not make huge profits. Today, with just about half of the total health care market, they are *extremely* profitable. There is little wonder that the private interests might wish to buy-off politicians to push for the privatization of Medicare. If this were to happen, they could have all-of-the-business without having to compete with federal government programs. It could be very profitable for the entire industry if this were to happen.

Before the Medicare reform package passed the House of Representatives in the fall of 1995, only one day of hearings were allowed to be held by the Republican leadership. The AARP, American Association of Retired Persons, was noticeably absent from even those brief discussions, although it represents the largest special interest group for seniors. What was the reason for this absence?

Earlier in 1995 the AARP had been subjected to the threats of Congressional hearings on their tax-exempt status. Could this be the reason that AARP was not very early vocal against a Medicare "reform" that might raise costs tremendously for their members? It was reported that a "carrot" was offered along with the "stick" of a hearing. Rumor had it that the AARP had itself been offered a federal anti-trust exemption if it would play along with the House leadership.. With such an exemption, the AARP would be able to bypass the insurance companies by offering a health care plan directly to their members. In June of 1996, AARP sent out mailers to it's members announcing a new health plan called "Members Plus." While now only covering prescription drugs, is this the start of such a plan? Can there be any other reason for the silence of the AARP, normally the premiere spokesman for the elderly?

The fact is, Medicare is not solely a program of health care for the elderly. Medicare insurance does cover the elderly and the sickest segment of the population at affordable rates. However, Medicare also covers health care for those who are disabled without regard to age. Medicare provides subsidies to teaching hospitals and to hospitals in rural areas. Medicare subsidies keep many hospitals open that otherwise would have had to close. Ending Medicare subsidies would result in the closing of many teaching hospitals and hospitals in rural areas and in the inner cities. Medicare is to the benefit of the entire population, not just of benefit to the elderly and their families.

Even with all the charitable and worthwhile things that it does, Medicare as it exists is still the most efficient form of health insurance delivery. Medicare spends only about 2% of gross expenditures on administrative costs. Two percent of a lot of money– is still a lot of money. Ross Perot and his EDS made a fortune out of that 2% when they began servicing Medicare for the government under a contract with the Nixon administration. While Medicare spends but 2 percent on overhead, the average mark-up on private health insurance is 50 percent.

The average cost for the administration and processing for each $10,000 in health insurance claims billed under Medicare is therefore $200, two percent. The average <u>profit</u> that a private health insurer would make that same claim is $3000, thirty percent. This calculates to a huge 1500% mark-up, when compared to the costs of the government program. Yet, this already tremendous profit continues to increase, because it's dollar amount increases along with the size of the hospital bills. This doesn't even include the profits from the extra discounts from providers. Even this kind of exorbitant profit, however, is purely legal because of the anti-trust exemptions. It is also "risk free" because all of the money is collected in advance.

Insurance companies have always been able to scapegoat doctors and hospitals for the increases in their premiums. The rationalization is, if insurance companies are paying more, insurance rates must rise to cover the increased costs. On the face of it, this argument appears to be true. Insurers were, therefore, seen as being justified in starting programs such as the Blue Cross "Cost-Wise" program which set maximum rates at which doctors agree to bill the insurance company in order to participate in insurance company programs.

Doctors are initially encouraged to sign up because they too wish to "hold down cost" and perhaps also gain enough new business to make-up for any discounts to be given. However, what often begin as "voluntary" programs to hold down costs, soon becomes "de facto" insurance company discounts, or a give-back from the doctors to the insurance companies.

Because of their anti-trust exemption, insurance companies can then go to providers, doctors and hospitals and demand extra discounts for allowing their subscribers to become the patients of these particular providers. The initial approach, is to offer to direct more business to a provider if the provider will give an extra rebate or discount to the insurer. These providers are then approached a few years later with another proposal to increase the discount amount.

If a provider does not, and other providers will, that provider is dropped from the program. Meanwhile, all of the insured patients, including original patients of the provider who had joined the plan because of that provider, are required to begin using a new provider. In this way, the insurer now owns the patient and can move the patient from doctor to doctor. Some insurers have now opened their own clinics to take full advantage of this ownership.

To make the market even more anti-competitive, these insurers have opened their clinics to the *cash paying* public. A patent does not even have to have insurance with that company, to be able to purchase care. What they must have is money, however, as caring for the poor and destitute is left to others. The poor are forced to use the higher cost emergency rooms where their care can be underwritten by the state. In this way, insurers are not only increasing costs for the "competition" but also making the extra profits that can be made from cash paying customers and to recruit new patients from other physician practices.

Insurers are now in direct competition with every physicians practice. The anti-trust exemption given to the insurance industry allows this, and other anti-competitive practices. In what amounts to blackmail, doctors and hospitals must abandon the poor, and either have to raise prices to the patients who pay cash, or shift some of their costs to other patients, in order to be able to afford the discounts to insured patients.

Most doctors and hospitals are forced to shift the cost to others by increasing the prices that they charge to everyone for their services. This cost-shifting– due to the unfair competition, is what has caused health care expense to rise at double the rate of inflation. Increasing health care costs contribute heavily to increases in entitlement spending and to the growth of the federal deficit.

The federal government, through the highly efficient Medicare program, still spends just a small percentage on the administration and the processing of claims. However, the total cost of these claims continues to rise. Prices are raised to everyone, but then so are premiums and the dollar amount of the insurers profit. Insurers can make extra profit by shifting the costs on to the taxpayer. Federal health care programs, in effect, are asked to subsidize the profit of private insurance companies by paying expenses that should have been paid for by the private plans.

There is no way to achieve or to encourage "fair competition," when the playing field that the competition is to be held on is, itself, far from being level. In return for directing their business, insurers are now routinely demanding and receiving 50% discounts from hospitals and clinics. The only way that a hospital can give that much discount, is to inflate prices to everyone else, or to shift costs and cheat other payers.

It is in this way that insurers force hospitals to raise prices to everyone else. The government, already paying for half of total health care costs, is billed for still more, and at higher rates to make up the difference. But, in typical anti-competitive fashion, the more health care costs, the more the insurance companies can charge, the greater their discounts and therefore the higher their profits. In fact, Blue Cross encourages cost increases by giving hospitals an additional incentive— an annual rebate based upon the total of all of the hospital's expenses.

Another way that insurance companies use their anti-trust exemption to their advantage is by basically being able to lie to their customers about what the actual cost of care is. Most insurers require that the insured also pay a portion of the expense, a co-pay, of usually 20%. By requiring a 20% co-pay from the insured and then receiving a 50% reduction in that charge from the provider, the insured are in fact paying 40% of the true cost. The patient pays 40% of the true cost of their care rather than the assumed to have been agreed upon 20%. This is how HMO's and insurers can make more money without having to raise premiums, nor must they then reduce premiums to compensate for the reduction in cost. Some HMOs, like US Healthcare, asks outside providers for give back discounts of over 60 percent. A patient with a 20 percent co-pay would then unknowingly pay for more of their own direct health care costs than even the insurer.

The same thing occurs with insurance coverage of prescription drugs. Insurers demand extra discounts from pharmacies and rebates from pharmaceutical manufacturers. The co-pay that a consumer pays is often a higher percentage of the total cost than the patient realizes. Any discounts that the patient receives are most often the result of give backs from pharmacies and drug companies. In many cases, the discount given by the pharmacy is a larger portion of the total price than what the insurer pays. The net result is that the insurer will often receive at or below-cost prescription drug pricing without much cost to the insurer. The pharmacy ultimately ends up shifting the cost of these below-cost drug sales to other cash paying customers.

The drugstore industry has traditionally been very competitive, which resulted in good deals for consumers. Prescription drugs have always before been priced competitively. Rite Aid Pharmacy, at one time, posted it right on the wall that they would meet any competitors price. However, give-backs to insurance companies have now raised prices to everyone else. – Now, cash customers end up paying more, often substantially more, to cover the below-cost sales to the insured. In Raleigh, a market that the Thrift Drug chain dominates, a cash customer pays $58.89 for a one month supply of a common drug At its counterpart in the Charlotte market, 150 miles away, where the chain is relatively weak, cash customers pay only $13.89 for that same prescription.[79] The Raleigh customer pays over $500 a year extra to subsidize the below-cost sales to the insured. A cash customer in Raleigh must not only subsidize below cost sales made in Raleigh but also those sales made in Charlotte.

Unlike Socialism, where those who can afford to pay more, are charged more to cover those who cannot pay as much, Social Darwinism encourages discrimination against the poor and uninsured. Those without insurance must pay higher prices to make-up for the discounts to the insured. Due to competition, prices are raised mostly on those drugs which people expect to be priced fairly. Yet, prices can only be increased on those drugs not usually "shopped" by consumers for the best price. Therefore, these price increases can be very dramatic. Usually it is the patients who can afford it the least, the retirees and those who cannot afford any insurance, who must pay more. The anti-trust exemption to the insurance industry hurts those who can afford it the least. The present system benefits only the insurance companies and those who really do not need the help.

What is worse, because of the anti-competitive nature of the system, all prescription drug consumers ultimately end up paying more. Because of the anti-trust exemption, manufacturers must sell to mail order pharmacies at a fraction of what retail pharmacies pay. They, therefore, charge higher prices to retail pharmacies to make-up the difference. These higher prices must be passed on to all retail customers, including those with insurance, on anything else they may buy in that store. All drugstore customers unknowingly subsidize the below-wholesale sales of drugs to insurance company and mail-order pharmacies through these higher wholesale prices.

Cost shifting, as a form of socialism, was tolerated before, because everyone knew they were paying extra for those who could not pay. Today, this socialism only benefits the corporate elite. It is the retirees on fixed incomes, it is families with children and others without prescription drug insurance who now must pay more. Like the Republican plan for privatizing Medicare, those who do not need the help are the ones who benefit, while those who truly need assistance— are denied it. The status quo in health care benefits only a few. It is no wonder the insurance industry lobbied so hard and directly spent sixteen million dollars to defeat health care reform in 1994.[80] Each of us, insured or not, are directly or indirectly paying more, either financially or through cuts in service for the resultant increases in profit for the insurance lobby.

Americans are told they do not want socialized medicine— by those who are fighting health care reform. As we know, under socialism, the means of production is owned or controlled by the state. Instead of a state ownership, Congress has allowed exemptions so big corporations can both own and control health care. The corporation which owns the largest prescription drug plan now also owns one of the largest drug manufacturers.

If your drug coverage is with that company, they will use this relationship to make even greater profits. This company now pays pharmacists to get doctors to change to drugs that are made by their company. Many doctors are so busy they will often say "just do it." These "different" drugs may treat the same illnesses, but are instead entirely different drugs, in fact, completely different chemical entities from what the doctor originally prescribed. There is always the possibility for increasing side affects or allergic reactions, however, the pharmacists are under a "Gag rule" from disclosing any of these facts to the patient. If your pharmacist is employed by a pharmacy that accepts this plan, they must attempt to change the drugs that your doctor prescribed to avoid a penalty, or even to face the loss of their job.

The Threat to the National Health

Worse than what it costs, is the damage that this anti-trust exemption is doing to the delivery of health care. Some Americans are paying for that insurance industry anti-trust exemption with more than money, they are paying for it with their health. Since the current health care system works against community based institutions, the poor and elderly must travel further to receive medical treatment or must visit the more expensive hospital emergency facilities. Very often, care is delayed solely due to problems with transportation.

What used to cost just a few dollars to quickly treat now costs many thousands to cure. Health care problems handled when they are small, always cost less than waiting until they become major. Today's system completely denies preventative and early health care to many, basically because the insurance industry makes a higher profit percentage from the larger, more expensive treatment options.

Community pharmacists and neighborhood drugstores were once a foundation of American health care. Local drugstores are the first place many went if they had any kind of a problem. Many American families still depend on their local drug stores for advice. After all, half of the doctor visits made today are unnecessary and most emergency room visits are for non-emergencies.

Likely, when you were a child, with a minor illness, your dad would take you down to that drugstore to see Ol' Doc. Doc would look at you, and either disappear into the back and return with something for you to take, or refer you to a physician, or even call for you. By forcing people into centralized, mail order plans for their prescription drugs, the insurance companies have almost totally eliminated the smaller, community based drugstores. By forcing extra discounts from doctors in private practice, most community based, independent physician practices have closed, as well.

In the community drugstores that are left, third party insurance claims cause increased delays for prescription customers and increase the chance of error, even for those patients who do not have insurance. Pharmacists must contact the insurance companies via computer modem each time they fill or refill a prescription for an insured. They must do this because many insurers reject or reduce payments on claims, or delay payment if at all possible. Therefore, if any line of the transmission is not suitable, the claim is rejected and must be redone and resubmitted.

This takes time, even if everything is working correctly. This extra time spent on insurance claims and their transmission causes most of the delay in prescription filling. Meanwhile a pharmacist may try to work on other prescriptions, increasing the opportunity for mixups, due to sheer quantity of partially finished work lying around on the prescription counter. To remain open, pharmacies are having to find ways to cut costs and services. Delivery service is a thing of the past. They must use more non-pharmacists and less total personnel to do more work. The public health and safety is thereby compromised. It is compromised solely to provide increased profit for the insurance companies.

Insurance companies now have three profit centers. The first is the traditional mark-up they have always added to cover profit and expenses. The second two are potentially much more dangerous to the public health. The first of these is the amount of extra discount or rebate they can get from the providers, doctors and hospitals. Managed care saves money only when costs are shifted to others. Insurers may receive discounts from providers, but these discounts can only come from reducing services or by forcing others to make-up the difference. The more people get into managed care plans, the less cost effective they can become.

If all of the patients in a hospital are on managed care, the only ways discounts can be given is to cut service, to raise prices, or to lie about how much discount is given. A pie may be cut into 6, or into 8 pieces, but the total amount of pie, itself, does not change. The combined total of all of the individual slices will still contain that same amount. The total, itself, is not changed. Any further division of that same pie will not result in more pie, but only in smaller pieces (read: less care) for each individual.

The third profit center for insurers is in denying care or by delaying payment for care. This option is a source of pure profit for the insurer. Insurers can accurately predict how much care a certain population will require. This becomes a fixed expense, to which they add their mark-up. In reducing fixed-expenses, by denying care, all of the savings goes straight to the bottom line.

Give backs from providers can no longer be expected to increase corporate profits. Health care providers have already given back as much discount as they can possibly give up. When a business operates on a 20% margin and gives back a 10% discount, they don't just give up 10% of their profit, they actually have cut their profit in half, and must now do twice as much, to make the same amount.

Physicians who must see twice as many people cannot spend the same amount of time in diagnosing and treating each problem. Less time being spent on each individual case usually means less care will be given to each individual patient. All patient care suffers under managed care, because even if they are not under a managed care program, their physician or hospital still must treat those patients who are.

Doctors are being forced to work harder and longer hours to make the same money. Most health care professionals, today, must do more work and are also being rushed to do it. The headlines are worse still: A man goes into surgery, and the wrong leg was amputated. A woman awoke to find that her surgeon had removed the wrong breast. An overdosage of chemotherapy medicine, mis-calculated by an overworked physician kills one patient, and seriously injures another.

The chances of error are only increased in a system that tries to get more work from already busy professionals, while offering them even less compensation. One surgeon remarked that going from ten procedures a day to thirty procedures a day takes a toll on even the best of surgeons. "It's like this," he said, "even Michael Jordan himself, would be less dexterous if he had to play three games every day."[81]

Cost are up, and care has deteriorated, because care is now being dictated for profit and not for people. Politicians are saying managed care is the answer. The Republican Medicare reforms rely on it totally for any savings to the system. Yet, even the stock market has discovered that HMO stocks are not as profitable as it first appeared they would be. There is even pressure within the managed care industry on the million dollar salaries paid to the top executives. The costs for layers of bureaucratic administrations on top of the salaries for hospitals and doctors does not leave much additional profit over what they could easily make just as insurers, even with the unfair advantage of the anti-trust exemption.

There is another reason that HMOs are not as profitable as they should be. It is because each cost saving measure that is implemented will soon become the new standard of care for the industry. Increasing quarterly profits become harder and harder to gain. Everyone else in the managed care business will quickly match any innovation and, therefore, few will long enjoy a competitive advantage. Mainly, each new standard of care just lowers the quality of care. Incentives such as paying physicians more to withhold tests and to deny care, have lowered costs, but mostly just lowered the quality of care.

"Gag rules" preventing doctors from discussing treatment options with their patients are not improvements to care. In fact, such innovations are the systematic violation of the rights of the patient. What's more, because of the lack of true competition in an anti-trust exempt environment, any costs that can be lowered– generally have been lowered only temporarily. Cost-shifting will surely raise them again in the next round of price increases.

Since the competition between plans sees to it that any competitive advantage will soon be matched, almost all of the savings in managed care situations come from the pre-negotiated discounts for service, or give backs, from providers or from the denial of care. Often in the competition for accounts, to get the health insurance business of large companies, the HMO, itself, must also give-back rebates to the employer. This puts the employer in the position of making money from the delay of care to its employees. If HMOs are the wave of the future, the future of health care will only get much worse.

Without any reform, the situation is bleek. Relying on ever bigger discounts is analogous to sitting on a big balloon. It goes down where you sit, but it pops-out everywhere else. For HMO's and the entire managed care industry to make any additional profit, they must rely on delaying payments or on denying any claim that they can get away with. How much further can we go with the managed care experiment before the balloon finally bursts?

Reform and Health Care

Some change is usually good for a society. With too much reliance on the status quo, society or whole segments of society can get fat, and non-productive. The growth of an ossified bureaucracy makes any civilization less efficient. Yet, an increasing conservatism makes for a society that is highly resistant to change. Members of an entrenched elite always become overly protective of their position, stature, and sphere of influence. Entrenched authority and the special interests which benefit from the way things are, can always be counted on to defend the status quo. They will fight to prevent reform, even when they know that some reforms are necessary. They will fight against virtually any change, even change which is both justified and required.

Change is a scary thing to many people. Change always carries with it the possibility of hurting someone and usually the most directly affected are those who are currently benefitting from the status quo. To be fair, users should not be abruptly denied the benefit of the system. The pain of dislocation should be shared by all, or as much of society as possible, because all of society will ultimately benefit from this change. It is important to lessen the impact on the individual by spreading the burden of change.

Needed change should be implemented swiftly to prevent the forces against that change from massing enough power to block it. Giving opponents of change enough time to organize a resistance is usually fatal. This point is well illustrated by the 1994 Clinton health care plan, which was in full public view and in the sights of it's critics for almost a year. The Republican Congress was elected in 1994 because they were successful in demonetizing and blocking Democratic reforms. The 1995 Republican Congress remembered this lesson, only too well. They were quick to limit the debate and to stifle dissent. This is neither right, nor is it good policy. The dynamic tension between opposing viewpoints can be a good thing. It can direct the thrust of necessary change in an appropriate direction, ultimately to the benefit of all concerned parties. All parties must be allowed to play at least some part in arriving at the final solution. Once the intended direction of change is set, however, the implementation may be phased in, so any pain is lessened or evenly shared. Sometimes, just a delay in the implementation of a needed change may be all that the opponents of change may require in order to be able to sign on to it.

Reforming health care, both to improve access and to reduce its costs, should be the highest priority facing our Congress. It is the largest and fastest growing segment of expense to the federal government and also to each of us as individuals. We, as Americans, are paying more and getting much less for our health care dollar. As a nation, we are paying at least 30% more for our health care than any other westernized nation.[82] Insurance plans that reduce the payments to providers of health care only cause the expense of that care to be shifted elsewhere, usually over to the federal government plans. We all pay more, ultimately because some do not pay their fair share. If everyone was covered by the same plan, this cost shifting could not occur.

Because of anti-trust exemptions given to the insurance industry, no true competition now exists in the health insurance system. The health care system financing system appears to exist solely to profit insurers and plan administrators. Doctors and other providers get less for their services. Consumers and their families must pay more for coverage. Consumers are likely to be denied their choice of plans. They very often do not have their choice of doctor or hospital. Managed care forces consumers and providers to fit into their systems, instead of utilizing the existing systems and allowing medicine to be practiced in traditional ways. An AP poll found that twice as many people rated their care to be fair or poor when they were unable to choose their doctor, as in HMO situations, than even in other managed care plans by a margin of 32% to 16%[83].

The level of service provided to the patient, the consumer of health care, has become much worse, and yet the providers of health care are also being squeezed. They are made to work harder and longer hours for a yet smaller share of the health care dollar than any other western industrialized democracy. Hospitals too, are being forced to lay-off nursing and other medical staff in order to pay for the increased administrative expenses. They are being forced to subsidize the profit of the insurance industry by giving back extra discounts to be allowed to serve those persons who have insurance. The only organized interest to continue to benefit from the status quo in health care is the insurance and managed care industry.

The Republican majority 104th Congress proposed a reform of Medicare and the health care financing system. It planned to remove expenditures of $270 Billion over seven years, mostly by lowering payments to providers, among other changes. We have tried this method of cost savings before, and know where those cost were ultimately shifted. Where these unpaid costs would be eventually shifted is anyone's guess. However, in the short-term, these lowered fees will only make it harder for doctors and hospitals in the traditional fee for service system to be able to afford to treat Medicare patients. The Republican leadership says that they want to give the people a choice.

Most Medicare recipients will be given this choice: to pay for more of their own care, or to sign up with a Health Maintenance Organization, an HMO. Under this plan, joining an HMO will be the only realistic option available to Medicare recipients of average means; if their health is good enough for them to qualify to join one.

The other proposal included in the Republican reform plan is to establish tax deductible Medical Savings Accounts, (MSAs.) Medical savings accounts are a "catastrophic" insurance based product that lets low-risk and healthy individuals gamble that they will stay well. If they do stay well, they will pay less and get some of their money back at the end of the year. If they get sick, they must pay higher deductibles and a larger portion of their expenses before the insurance starts paying.

That the MSAs have lower premiums and much higher deductibles makes them attractive to mainly the younger and healthier populations, leaving the older and sicker populations in the traditional fee-for-service program. This would only drive-up the costs for those remaining in the traditional program, because the costs per individual goes up, not down, as the group becomes increasingly older and sicker. In the end, the taxpayer would end up having to subsidize the Medicare program more— not less as the Republicans have predicted. These costs may even be increased enough to end the program.

MSAs are a flawed concept. With their higher deductibles, they are designed to benefit only the "well-est" and the wealthiest of Americans and to take their contribution out of the pooled resource that benefits everyone. Perhaps, this was an attraction to the Social Darwinists in the Republican 104th Congressional Majority. However, there is currently only one company, Golden Rule Insurance, that promotes and offers Medical Savings Accounts. Golden Rule has some of the highest profits in the industry. To get these high profits, according to Consumer Reports, it rejects 20-30 percent of all applicants who are 65 and as many as 50 percent of those who are 70. Golden Rule can "cherry pick" applicants because it is the world's largest insurer of individuals.[84]

Why else would the Republican Congress push a solution offered by only the one company? According to reports filed with the Federal Election Commission, The Golden Rule Insurance Company was third in soft money contributions to the Republican National Committee, behind only Amway and Phillip Morris. It gave $416,000 to the RNC for Republican candidates for Congress in October of 1994 alone, with total contributions of over a million dollars. Newt Gingrich and GOPAC received over $200,000 from Golden Rule.[85]

We do need to reform the health care financing system. However, we need to reform the _total_ health care financing system to avoid cherry picking and other cost shifting schemes, that have inflated the cost of our current system. The simple and incremental first step to a national system would be to open up Medicare to a younger and healthier population. This is a "win-win" solution, but one not likely to be on the table in a Congress that has been bought off by the special interests. Those aged 45-59 who have recently become jobless due to "downsizing" by big business would become ideal candidates to be first included in the Medicare program. Many such "early retirees" now find it difficult to obtain a new job that offers any kind of benefits.

Even by paying higher rates than the older and sicker Medicare recipients, these unemployed or underemployed would save substantially over the private plans. Costs would go down with this open program, both for existing and for the new subscribers because the costs associated with the older and sicker population would be spread-out over more and healthier subscribers. As more subscribers leave a private health insurance system that has been shifting its costs to Medicare, the spiral of cost escalation that comes with this system would also be reduced. The cost of care would, therefore, go down for everyone, to the insured and to the un-insured alike. Those individuals who would like a level of care that is higher than the basic coverage of this public plan would be free to purchase a supplemental policy on the open market.

Health care reform need not be complicated. There need only be strength in numbers. If there is to be no national health care system, a co-op of individual citizens can easily be formed. A large enough co-op could receive almost the same discounts that the drug manufacturers and health care providers give to the HMO and managed care companies, but instead, pass the cost savings along to the consumers. In theory, this takes only having a sufficient pool of subscribers.

If there are enough individuals who would like to be able to purchase prescriptions at wholesale or less, and receive at least 20% off of doctor and hospital bills, a public or private group could readily be formed to accomplish this. Under existing law, individuals who do not have health care coverage could legally join together to form this type of association. The main reason for the complexity of the 1994 Clinton health care plan was to allow it to accommodate all of the various, politically active special interests that must be accommodated in Washington, today. You and I, joining together as individuals, however, need only accommodate ourselves. The basic idea is simple. In America, individuals with common goals and united can accomplish anything.

There are also other avenues for health care reform. The most cost-effective and competitive form of health insurance is "catastrophic" health insurance coverage, although the deductibles are much higher. In catastrophic insurance plans, the subscriber pays for all of the smaller problems and the insurance kicks in only for the more severe illnesses. By at least leveling the discount playing field while adding the much cheaper catastrophic coverage, a health care co-op could offer much lower overall premiums to the consumer.

The total amounts of discount could vary, but would represent a portion of the give-backs from providers that insurance companies receive and the extra profit that insurers enjoy because of their anti-trust exemption. Overall, just by forming a buying co-op, consumers could save a large portion of their health care costs and guarantee that they will always retain coverage. See http://www.charweb.org/health for more information on Health Insurance Co-ops. Further savings can always come from the cooperation of consumers and providers.

The original mission of Blue Cross and Blue Shield was very close to this in concept. Blue Cross and Blue Shield was first established as a "not for profit" organization to protect doctors and hospitals. However, that mission was changed. In 1986, the Blue Cross and Blue Shields won the right to exclude "high-risk" subscribers and to raise rates to what the market would bear. Today, they are not much different than everyone else in the insurance business. According to Patrick Hayes, president of the Blue Cross and Blue Shield Association that franchises the name, "They are definitely not charities." [86]

Almost that same thing can happen with government systems. The New Deal, as a social contract, was corrupted because some politicians, seeking contributions, sold-out to the various special interest groups that had evolved only to insure more for themselves. New Deal programs may need reform, but those kinds of reform that will fix the true problems, and not that which benefits only the special interests. We may need reform, but certainly not that which is counter-productive or which simply names a scapegoat.

Everyone benefits when they pool their resources for specific purposes. This is the principle behind the original non-profit Blue Cross and Blue Shields. This is the principle behind paying taxes. The government pools the tax money to build things like roads and schools that we all can share. We each not only do not have to build our own, but individually do much better than we could have done by ourselves. This concept also works for social stability. It is simple, really.

In the New Deal, the social stability of a purely collective system was used to balance the extreme volatility of an unregulated free enterprise system. In a dynamic tension between those two extremes, the poor could be cared for without the markets even noticing that burden. At least before the insurance companies abused their anti-trust exemption, historically, it had never before cost the taxpayers more than 1-2 percent of the entire federal budget to provide the welfare and social safety net programs.[87] This truly infinitesimal amount provided for a cultural and social stability. That small amount was not noticed, at all, for as long as the economy was allowed to grow. Economic growth more than covered the expense.

Just as in growing economies, we are all able to share in the increase, a stagnant economy puts pressure on everyone. In growing economies, small businesses have the equal opportunity to enter markets as have their larger competitors. However, only in stagnating markets are larger companies able to use their size to overwhelm their smaller competitors. Special treatment to large corporations and the anti-trust exemption to the insurance industry is more than just being unfair to small businesses and working people. More expensive health care insurance can only hurt those who can least afford to obtain it, just as it can only help those who hold the monopoly on providing it. The situation cannot be made fair, even when everyone pays more, equally. Those who can afford to pay more for insurance, will. Those who cannot pay more, will do without it, and the state will pay for their care. The health care market is different from any other. Everyone gets care, whether or not they can pay, just as everyone ultimately shares in paying for increases in the cost of the total.

An anti-trust exemption for the insurance industry is wrong because anyone can be denied or rejected for health insurance for any reason. The insured can be charged at any rate, and that rate can be changed at any time. It is wrong because it results in the unfair shifting of costs on to others. Increasingly those without insurance, the uninsured, are charged more for drugs and medical services to offset the discounts given to the insured.

The nation's total health care cost in total, the cost for everyone, is much higher due to the exemption of insurance companies from our nations anti-trust laws. The cost are higher, and the standard of care is lower, but it allows greater profits to the insurance companies. We need health care reform and the end to anti-trust exemptions. Unfortunately, the industry has friends in the Congress who will help them to keep it. Special interests and the insurance industry defeated health care reform in 1994. They will continue to use the control of government to benefit only themselves, unless we act together as a nation to end it.

The very wealthy can buy insurance coverage. The poor can get coverage that is paid for by the rest of us. However, the underinsured or uninsured middle class family stands to lose their homes and their life savings if a family member suffers a serious or catastrophic illness. This is the very reason that

President Johnson proposed national medical insurance for the elderly, in the first place. President Johnson proposed Medicare because traditional insurers would not cover the elderly, at any price, and this lack of affordable health insurance had caused financial catastrophe for many seniors and their families.

I know of at least one family who lost their home due to the illness of a family member. Although this particular family had other family to rely-on and was not ultimately forced to go onto public assistance, many others have been. There are many more families who have suffered serious financial setbacks, because they could not afford insurance, or could no longer afford to continue their insurance coverage.

While 37 million working Americans are without health insurance in 1995 (two million more than there were in 1994), through their taxes they help to subsidize $43 billion dollars of corporate health plans, most of which provide lavish benefits for top executives.[88] If these uninsured Americans do get sick or become ill, as is the usual, the middle-class taxpayer will be forced to pick up the tab.

10. Our Pooled Resources

At one time in this country we took great pride in our system of national parks, our public libraries and museums, and our public institutions. That we held these things in common and that we paid for and maintained them by contributions from our taxes did not bother us in the least. In fact, we took much of our identity as a great nation from our public works. We used and enjoyed the roads and public parks. We took pride in our universities and the education our children received in public schools. The private sector had little to do with the success or failure of our community systems, our pooled resources, except to contribute to it in the form of taxes.

When individuals pool a portion of their money and resources for a specific goal– that all will benefit from, each gets more for less. Individuals alone, cannot afford to build their own roads and their own schools. People coming together and working together to improve their own communities and the pooling of resources is basic to our advanced society. Our democracy allows for the incorporation of many and differing ideas into the community, if the individual will take the lead. It does not demand, nor will it allow for an ideological purity.

No one ideology has a "lock" on all of the good ideas. The private sector does not have all of the answers. In private sector solutions of public problems, some will gain and others always lose. A society that is run by and for the elites is little different if those elites are communist elites or corporate elites. In a democracy, especially in the public sector, we seek to arrive at a "win-win" solution for everyone, if at all possible.

The dynamic tension between the extremes of the left and the right have given us some of our most innovative solutions. Although out of favor now, the concept of liberalism was a meld of thought from both left and right. It led to creative policies and to the glory days of our republic in the post-war era. Each side gave up something and got back more than either side had brought to the table. The communist threat forced them to work together. Together the left and right in American politics worked to accomplish their mutual goal of making the world safe for democracy. In the 1960 presidential elections, there was so little difference between the stands of Nixon and Kennedy that Kennedy was forced to invent a "Missile Gap" with the Russians in order to have anything at all to talk about.

We need to maintain a strong free-enterprise system. However when free enterprise is allowed to enter the public sector, to handle our pooled resources, some gain and others generally will lose. The charge of government is not to decide who profits, and how much. That is the goal of the free-enterprise system. Government is there to do for us what we cannot easily do for ourselves. Government exist solely to protect the common interest, not to provide a profit or to protect the profits of those individuals who would seek to influence it.

That some Members of Congress will take sides depending on the amount of money that will be contributed is not an extreme case. No matter which party is in charge, it may be corrupted by those special interests who are looking out only for themselves, for their own interest, first. Some will gain under their proposals and some will lose or gain very little. However, when the public policy is decided by the private interests, then the public interest will always lose.

To gain the most from dynamic tension, to enjoy the benefits of this association, the public and the private sectors must be kept strictly separate from each other. After all, the goals of public and private sectors are different. The goal of free enterprise is to produce profits while the goal of the public sector is to efficiently manage the public resources. The bottom line of government is not to show a profit, but to efficiently do the public's business.

Free-enterprise should dominate the private sector, and be left alone, except when government regulation is necessary to protect the public interests. However, none of us want free enterprise to dominate the decisions that need to be made for us by our public officials. Public officials need to be influenced solely by that which is in the public interests. Our current system of campaign financing, of raising money for candidates, however, works against our elected officials being totally unbiased when dealing with private interests.

People generally do not like to pay taxes. The profit motive applies to individuals, as well, and most of us wish to keep as much as we can in their own "private sectors." But, people also have an interest in the larger picture. They are not generally against pooling some of their money as insurance against catastrophe and for the benefit of public works. People do not mind paying fair taxes, if they think they are being well spent.

Taxpayers just do not like to think they are being taken advantage of. It does not inspire the confidence of taxpayers when the private sector uses their trust in the public sector to earn tremendous profits for themselves. The insurance industry is only one example of those who have benefitted at the expense of the public treasury and our pooled resources. The insurance industry has used their Congressionally granted anti-trust exemption, just as the defense industry has used the importance of their position to reap huge profits at the expense of the public trust.

Perhaps worse than misuse of the public trust, is the misuse of our personal and professional trust. There is now a slickly produced video being circulated to physicians about a new kind of marketing, an "investment" opportunity for the nineties. This tape is hosted by Gary Collins and Sarah Purcells and features the highly positive testimony of three doctors and an accountant. Nowhere on the box or during the program does it even *once* mention the sponsors, but it does, however, make compelling arguments for contacting the individual who sent you the tape.

According to the "salesman," who sends the tape, the intended audience is the overworked physician who is working sixty hours or more a week, and who is less financially secure than he or she used to be. It is not mentioned, but is also preferably one who is bitter about it as well. Doctors are targeted because they are generally earning much less than they once did, and are now less financially secure. After all, it is they who are bearing the brunt of the cuts in payments for health care, both from the federal government and the insurance companies.

Doctors also have many patients who trust them, and also a reputation for being too busy to look out for financial details. The general appeal of this marketing is to achieving fairness and the recovery of lost income and financial stability rather than solely to greed. One of the anecdotal stories used during the interview was of a practitioner who just gave his share of the practice to his partner because it was no longer worth anything.

In the beginning of this pitch, the physician is told there is normally an investment in time required of perhaps 15-20 hours a week with a pay-off of huge amounts of money at the end of two years. However, the physician is also told that with this type of marketing, the "salesman" also gains when the physician gains and therefore the "salesman" will do most of the work.

After several sessions of marketing basics, lessons in exponential math and interesting possibilities for financial security, the physician learns all that is required for them to do is recruit from their patients, to tap a resource which they had not thought much about, the trust of their patients. By using this untapped asset, the physician could re-gain the financial stability of the practice which had been taken away from them.

The idea is sold to physicians as a way to reclaim that which they had lost. Once the physician is really sold on it, then, and only then, are they told that the program sponsor is Amway. However, just who was it that took the financial stability away from physicians practices, and who put them in a position to want to sell out for extra cash? Was it, ultimately, the federal government, the same federal government where a Republican majority Congress gave an anti-trust exemption to insurance companies? Is this the same Republican party who took money from special interests to block health care reform, favor managed care and big health care corporations, and which also received millions from Amway? Is this not also what made life much less secure for doctors?

America's anger is not directed so much at "failed liberal policies" or fraud, waste and abuse as it is against influence peddling by our elected leaders. The American public demands fairness and equal treatment from government. Yet, conservative Federal Reserve policies are what reversed the creation of more economic pie for all to share. It was *Social*

Darwinism in government that slowed the historic growth rate of our economy to benefit the elites. Social Darwinism seeks to further advance the elites, stealing much of the opportunity for advancement from our middle class, including America's doctors. Slow growth initiated the debate over how to all share in that same pie, not waste and abuse. Waste and abuse became the scapegoat while the true causes of the squeeze on the middle class were hidden from the general public. However, the public will find out. The American people will be much more than angry at those leaders who sought to profit from their control of our shared pool of resources.

Control of what we *will* share is just as important as what we already *do* share One reason that executive salaries have risen so extravagantly, is because our leaders adopted policies which encouraged it. Top executives take more compensation in salary because their salaries are, in fact, subsidized by everyone else. Big earners not only pay income taxes at a lower rate, but also are exempted from paying Social Security and Medicare taxes on most of it. Employers further do not have to match an employee contribution. The net result is at least a 15-20% taxpayer subsidy for obscene salaries. Americans can no longer support the historic governmental role in the pooling of our resources, unless all will benefit from it.

Our leaders have a fiduciary responsibility to us. The American people expect them to be good stewards of everything which is entrusted unto them. This includes *all* of our pooled resources, including our land, air, water, public safety *and* our financial resources. We hold our leaders to a much higher standard, expecting them to make wise investments with the public assets. We expect the leaders of both parties to work together in good faith. We want them to come forward with policies which will benefit the entire country, not just those to benefit the special interests.

Social and Economic Policy

The conservative "think tank" and it's attempts at engineering social policy has been very effective in the promotion of conservatism, just as they have been very hurtful to society as a whole. What they are advocating is not new, but is now intended as a means to gain political advantage over the other philosophies of government. Just as we all recognize the need for religion to play a greater role in our lives and in our personal decisions– it does not then become an excuse for non-mainstream religious ideologues to dominate the government and force their values upon the rest of us.

There *are* traditional values that we can all agree on as being important. These include looking after the interest of children, of women, and the elderly. These interests are important. Together, they truly are the values of American families. However, these are the interests that have been allowed to further erode once conservative administrations took control of the social welfare system. Their decline has, in fact, greatly accelerated under conservative control.

Conservative involvement in rule making has made the problem of illegitimate births much worse. Rigidly adhering to a rule of marriage before sex has worked to prevent marriage. Insisting there be no father present in the home, in order to give aid to the dependent children, has removed fathers from homes. Fatherless homes, then and now, become a major source for future illegitimate births.

Most women, whether rich or poor, do value companionship. Most are seeking to form some type of relationship. It is hard enough for an unwed head of a household to form a relationship that can lead to marriage, as it is. Any father present is better than no father present at all. Conservative economic policies have slowed job growth. Therefore, fewer men can marry and take the responsibility for raising a family. Excessively conservative and mean-spirited social policies have made things much worse today for poor families and for unwed mothers than they have ever been before. Putting women into much lowered circumstances, only makes them more vulnerable to further sexual predation.

Rates of illegitimate births rise dramatically in the teen years and decline steadily with age until they are almost non-existent by the thirties. This suggests that even relatively uneducated women wise-up to the promises made to them. They must be learning from experience, because very often the community has neglected to protect, or to educate them in the first place. This also illustrates the importance of education and of community support of these goals in the self regulation of behavior.

The government does not have the duty to oversee every move that our children make. We do, however, have the duty to warn, to protect, and educate our children so that they do not have advantage taken of them. Knowledge is not always pleasant, but lack of knowledge can often be quite unpleasant. Conservative objection to sex education, very often, quite simply makes those who are uneducated into parents.

Some parents genuinely believe it is their responsibility to educate their own children, but most of those who object to the teaching of reproduction in public schools, do so, on religious grounds. However, if it is not taught at home or at school, then the number of students who can get good birth control and disease prevention information is needlessly restricted. People need good information with which to make good decisions. Withholding this information can only lead to poor decision making or to simply going along with someone else's decision. There can be no religious grounds to condone that.

At best, without education, innocent and ignorant adolescent girls are left to their own defenses against more experienced, older males. In what in most cases amounts to child abuse, teen moms are made pregnant by men averaging better than five years older than they are.[89] Such men, likely, are paying them male attention for the first time, since girls who find themselves in this position were likely from and raised in fatherless homes. Fatherless homes thereby become the prime breeding grounds for future fatherless homes. Additionally, fatherless homes provide little protection from sexual predators for women and for their daughters.

In his book *The Selfish Gene*, Richard Dawkins describes the biological and sexual strategies that have been genetically evolved by men and women for mating and reproduction. In a nutshell, the most successful biological strategy for a male is to invest as little time and resources as possible into mating with as many females as possible. The reverse strategy is true for females, where the biological contribution and time investment is much greater. In summary; biologically, men are rewarded for statutory rape and for spending as little time as possible being husbands and fathers. Society needs to develop the necessary tools to once again reverse this sexual bias.

Since the traditional stigma is largely gone from illegitimate births, we need to ask ourselves to what purpose did that stigma serve. Originally, this stigma existed to encourage marriage and to promote the formation of families. Families, in turn, protect the rights of, and are crucial to the proper upbringing of, *the children*. In the Neo-Conservative system, one unguarded moment puts a female on the path to be abused again and again, while the needs of the children are ignored totally. The opposite of caring is not hatred. The true opposite of caring is indifference. Neo-Conservative systems solely exist for the powerful to remain powerful, and yet, even to increase their power. In this system, the weak exist only to be used by the strong. They do not count, nor do they matter.

Our children should, instead, be a priority for all of society. The proper upbringing of the children should not be an afterthought nor should it be considered a charity. As the twig is bent, so grows the tree. It is in the interest of society as a whole that the children be given the opportunity to become good and productive citizens. We must replace that no longer effective tool of stigma with something else, and we must develop a social support system to accomplish that goal of protecting the children.

Scapegoating and blame will not work. Perhaps, the fathering of illegitimate children should finally be made illegal. Such a law most certainly would have been handed down to us in English Law had there earlier been the ability to determine parenthood. Fatherhood can now be easily and accurately determined through the genetic testing methods that we now have. There is only one other option: prevention. We can replace stigma with education and community involvement in the protection of our young people from sexual predators.

Neo-Conservatives show favor to a rigid anti-abortion social policy, although it increasingly turns ignorance, rape, or a momentary lapse of individuals, into a permanent under class. That a noted Conservative Television Preacher's first child was conceived before he and his wife were married indeed shows that we all are human, and is yet a further example of how rigid is the ideology. Ideological purity is not the object of leadership. The duty of leadership is to help individuals in society to make good decisions, to learn to make good choices on their own. The object of good government is to lead people in the right direction, yet stay out of their lives, as much as possible. Successful leaders provide leadership by example, and do not try to dictate their choices to others.

The "system" under conservative administrations, however, has ignored teen sex and sexual predation. In some areas, children having children is a badge of maturity. It proves an individual to be an adult, and rewards them as such. For the community it is a tragedy. However, it was easier and much cheaper for the government to just send a monthly check than it is to provide protection for young girls, to teach job skills or provide job training, or to provide day care for working mothers until they get on their feet. The system of today perpetuates an uneducated, unmarried, unproductive, social underclass. This is just fine with conservative elites, those same conservative elites who have been working within the system to help to destroy the system.

During the Bush administration, gag rules for doctors and nurses were instituted. Doctors in federally funded clinics were prohibited from even mentioning the existence of abortion as an option. The choice to have a child was made in advance for many young girls, with the unwritten promise of what would amount to lifetime federal assistance. Given no other choice, what poor, undereducated young girl could object to living independently, possible escaping an abusive situation, probably in her own apartment, by going ahead and having her baby. Economic incentives such as these, while less expensive in the short run, have also gone a long way in erasing the stigma that was earlier so effective in discouraging illegitimacy.

Most teen moms want a normal life just like anyone else. They may not be as mature or as well educated as others, however, they too want the best for themselves and their children. They simply do not have the tools with which to make good decisions nor do they have the ability to look ahead or even comprehend fully the future consequences of actions taken today. Many reasons are given for having children. Very often, those who are asked to make these decisions are not yet mature enough to make them The fact is, most social ills are directly traceable to poor decision making and to the lack of education. Correcting the problem, long term, requires education and job training and most of all, protection of our young people from those that would abuse or take advantage of them.

Under previous administrations, economic policy was tilted to favor the rich. Economic policy since the early 1970s, favors old money and existing wealth over the young and those just starting out. Marriage and the formation of traditional families by the middle class is declining due, in large part, to excessively conservative economic policies that hold down opportunity. There are now fewer young adults who have the confidence in their long-term ability to support a family. Indeed, the opportunity for the full employment of all citizens has declined.

Wages are stagnant for most Americans, and the standard of living has been declining for many years. Competition from imported goods have eliminated whole legions of American workers, especially those in the higher wage and lower skilled manufacturing jobs. With less jobs and therefore less opportunities for advancement being created today, there should be no surprise that less of the traditional "family values" are being exhibited by our young people, and that one result of this may be the increase in non-standard relationships and of illegitimacy.

Because of the high cost of health insurance, fewer of us can get that coverage through our places of employment. In fact, loosing health care benefits for yourself and your family may be the worst aspect of getting off of welfare. The high cost of employee benefits is a major part of the reason that fewer jobs are created in America today. It is much cheaper for many employers to pay time and a half overtime than it is to hire an extra employee and to pay those benefits. The high cost of benefits keeps both raises and wages down.

Because the high cost of health insurance makes it hard for small employers to afford it, the high cost of insurance favors larger companies, who can negotiate benefits, over smaller companies in the competition for skilled workers. The giant retail chains gain an advantage over other retailers in hiring mostly part time workers, because employees who work less than thirty hours a week are exempted in federal law from having to be covered by benefits. The downside of this is, if these part-time, uninsured employees do get sick and then cannot pay, the taxpayer must foot the bill.

The changes that are occurring in the jobs market call for an increased investment in our citizens. Those who have skills that lag behind those which are needed to earn a living wage need to be retrained to improve their job skills. Every adult citizen should have the tools with which to earn a living wage. Education and retraining for new work are the most important things that we can do to revitalize our society. By insuring that individuals have the skills to compete in a changing job market, we insure that everyone earns their own way.

Private industry is reluctant to spend money on worker training, because, once trained, they may use their new skills to obtain a higher paying job elsewhere. The states are almost in the same position because people often move from state to state for better employment. Therefore the federal government, if only by default, must make the primary investment in education and job training. Instead, our government now spends a lower percentage of GDP on job retraining than any other western civilization.[90]

At a time of crisis in the job market, when workers need to be retrained for new work, the federal government should be investing heavily in job training. Instead, according to the Congressional Record, the House of Representatives voted to cut $9 Billion from even the then current spending for job training and vocational rehabilitation programs. In contrast, they proposed $13 billion in extra military spending that even the military did not want. However, the lobbyists for the defense contractors did want it. Unfortunately, there are no lobbyists for job training programs nor does the military or anyone else in Washington seem to have the clout of the defense industry.

The big-business lobbyists have the ear of the Congress and therefore get special treatment. Highly paid lobbyist make the difference when it comes to getting special favors for a particular industry. Large corporations have the edge when it comes to hiring lobbyists to state their case. Big retailers have gotten an unfair advantage that has driven many small retailers out of business. Owning your own small business and advancing by industry and thrift or by just plain hard work is all but impossible today.

People are working harder and longer hours, just to maintain the lowered standard of living that they now have. People are spending more and more time just earning a living. This leaves less time that can be devoted to higher level social and learning activities. People have less time for both civility and the good manners that in the past smoothed everyday social intercourse.

The general level of daily social interaction has become much coarser. A powerful elite minority has arisen. The elite was able to develop because it now had acquired all of the money, time, and opportunity the rest of us no longer have.

The chief benefaction of slavery in the pre-Civil War South, was that it allowed slave holders the time to become involved in education, politics, civic and social affairs. Having the time and the money for this involvement gave rise to the establishment of a powerful conservative elite, an elite that could argue effectively for the conservative cause, and for slavery. In defending the status quo, the elite made many "state's rights" arguments that ultimately got even non-slave holders involved in their cause. Many poor-white Southern men lost their lives in the Civil War because they were convinced that a rich, white-male elite also best represented their interests.

Today, too– the federal government is accused by conservatives of "grabbing power" from the states. This "power grab," however, resulted only because some states refused to pass or to enforce laws guaranteeing fair and equal treatment to all of their citizens. In some states, the poor and minorities were not included in basic public services such as running water, sewer, electricity and paved roads. It was important the federal government step in, especially in areas where segregationists had tried to deny educational access to the children of the descendants of slaves.

Individuals need to be treated fairly, and no one deserves to be treated any better than all of the others. The American people expect a basic fairness. Our system is based on the worth of the individual. In it, everyone deserves the chance to advance themselves. People who feel that things are going against them and will only continue to go against them become increasingly cynical, bitter, and anti-social.

The American dream is to gain a better life for ourselves and our children. We realize that this may not always be easy, and do not mind working hard and long hours to acheive this goal. As good Americans, we feel that our government should at least be neutral in its dealings with us. We feel everyone deserves at least a shot at the American Dream. However, for most of us, those not among the elite, the system is broken.

The Public Health and Safety

A most frightening statistic, is that of what will often happen to the children born of teen moms. In North Carolina 98% of the boys with learning disabilities and in trouble with the law, the "Willie M." children as they are called, were born to teenage mothers.[91] Data as overwhelming as this, can only suggest *all* children born to teenage mothers may also be at a greater risk. It further suggests that even well-meaning teenage mothers may not have the maturity or the education to properly raise children. Fourteen year old girls, especially, have no business being parents. When fourteen year old girls are having babies, and fourteen year old boys are roaming around and killing one another with machine guns, society has only itself to blame.

According to FBI statistics, in 1995, crime was down for the third straight year, overall. While overall crime was down by 3 percent, crime committed by those who were under 18 years old was up by 7 percent. The tremendous rise in the juvenile crime rate over the last 20 years corresponds almost exactly with the start of conservative control of the welfare system. This indicates to many that the two factors may somehow be related. In the very least, indifference to the problems of youth do not make these problems any less significant, either for the children involved or for society as a whole.

Crime hurts all of us, but it hurts poor neighborhoods more dramatically. Crime hurts poorer neighborhoods much worse, both in physical and in economic terms. Most of the wealth in middle class American is tied up in home equity. Even less wealthy homeowners take pride in having a share of the

American Dream. Their homes may be worth less than equivalent homes located elsewhere, because homeowners in a crime ridden neighborhood suffer the economic impact of crime on real estate values. Crime lowers real estate property values and therefore lowers the net assets of those homeowners who live in that crime ridden neighborhood. The investment of these homeowners would climb in value, rather than decline, if their houses were located in safer neighborhoods.

Crime also hurts poor and minority communities, economically, in other ways. The free market demands higher prices for allowing stores and businesses to remain open in crime-ridden areas. Shoplifting and theft raise the prices which must be charged in stores located in these areas. We all pay more due to crime, especially those who can least afford to, those that live in poor and crime- infested neighborhoods. Crime prevention is important to all of free enterprise. It must be vigorously pursued, even during times when the overall crime rate is down.

It costs the community at least thirty thousand dollars a year to keep a criminal in jail. The community could spend the same money on a thousand children, to fund programs like Scouts, Big Brothers and Big Sisters, and Indian Guides– programs that build character and promote citizenship. We need to expose children to good role models. We would be much better off to spend the money spent on jails on such basics as good day care for children. The State of North Carolina reports that it now spends $2 million on every murderer that it executes, due to the additional trial and appeal expenses. That same money would be better spent on prevention programs and on programs that put children on the right track.

Keeping the perpetrators of crime in jail is the only sensible course of action for a community. However, we can and must do both. A few dollars spent to put a kid on the right track is at least worth the many thousand dollars that it costs to keep him in jail. It is important to both prevent and to punish crime. We can do both, but only if we as a community, together, will become involved in finding solutions.

Social problems such as homelessness and crime; public health dangers such as TB, AIDS, and teen pregnancy have all been made worse either through design or through failure to act because of the ideological rigidity in conservative administrations. AIDS was ignored, because it first appeared in the gay community. The resurgence of tuberculosis was permitted because the poor and homeless were the first to display it. Now, everyone, no matter what their station in life, risks exposure to these dreaded diseases and all must suffer from the effects of crime and negligence on the social fabric of the community.

The general public is pragmatic in their view of these problems. Public health and the health of the community is important to everyone. People really do want clean air and water, but we don't want to feel that we, alone, are making all of the sacrifices necessary to obtain it for the community as a whole. We also do not like to see some being allowed to pollute or exploit our shared resources at the expense of the rest of us. We as Americans expect equality, balance and fairness. Free market solutions to problems are sometimes the best and only solutions. However, sometimes we must also use our pooled resources, the tools of government, to solve that which can only be solved in working together.

The Reagan and Bush administrations might have prevented the degradation of the environment that occurred during their administrations through simple regulation. However, they were uninterested in doing so, since they were ideologically against *any* federal regulation. The natural resource extraction industry hastily acted to take advantage of that change in the regulatory climate. The result was many unadvised and inexcusable abuses of the environment. The resource extraction industry, therefore, had to be quickly controlled to prevent massive destruction of the environment.

Instead of the Republican administration and the Democratic Congress working together to write good legislation that all sides could agree to, all progress in preserving the environment had to be pursued though Congress. The legislative branch responded with some complicated laws which provided less than perfect solutions to the problems. These laws were effective in reversing degradation of the environment but have been accused of being burdensome, complex, and in a few cases counterproductive. Simply in working together, this could have been avoided. Today, things have become much worse and the prospect of working together is just about gone. Instead of working together we are now working against one another and against our common interest.

A special interest group, Project Relief, an alliance of 350 powerful corporations, was organized to roll back enviromental regulations that its members thought to be onerous. The April/May 1996 issue of *National Wildlife* reported that, in the 1994 campaign cycle, Project Relief directed more than $19 million in contributions, including $87,126 to House Speaker Newt Gingrich, and more than $330,000 each to Senate Regulatory Task Force members Kay Bailey Hutchison (R-Texas) and Larry Craig (R-Ohio), all leaders in the regulation-reform movement. The same article reported that industies lobbying to weaken the Clean Water Act made campaign contributions of $57 million between the 1990 and 1994 elections. These donations came from political action committees organized by chemical, pesticide, agricultural, oil-and-gas, and real estate interests. A similar link between donations and votes can be found on measures to relax pesticide restrictions, revoke endangered-species protection and to reduce wetlands protection.

As concerned citizens, we should be more willing to work together to protect our environment and natural resources. We are willing to work together to solve those problems which could have been easily and cheaply prevented yesterday. We want laws that will end pollution without excessive regulatory control. We insist on regulations which give producers the freedom to choose the most economical ways to prevent pollution, not simply to end pollution by putting companies out of business. The American public, demands "win-win" solutions.

Regulations have been blamed for the decline of our industry, however, most decline may be instead due to the increased foreign competition and to product obsolescence. Ultimately, governmental regulations protect legitimate and non-polluting industries because the initially cheapest product is not always the most cost effective. Sometimes a challenge to the status quo may be what is necessary to spark a better technology and to stimulate the innovation that will bring costs down.

If a product needs to be produced, American ingenuity can usually find better ways to do things. OSHA is a good example. Before President Nixon signed it into being, many workers were killed or injured on the job, at very high cost to all of us. Today, insurance and other cost of worker protection has become much less of a problem, as we have found new and better ways to do things. American workers are now far safer and have a higher productivity than any other.[92]

In 1975 the regulations limiting workers' exposure to vinyl chloride led to the automation of some steps, resulting in higher productivity and cheaper ways to make plastic. In 1978 regulations designed to reduce brown lung disease helped to speed up modernization of textile mills, boosting productivity and making us more competitive in the world wide textile market. In 1987 costs due to a new federal standard for worker exposure to formaldehyde were predicted to cost $10 million per year. In fact, the costs were negligible, what's more, the changes made to comply with the ruling boosted the global competitiveness of American firms, making the regulations a large net plus. In 1990 the price tag for reducing emissions of sulfur dioxide- the cause of acid rain- was pegged at $1,000 per ton by utilities, the Environmental Protection Agency, and Congress. Yet, today the cost is $140 per ton. The reason: low sulfur coal became cheaper, due to improvements in both production and transportation stimulated by the increased demand.[93]

Some conservative Members of Congress are trying to end worker protection programs, such as OSHA. They say that these programs are wasteful and too expensive for business to comply with. They say that OSHA and the burdens of complex regulations are what is hurting America's industry and competitiveness abroad. Many CEOs who complain about regulations do not understand that without any regulations, the market would allow cheaper and less qualified producers to compete unfairly with them, and put *them* out of business. This is what happened in the airline and trucking industries. They forget how things used to be for the American worker, when the labor union was all that stood between workers and exploitation in the workplace. Labor unions have been on a steady decline in America since OSHA was established. Perhaps this is what Richard Nixon intended by signing the program into law. If OSHA were to no longer be at the side of the American worker, then the labor unions most certainly would be.

11. A National Psychosis

The real beauty of the free-enterprise system is that it works without external input. It works because, universally, people wish to improve their lot in life. When given the chance, they are willing to work hard, without constant supervision, in order to get ahead. People need only a positive goal, and a job that they can use as the vehicle to accomplish that goal. Today, this is not as easy as it had been in the past. There are not only less jobs for young people in the community, there are less positive role models for them, as well. In many communities, there is not much at all for many young people to do, except to "hang out" and be with others who like themselves have nothing to do.

Too much unsupervised time usually promotes childish, if not destructive and anti-social behaviors. In many cases, idle hands really do become the "Workshop of the Devil," especially if those idle hands lack the direction and guidance of responsible adults. Television, with its one way dialog of violence and sex, is now what sets the standards for the community.

Television has been blamed for much of what happens that is bad in America. Other countries, Canada for example, have virtually the same television shows, but Canadians are much less prone to civic violence. Japan has even more violent television shows than we have, yet has much less crime. That they also still have positive adult role models in the community for their children to emulate is the reason for this difference. Those role models who used to work and live and operate businesses in our neighborhoods, providing jobs for our teenagers are now a part of our history. Moms are increasingly working away from the home. Television is now relied upon as our babysitter. After all, television has less effect on children if it is not the only influence in a childs life. Solutions to problems offered by characters on television shows are usually not appropriate to be used in real life. Television also greatly raises expectations by promoting products that promise happiness. Many of our young people lack the maturity to understand the underlying misrepresentations. They may feel frustrated that they cannot obtain that which is offered. They may turn to drugs and to crime as methods of achieving the goal of purchasing items that they desire. Even if the funds for their purchase comes from legitimate sources, very often the dream when it is bought does not match their expectations for it.

Advertisers encourage us to be consumers, but without the accompanying community interaction the purchase may yet be un-fulfilling. Sadly, the lifestyle depicted in the advertisements as a result of using the product would more than likely be unobtainable for that purchaser. Often, the purchase, itself, does not validate the decision to purchase it and the purchaser leaves the store feeling empty. The phenomenon of compulsive shopping has been growing in America, and is now recognized as a social and psychological addiction.

Many will get themselves in overwhelming debt trying to fulfill their primeval role of hunter-gatherer in our modern free enterprise system, or by trying to maintain a former lifestyle that the present economics do not allow. They are likely only goaded on by the advertisers message to consume, consume. Like those with eating disorders, this compulsion may be a direct result of the biological stress of today's civilization. This disturbance most often affects those persons who lack a sense of direction or of purpose or those who are no longer allowed to compete fairly in the marketplace. Everyone must feel that they have a purpose or a role to play, or a place in society for our interactions with that society to have any meaning. If the sense of "place" is important in our society, Columnist Dannye Romine Powell, stresses that it is particularly so in the South.

The tragedy in Union, South Carolina, where Susan Smith drowned her two young sons, is a result of the importance of "place" to many people. Smith was of a "good" working class family in the small town of Union. Upon the death of her father, her mother remarried into a "better" merchant class family which gave her access to that group. Susan Smith, as a recent divorcee, had found a man who would be interested in her, if only she did not have the two children. She appeared to view her boys as obstacles to her marrying "up" in class. Who knows what she was thinking, yet, the result was that she rid herself of these two little obstacles by rolling her car, with them still strapped into their seats, into the nearby John D. Long Lake.[94]

Those politicians who use the tool of scapegoating, attack the effect or the result of the problem and do not address the true source of the problem being scapegoated. It is interesting to note that Newt Gingrich first scapegoated the Susan Smith case as being caused by the Democratic Party's tolerance of a "decline in family values." As is usually the case, there is more to the story. Susan Smith had been sexually abused at an early age by her stepfather, and the relationship was ongoing. She had learned from him at an early age to use sexual favors as a method of gaining her "place." That the stepfather was once the head of the local Christian Coalition and is still an official of the South Carolina State Republican party, indeed, shows the "decline in family values" to also be a Republican concern.

Divorce, more than anything else, affects the sense of "place" for individuals within society and within families. That much of the top Republican leadership is divorced or has even abandoned their families leads many to believe that "family values" may be just a campaign slogan. A rise in divorce rates since the 1960s, however, is easy to understand. Birth control pills allowed women to control their own fertility for the first time. The higher divorce rates initially, indicated that the lot of women was improving, that women no longer had to tolerate abusive situations, anymore. The continuing higher divorce rates are mainly due to the economic stress that we and all of our institutions including marriage are increasingly under.

As we are all looking for our proper "place" in an orderly society, for most of us, that "place" is lower than what we ever thought it would be. Our expectations, both socially and financially have, for most of us, somewhat lowered. When many things are changing and when things that you felt would always be there for you are no longer there, the increase in stress is the natural result.   Stress, some of it pathological stress, is increasing in the workplace and the community at large, as well as, in marriage and in the family. The decline in the traditional family, today, is very real. The economic pressures on the average working class American family, even if it can stay together, is intense. The costs of raising a family: education, isurance, medical and dental care have all risen sharply just as real wages have plunged.

The nuclear family with a husband as sole breadwinner has become a shell of what it once was. Both parents are having to work, and to work long hours, just to just keep up. Parents are spending 40% less time with their children than they did 30 years ago. Because both parents are working, children are supervised by people paid to care for them. However, more than 2 million children under age 13 have no adult supervision either before or after school.[95]   Not only are these children deprived of learning by example in following their mother on her daily errands, those children who are left at home alone are most often victimized by others.

Children are left alone, because paying for day care would eat-up most of the mother's wages. The cost of day care is a major problem for many working mothers. This is primarily because real wages are so low. It is estimated that the true economic value of welfare is equivilent to a wage of $8 an hour (almost twice the current minimum wage) to working mothers– if only because of child care expenses. To go off welfare would require a job earning much more than those minimum wage jobs which are available, and the family would still have to give up, or somehow replace their state sponsored health care benefits. We are in a economic situation where we can either create jobs that pay a living wage or we can plan to pay welfare. Situations such as these require innovative solutions, rather than scapegoats.

The most important thing that we can teach our children is how to make good decisions, yet cuts were made in education, because some taxpayers demanded it. Children, today, need the best education they can get, but the system works against them getting one. Children are either not taught the basics or they could never really learn them. Many children are left to fall through the cracks in our systems and there is no one there to catch them. The extended family is no longer always nearby to help care for and teach the children. The system is indifferent to their plight. Too often we simply fail to meet the needs of our children. In doing so, we are also failing to anticipate our own futures.

As a nation, we have forgotten the most basic rule of all, the Golden Rule. People have lost the bond, the connection with one another. It, therefore, becomes much easier to justify to oneself to take advantage of another or to ignore their need. Television and the press elevate as role models for our children those who have become rich or successful by exploiting others. Politicians who would hurt those who are somehow different are applauded. The reason for moral decline in America is that we have become polarized. Today, it is "us against them." We have become self-centered and selfish. We care less about the plight of others, because we are ourselves having to work harder. However, when we ourselves are old and helpless, can we expect those who we did not care for, to care for us?

Our society has ceased to function as smoothly as it once did, although the Ten Commandments are still as valid a formula for a smooth functioning society. There have been tremendous changes in our society over the past thirty years. Rules of behavior that worked well in sparsely populated rural areas do not work as well in a crowded city. Many things, indeed, have changed. We cannot return to the small town innocence and the simple government of yesterday. There can be no simple answers to the increasingly complex problems. Politicians who tell you so, are only lying to get your vote. They are trying to cover-up the real reasons, the increasing unfairness and inequity of a government where the laws are passed to favor an elite.

Many things have changed. However, there is something that we can do. We can spend less time in front of a TV and spend more time with our neighbors and friends. Individuals again need to read, to read their bibles and books on citizenship. We must, each of us, drag the old chestnuts out of the fire and put them back in our hearts where they belong. But we must do more. We must all work in our communities to make things better. We must become involved in the politics of fairness. "DO UNTO OTHERS, AS YOU WOULD HAVE THEM DO UNTO YOU" are not just words. They are a code to live by, and a lifestyle to practice. We should again live by them.

Creeping Barbarianism

The people know that something is up. Many are just plain mad but don't know why, or at exactly what. They are looking for scapegoats and the free market has provided them. Many scapegoat the government, therefore, trust declines in our system of laws. In the elections of 1994, campaign ads impugned the integrity of the opposition much worse than ever.

This only increased the mistrust of government. People were angry and they vented their anger against the politicians. In many cases anger against the government made them strike out at all who were serving in government, both the good and bad. Many voted with their emotions, not with their heads, if they bothered to vote at all. The very success of stimulating anger, of the Scapegoating of government will cause that tool to be used again. Those who have spent so much time and money making people angry, had best be very careful now that they themselves have been elected to office. There may be no way to harness the power of intolerance and rage once it has been released.

Barbarianism and intolerance ends civilizations. It can come from inside or from the outside, but it always results in the breakdown of civilization. Truth declines first, then trust, then tolerance and then cooperation. When this happens, civilizations will always fail. The perceived lack of fairness is just as effective in evoking the return of barbarianism as actually stealing from and lying to the people. The perception of unfairness is just as powerful in stimulating intolerance and the scapegoating of others as is actual unfairness.

Some of the very early signs of creeping barbarianism are such subtle changes in style and fashion that one cannot easily put a finger on, yet you know that it is there. Tattoos and body piercing are moving into the mainstream. Religious fundamentalism and primitive religions practices such as snake handling are on the rise, as are an increase of zealotry and ideological rigidity. The freedoms of speech, religion, and the right to bear arms are exercised, by some, to the maximum that the law allows. These rights are staunchly defended only for themselves, by those who would try to force their beliefs on you. These same people are equally intolerant of any views that are not exactly like their own.

Other signs of barbarianism, like increases in violent acts, are more obvious. Youths especially are using guns more and more to settle disputes. We definitely have a trend of increasing murders, rapes, and drug violence. The United States leads all industrialized nations in the number of rapes and murders committed each year. A 1995 FBI study showed that of those serial rapists who could be apprehended and studied, 76 percent had been sexually abused and 73 percent had been psychologically abused as children.

Physical violence is tolerated more and more in our society. Flogging is seen by many as a fair punishment for minor crimes. The country of Singapore, with all it's brutality, is seen as a model of law and order. Tuff-man, no-holds-barred fighting contests and full contact karate are now joining Hockey, Boxing and Football as spectator sports. Even a "tame" sport like figure-skating had a top skater involved in a plot to knock her main rival out of competition.

Americans are urged to ignore inhumanity to man in Bosnia, Africa and other places. Political leaders argue against American involvement in even peacekeeping missions. Goods made with slave and child labor in China and elsewhere are allowed in our country to unfairly compete with U.S. made goods. In the 1996 Republican primary, Presidential candidate Phil Gramm wanted to emulate China and turn our prisons into factories. This would only further depress the wages of those who now have low skill manufacturing jobs. Many of those who are now in prison, only turned to a life of crime because they had poor role models and little education or social skills with which to get legal work in the first place.

Laws that protect the rights of the elderly and protect the helpless from abuse were struck-down in the 104th Congress for reasons of ideology and to free up funds to be spent on more powerful constituencies. There are never any good reasons to retract the federal protections of the Constitution from our citizens, and these reasons certainly are not good ones, either. Neo-Conservatives in the Congress, by voting to remove the protection under federal law for nursing home residents, also, ignore the fact that they were signed into law by a conservative, President Reagan, and that there were good reasons for them.

The only individuals who will benefit from the repeal of these laws are those shady nursing home operators who can now use drugs to sedate, or even tie residents to their beds- to keep them isolated against their will. These rule changes may, in fact, save some money for nursing home operators. They may also reduce nursing home costs to Medicare. However, in the haste of the ideologues to justify another tax cut for the wealthy they trample all over the Constitutional rights of the patient.

It is hard for us to criticize the Germany of 1939 for establishing an Aryan Elite; as we ourselves institute an Economic Elite in our own country. No one stood up for the small gasoline station and convienence store owners– as big oil distributors first set prices and therefore the profits that they could make on gasoline. No one objected as the smaller operations were unfairly competed against by the national chains and company-owned stores. No one paid attention to the plight of family farmers as "Big Agriculture" forced them off of their land. No one else cared when 5000 hog "Hog lots" used agricultural zoning to move in next door to family farms. No one listened to the environmental complaints, or even cared about the odor.

Social Darwinist feel that they are justified in allowing the establishment of elites due to Darwin's Law of "Survival of the Fittest." They even feel justified in cheating to achieve it. Although, lies and dishonesty are not tools that would be needed by a true elite. Our system *is* based on the profit motive. However, a stable society cannot long remain stable by giving the dishonest the control of government or by justifying the flawed ideology of greed.

A New Dark Ages

As a civilization matures, more and more vested interests naturally develop. These special interest groups like things just the way that they are. By and large, they are resistant to any and all change. They become increasingly conservative. They are very protective of their position and influence in the community. Often they are very over-protective. They will actually try to sabotage needed change or strive to hurt those who would bring it about. Just as some professions form their select societies or associations to exclude newcomers. The vested interests, too, try to dissuade competition. They will argue for the rights of monopoly and for laws to protect their positions. Under their influence, all progress will slowly wither, or be allowed to "die on the vine."

The earlier Dark Ages were much like this. The insiders of the Court, the sorcerers, magicians and charlatans that they were, zealously guarded their insiders knowledge. The state of their art was relatively modest, however they were still very protective of that which they did know. They went so far as to block the spread of literacy and actively withhold knowledge from the common people. This, in fact, soon became the primary interest of the elites in protecting their interests. In this conservatism, in protecting their secrets from others, they also protected their power. The leaders and insiders cloaked their actions in superstition and fear. They knew that they could only continue to retain their power over everyone else, by slowing the advance of civilization and by preventing the spread of knowledge.

On the other hand, when once-vested interests have been overthrown, new challenges arise. In the haste to embrace change, little thought may be given to the consequences of change. The Bolshevik revolution that led to the formation of the former USSR is a good example. The Bolsheviks were made up of two groups, much like the membership of our own Neo-Conservative revolution. One group was very religious and ideological. The other one was more pragmatic in their pursuit of power. They too, were interested in change, but change mostly as the method of gaining power for themselves. Together, these two groups provoked the revolution that led to the change in Russia. Working together, they worked to cause the revolution that led to the downfall of the Czar. However, as could be predicted, the inevitable purge came. When it became time to establish a new leadership, a new elite emerged. Trotsky and the other idealists, since they were no longer needed, were executed, or imprisoned.

Conservative pundit P.J. O'Rourke argues "that conservatives do not attack liberals for saying things that are bad. Rather, the fight begins when liberals say, "Government has enormous power. Let's use some of that power to make things good."" He would rather that government not be involved. His is a true conservatism. The Neo-Conservative revolutionaries of twentieth century America still want the government to remain involved, but involved only to aid them, rather than to aid the others. They would use the power of government to help themselves to the bounty of America, while using this power to do mean things to their political enemies.

Neo-Conservatives have adopted the ideological conservative rhetoric, however, none of the principles of a true free-market conservatism. In a true free-market, in a democratic society, politics should not be used as a shortcut to power, nor should it be a way for an elite minority to dominate the others.

Many who backed the Bolshevik Revolution were disappointed in the final result. We too, must learn from history and from the mistakes of others. Revolutions are one thing, however, the long-term effects of even small changes must be considered. Changes which are now merely considered as "time saving shortcuts" necessary to reach our ultimate goal may not be in our best long-term interest. Just as the small additions that conservative "think tanks" often suggested to traditional liberal programs, often ended up in dramatically changing their impact.

Change can be for the good. However, all change is not always for the best. Change, especially, change that is hotly demanded, can usually be counted on to be counterproductive. Moderation is called for, in virtually every circumstance. Slow, steady, well considered change is usually good. If it is sustainable, we know that the direction of the change is the correct one. Shifting too far, in either direction will ultimately, only lead to disaster, both for the individual and for the nation.

The threat of a new dark ages is very real. Civilization stands on the very shoulders of those who have gone before. No one, today, must relearn all the things that have been invented through the ages to be able to benefit from them. Education is the key. We need simply to add to, to build on, that which has gone before. If we do not produce a new generation capable of understanding, the ability to preserve and expand upon the civilization that we now have will be lost.

Can this be prevented? The answer is yes, that it can be. However, the problem gets worse, potentially much worse. Knowledge may disappear and vanish, entirely. This is more likely to happen today, than it could even a hundred years ago. Most knowledge of human progress made in the last fifty years is stored on magnetic media, floppy discs, disc drives, and video tapes. To wipe it all away, would only require a good size magnetic storm, such as from a large sunspot.

The printed word, our hard copy back-ups of what is stored on electronic media, is in not much better shape today, either. Xerographic and Laser and lithographic printing have projected lives of 10, 15 and 75 years respectively. Each of us has in the past, at least once, received a letter with the print flaking off the paper along a folded line. It was printed on a laser printer or copied by xerography. Most other printing today is done by the offset process, or on the surface of the paper. It is fast and cheap. Earlier books were printed by letterpress which stamped the ink under pressure into the fibers of the paper. Letterpress printing has a useful life of hundreds of years. We are mistaken to assume that all other printing does too.

Change can be good. We must embrace change when it is necessary. However, we should not risk placing all of our eggs in one basket, either. We must make change our friend, but know that it can be an enemy, as well. We must not embrace change for the sake of change, nor should we resist all change. We err to think of what is new as always being something better. We err to believe that the latest idea is in every way an improvement over what we now have. We err when we believe that changes in government programs, when sponsored by an elite group, are intended to help anyone except for that same elite group.

12. Enlightened Self Interest

The first and most important step in solving any problem is identifying the true problem. Today, there are many signs of an impending decline. We, as members a society, seem to look out only for our own short term interests. We do not give much thought to what the future consequences of those decisions will be, either for us, individually, or for our country. There are few true patriots anymore. Everyone looks out for number one, and for number one only. We are, therefore, very often totally influenced by those who claim to be on our side. We may completely agree with all of their arguments, and may even be willing to let them make our decisions for us.

Self-interest is what drives our system, however in the extreme of being selfish, we are also most easily misled. We are the most easily manipulated when we are being greedy. Con men know just how to appeal to greed and self-interest. They flatter our decision making ability. They, first, get us to agree with them by stating the obvious. The ultimate goal is to gain our trust. If our judgement is also clouded by greed, then this becomes much easier. We do not then focus on that which we need to be focusing upon. The saying "If it sounds too good to be true, it usually is" is especially true in politics. There is no way to realistically increase defense spending, cut taxes and reduce the national debt without someone being hurt or, at least, someone having to pay more.

The debate is further complicated because there is no single source of truth on every issue. Different individuals may have differing ideas on a subject and still be correct. It is the combined viewpoint that matters. Different viewpoints may correctly represent the different aspects of a particular problem. In the end, it is the whole that matters, the whole that is our American civilization. Unlike in communism and totalitarian societies, the actions and the viewpoint of the individual is important in our society. Each individual makes a contribution to solving the puzzle by providing a particular piece. In a free enterprise society, all individuals are important.

It has been said that Americans lack direction, or that we lack consistency of purpose. Of course, no one goes around asking "What is our national aim?" or "What are our long term goals?" But then, How *can* you know when you get there, if you don't know where you want to go in the first place? In America, each of us have differing individual goals, talents and needs. We all have similar, if differing, personal values. Some of us only care about where we live, or what kind of house we live in. Others, may only care about what kind of car that they drive or whose clothes they wear. Some of us care about little else other that where we will take our annual vacation. We are all different, yet we should all share the American ideals of honesty and fairness.

As Americans, we are also interested in solutions. We cannot solely be interested in short term solutions, either. To view the larger picture, we must become more involved with one another and within our community. We must spend more time in meeting the needs of the community. Individuals who are not sure what they can do to help rebuild our bonds of community, should pray for guidance and inspiration. We must all decide what is really important to us, both as individuals and as citizens of our country. Each of us needs to ask, "How do I fit into the plan?" Then as individuals, working withing the group, we must resolve to make a difference while working towards the one goal that we have chosen that also advances the group.

We are a free-enterprise system. The primary goal of this system is to fill the true needs of the marketplace. The appeal of the short term, selfish interest in our country can be changed. We can easily just set other goals. We must first, however, know where we are came from, before we look ahead to where we may want to go. The first lesson is to learn from history. Those who do not learn from the mistakes of the past are doomed to repeat them. We, as Americans, are all in this together. We stand or fall together. We must learn from, and follow the examples set forth by the first patriots. They put consideration of the future ahead of their own fears and ahead of short-term, purely selfish self interests. True patriots are not always solely interested in self. We as citizens, should be more like this as well.

The original patriots talked with one another. They were brave enough to risk their very lives to engage freely in public debate. They found out what was bothering their neighbors. They interacted with each other. They discussed possible solutions. The entire country was involved in the discussion. A dynamic tension between ideas developed as ideas became cross pollinated with other ideas. A common bond, a sense of community, grew among the people. We set common goals. The patriots knew that, together, they would stand or fall, that they would only stand or fall as a group and a society, together.

Today, many do not see it this way. Few even bother to talk with one another. We have not actually defined what the true issues are. We have increasingly let ourselves become divided by what have also been increasingly petty differences. There has been no national debate to give voice to that which is disturbing to many Americans. Taxes are given as a reason for alarm by an increasing number of citizens. Politicians have been very quick to respond to tax issues. Each seems to have a different proposal with which to carry forward their own agenda of tax changes. However, someone must first define exactly what is wrong with our system of fairly collecting taxes before those quick-fixes should be attempted.

Medicare is a tax. Social Security is a tax. They are both taxes. They are not, as some would have us to believe, individual contributions to a retirement or health insurance plan. Like all of the revenue collected by the government, Social Security and Medicare (together known as FICA) are taxes intended to aid all of the community. These particular taxes go to help insure income and social stability. Yet, they, too, go directly into the public treasury. This money goes into the pool of public funds which pay for the rest of the public programs, or for tax cuts.

There is no Medicare trust fund. The Social Security trust fund consists entirely of treasury bills, simply federal IOU's. They are instruments of the public debt, which when they come due will be paid back from the general revenues of the public treasury. The proceeds of Social Security and Medicare tax collections go straight into the treasury as yet another form of federal income. This way, it can be counted as revenue, revenue which will make the national debt appear to be smaller.

Since there is no real "Trust Fund," two items never discussed are exactly *what* we are obligated for in the future and *who* does not have to pay it. The generally accepted figure for our federal debt is $5 trillion. However, we are also obligated to pay at least twice that amount in future payments for Medicare and Social Security benefits. As the money to pay these obligations is not really there, this places our true federal debt at closer to $15 trillion. To make matters worse, the wealthy are not obligated to pay towards this debt. Since the income cap for Social Security tax purposes is around $65 thousand a year, the rich end up with most of their incomes exempt for Social Security purposes.

In his reelection bid, George Bush called for lower capital gains taxes and for lower marginal rates of income tax. These tax reductions would continue to benefit mainly the rich. Lower taxes <u>was</u> a key component of mood of the electorate in 1992. However, it was only a portion of the more complex issue. The messages of fairness gained the majority of votes cast in the referendum for change that was that year's presidential election.

George Bush is not now the President of the United States because he did not view basic fairness as a concern to the average voter. The other two candidates for President were not exactly on target either. However, just the public acknowledgment of the debt and slogans such as "It's the economy, stupid" were closer, in the minds of many, to the fear and anger that they felt over the continuing economic unfairness.

A 1990 *Money* magazine article reported that George Bush paid 23% of his $453,000 income in federal taxes, versus the 28 percent paid by an average two wage earner family with an income of $52,000– over four-hundred thousand dollars less income. Bush faced a top marginal tax rate of only 31 percent, versus the marginal tax rate of 54 percent that this average family would have to pay. The main reason for this disparity is that Social Security and Medicare taxes hit the average family much harder than it does the Bushes and other wealthy families. FICA taxes had more than doubled under Reagan and had increased an additional 9% under Bush. Any tax cuts that the middle class may have gotten in the eighties was taken back from them in FICA tax increases. [96]

The 1994 Clinton health plan debacle represented a similar misreading of the public's concerns. The Congressional Democrats represented the demise of Bush as evidence that the tax aspect of the public mood was unimportant to the voters. What the people were looking for in a national health care financing reform was not what was offered to them. What the people really wanted was simple and honest change in the fairness of the financing of our system of social stability. In 1995, the Republican Congress tried to exploit the dis-ease that the public felt toward the Medicare system as a method to provide yet another tax cut for the wealthy. They too, misinterpreted the public displeasure as being with the stability of the system and not at all due to concern for the massive debt obligation and the underlying imbalance in taxation.

What the American people want is fairness. They also want systems that are efficient and provide real value for the public investments which are made. Our current health care system is operated by the private sector, but is paid for through a combination of public and private funds. It is much more than just wasteful and unfair, it combines the worst aspects of either system.

As currently constructed, our system of health care provides excessive profits for the insurance industry at the expense of the Medicare system and of our pooled resources. Many of the costs of private health care are shifted onto the public, to the rest of us, by the current system. The need for care of the poor is often left unmet. Most of the cost of social stability are borne by the middle class, when, indeed, everyone benefits from it

The American people want a system that is fair. They want a system that keeps costs down, yet will keep people from losing their homes and their life savings due to the illness of a relative. This can be easily done if we will only pool some of our resources. The current system cost a lot, yet many elderly must sell their homes and lose all that they have before they receive help to care for a spouse. Many families are destroyed due to the debt that a serious illness can bring. Those who can afford some insurance, however inadequate it may be, are only a little better off. Those totally without resources are covered through our pooled resources of government. The rich can afford coverage on their own. The poor are covered. The rest of us must lose all that we have in order to receive help from government. Should we require that the middle class be bankrupted before we can be allowed to act on beginning an honest pooling of our resources?

We are a free-enterprise society, yet our pooled resources should be kept from those who would use them for personal profit. We are already paying more than enough to cover everyone's health care insurance. If the private sector profiteering were removed from the public system, what we spend now would cover everyone. Our Medicare taxes, alone, would be enough to provide health insurance for everyone, that is, if the wealthy were to pay their fair share. If the wealthy will pay the same percentage of tax as the middle class, we would have enough revenue to have both universal health coverage and to balance the budget.

Those individuals who cannot easily afford to pay more for Medicare insurance are the ones who are already paying the lions share now. The ones who really can afford to pay, now pay much less of their incomes as a percentage. If we are not to have a graduated system, we should all pay taxes at the same rate. That's it. That's all we have to do to both provide funding for universal health insurance and balance the budget. We could even greatly reduce the total tax rate for the middle class. All of the arguments come down to that.

Government tax policy is seen by both sides in the political debate as a mechanism to direct investment in ways that will benefit the public good. Tax deductions for charities, increase charitable giving. Home mortgage interest deductions stimulate the housing industry. However, too much of a good thing can be just as harmful as doing nothing. If too much mortgage interest is deductible, then it will inflate the price of homes. The same thing applies on tax deductions for the rich.

Under "tickle down theory," tax deduction for the rich spark the economy. Once the economy is sparked, however, it should continue unabated. Further increasing tax deductions will not help, nor will slight decreases in deductions hurt. Those who are making the most money will not quit just because they have enough. If this were true, we would not be experiencing the great increases in the number of billionaires that we are now seeing. Simple fairness should dictate that the wealthy should at least pay the same percentage of their incomes for tax as the middle class.

Looking Out for One Another

Our shared culture is what holds us together. We are not a tribe related by blood. Diversity is our greatest strength. We each have different and equally correct ways of approaching our common problems. When creative solutions are needed, our diverse population has tremendous creative talent. We must be able to count on one another to help solve our mutual problems. We have been divided by those who put special interest over our common interests. Even when we think that we are finding common ground, today, we may not be.

According to Machiavelli, to make someone think you are on their side, claim to share their heros. Newt Gingrich claims to revere Franklin Roosevelt. Does he, or is this just a method of disarming Democrats while he undoes Roosevelt's New Deal? We need leadership that we can count on to bring us together, not to divide us. We need leaders who will serve the public interest, not those who will serve only the special interests. We cannot neglect our common interest.

Stable societies encourage interaction among groups. No class or income strata can exist on its own, without all the others. We are all interdependent on one another. In the very least we are dependent on each of us being good citizens and not going around killing each other. Societies that once were stable, but now are not, should first look to fairness and then look at themselves.

Many wealthy conservatives blame society for all of it's problems. They think of themselves as blameless, yet they also think they have accomplished everything entirely on their own. They think that being part of a stable society had nothing at all to do with their success. This is a common conservative fallacy. If one is allowed, by his or her situation, to call the shots for the group, then he or she must answer to the group, and allow the group to share in any gain. Every CEO who has ever had to face the stockholders knows this rule very well.

Americans, today, miss the lesson of Henry Ford. Henry Ford is credited with putting America on wheels, of creating a mobile society, and all of the things that were appendant to it. He is also seen as the father of the assembly line. This is not the point. Henry Ford had an idea. Prior to his Model "T" Ford, automobiles were rare and most were quite expensive. The market was quite small and highly competitive among many builders.

Henry Ford figured, if he could build automobiles at a price that the common man could afford, he would sell a whole lot of them. This was the innovation. The Model "T" Ford was not, itself, an innovation. It was based on prior designs. In fact, the front suspension was identical to his previous Model "N" Ford. His innovation was, that he had a good idea, and then got others to sign on to it. He had Pontiac and the Dodge brothers building bodies for him. Dodge even spent their own money setting up for production. Many other competing suppliers cooperated, and worked together on Ford's project. They worked together, because it was in their own best interest to do so. The public was already sold on Henry Ford's idea. He had firm orders in hand for more than he could easily build alone. In working together, the automakers all benefitted. Together, they built an industry, a larger pie for all to share.

Americans were known for this working together, for this team building. Alexis DeTocqueville identified this as the "one thing" that made Americans, different from everyone else and identified it as the source of our social cohesion. But, all of that is changing, now. In what Columnist David Browder has termed a "classic" essay– "Bowling Alone," writer Harvard University's Robert Putnam, uses the decline of the bowling leagues in American as the metaphor for a decline of community, and of the decline in participation in those voluntary and civic associations which have traditionally held us together. All of the scapegoating, violence, division, and greed have left us a nation of individuals, each "bowling alone." Before it becomes too late, we must once again find and reaffirm our ties and common bonds as Americans.

We must, once again, join with one another, and find common interest and goals to pursue. We should attend our churches and spend time talking with neighbors over the fence or at the corner store. Also, think about joining a club or civic organization, volunteering for a cause, or attending city council meetings and getting involved in politics. We need our good people, to do good things, to reaffirm our common bond as citizens.

Too many have just given up. We are not noted as a nation of quitters. We need people of differing backgrounds and beliefs to find common ground in something totally different from what is safe and comfortable for them. Our children need good role models. We need the positive interchange of ideas and understanding that makes for healthy civilizations. Because our civilization, and we as individuals, all ultimately depend on one another.

People generally need only two things: love and meaningful work. Without both, individuals cannot grow and thrive. We all need affection from someone, whether we earn it or not, and a job that lets us participate in the orderly marketplace that is so important in our free market society. The desire for love and affection has led to many ill advised relationships. Let us try to understand the foibles of others. Promises are often made to manipulate those who desperately want that which is promised. We know, as a society of individuals, that it is not a good idea to go looking for love, but we should always be looking for meaningful work. Work done that is not paid for in money is paid for in other forms of INTANGABLE income. Volunteer or unpaid work is just as important as paid work, when it is meaningful to yourself and to your society. *All* meaningful work allows you to be validated as a participant in the progress of society.

Meaningful work is very important to the well being of each of us as individuals. Work like this does not always exist today. Many tasks are so complex that the portion done by an individual seems to have no relation to a finished product or service. Many of us have lost the sense of fitting into the unified whole. With a true level playing field, all can find meaningful work, every adult will earn a living wage.

Everyone needs something, part time or full time, paid or not, that they find meaningful. Welfare mothers too need to work. We all need to work at least part time at something that makes us a part of the larger society. We each need to find a good or a service that really helps others, and to work to share it and to promote it. If you don't know how to do what you want to do, go back to school. If you already know how and what you want to do, learn to do it better. Meaningful work is to the benefit of yourself and to the whole of society. That everyone gains when you gain is the whole point of enlightened self interest.

True Patriotism

Many people, today, say they hate politics, and with some justification. It is truly fortunate that being actively involved in politics is not the only way to serve your country. Public service was at one time emotionally rewarding to those who served. Today, however, those who are serving in government often receive the majority of the hatred and abuse that has been directed at government in general. Therefore, only those who would seek to use government for their own ideological or monetary ends will be more attracted to government service.

There is a special need for true patriots in government, today, but also in all careers, and in all walks of life. Each of us has a place where we can be of service. Each of us has a task that we can accomplish in order to help to rebuild the core of our country. No matter who we are, we can all have a part to play in renewing and revitalizing our society. We must each put the practice of true patriotism into our daily lives.

What is a true patriot? A true patriot is that individual who puts the good of society, the future of our civilization, and our mutual goals, ahead of their own immediate, personal wants and needs. It is not always a major thing, either. There are many small things that add up to be big things when everybody is doing them. Looking out for your neighbor, is one. Buying American made products whenever possible provides jobs for your neighbor. Showing little children how to be good citizens, so that we don't have to put them in jail some day, is another. Taking care of your health and staying healthy will prevent illness and expensive hospitalizations, that in the long run, even if insured, cost all of us more.

There are three things that can always be counted on to kill a society or to end a civilization. They are: a decrease in trust, the lack of perceived fairness and an increase in barbarianism. All of these factors are present in the social fabric of our society. Each of them can be found in every one of our neighborhoods and communities If we each want to do something that is really important, we can help to reverse this trend. We should try to find ways to increase the positive interaction of individuals and thereby also the inter-dependance of one with the other. We each have a role to play in reawakening the Spirit of America.

Neo-Conservatives criticize government for taking from one and giving to another. On the other hand, once those same Neo-Conservatives gain power, they want special tax breaks for their friends and campaign contributors. They want to take from the public treasury and use it to advance themselves and their friends in the conservative elite.

What we really need from government is to maintain balance and fairness. We need policies that truly correct the abuses of the past, not just redistribute the booty. The people, in electing a new group to the Congress, expected them to at least be neutral to their interests. They did not expect the new Congress to either excessively punish those who had been helped by the Congress in the past, or to excessively favor a entirely new group. Instead, public policy continues to be bought and sold by the lobbyists and insiders, only now it is much worse.

Many have advocated changes in the way that the government delivers services to the people. We can all agree that changes were needed. However, the Neo-Conservatives did not wish to just make needed changes. Instead of changes that would level the playing field, they instead tilted it to favor their own special interests and the interests of those who supported their election. Instead of ending prior abuses, they created new abuses of the system. They then proceeded to help only themselves. They then delivered on the promises of subsidies and tax breaks to the few, that in the end will hurt all of us. Changes indeed needed to be made. But not these changes. Change always involves pain, however, pain should be evenly shared by society, not just heaped upon the allies of your political enemies.

The 104th Congress voted to roll back decades of progress in the protection of the environment. They voted to allow more toxic chemicals in our drinking water and to remove federal protection from wetlands and aquifers. They allowed wavers, loopholes, and exemptions to corporate polluters who would use our public rivers and streams as their own private sewers. Who gains and who loses from these changes? Who will be stuck with the bill for the clean-up, or who must pay the environmental costs? Not them, our children and our grandchildren will be the one's who must pay.

Previous Congresses were also mired in the status quo. They also took money to protect those special interest that no longer deserve protection, yet make campaign contributions. Laws that favor virgin over recycled plastics or paper is but one example of programs that no longer make sense but were bought to promote a special interest. That virgin material is subsidized and cost less to ship than recycled is unfair both to the consumer and to the environment.

Yet, in the Neo-Conservative Congress, this tendency and the types of political favors that are returned is much worse. Selling out is now obligatory and expected. For a contribution, those industries who would abuse workers can change the labor laws. For the help with a campaign, lobbyists for polluting industries can re-write environmental laws to suit themselves.

We all share the environment, like the village commons of an earlier time. It is indeed the largest and most important of all of our pooled resources. Letting some spoil the "Global Commons" in the name of more profit for themselves, in spite of the cost to society is unthinkable. We need laws protecting the water and air and even laws that preserve birds and trees, in order to protect us, the human animals. As children, we learned to pick up after ourselves. As adults, we should continue to do it, as well. Americans love our land, our soil, our air and water. As good stewards, we each have the responsibility to care for it. Ultimately as the joint consumers of all of our shared resources, we each deserve the purest and the best that we can have.

The essence of the free-enterprise system is to allow good ideas free access to markets. The best ideas will win in free and fair competition and everyone then benefits. The free enterprise system does not exist to give unfair advantage to any group or philosophy. It is not there to allow the strong to take advantage of the weak, nor to promote the interests of a few. Especially with regards to elections, we need competition that is both, free and fair. Those who are once able to gain control of the government, should not be allowed to change the rules so that they may stay in control, forever.

We do need a progressive government, willing to make changes, willing to challenge the status quo. Sometimes it becomes necessary to offend the powers that be, in the name of more efficient and fairer markets. However, efficiency of the markets is not the only issue. What we absolutely do not need, is to restrict the freedom of others, so that we ourselves can have *more* freedom. This will never work in our system of laws. Yet, this is what conservative administrations and Congresses have tried to do, in repayment of campaign debt to fundamentalist interests. In the repayment of these campaign debts, all of us lose our freedoms. The most important thing that true patriots can do as an individual is to work for national campaign finance reform.

Too many politicians come to Washington, pre-bought by the special interests. Too many laws are made to favor one company or one industry over all the others, in payment for help during a campaign. Campaigning is expensive, and getting more so. It is easy to see why politicians become tempted. The temptation some politicians feel is to sell the rest of us out, just a little bit, because of all of the other good things they feel they do for the country. Term limits could help, but even the 104th Congress which was elected with that as a stated goal could not deliver on them. Campaign finance reform would end business as usual in Washington. In fact, we could come out way ahead, as a nation, and as individuals, if we let the public pick up all of the costs for national elections.

As consumers should never buy on price alone, but should take into account the *total* cost of a good or service; the same should apply to government. We are paying too high a price for our system of elections. Our laws are often changed to help the contributors to the campaigns which elect the lawmakers. It cost us much more in revenues lost in the protection of industries from taxes and in the government subsidies to them, than we could ever save by continuing to let our current spoils system of elections. We all lose by letting politicians continue to be bought and sold. Special interest through their campaign contributions unfairly tilt the playing field of free market competition. This unfairness cost all of us more in the long run.

Just as we can build schools or build prisons, we can pay on the front end or we can pay *more* on the back end.

We need real anti-trust reform in specific areas such as in health care, in order to make progress on reducing our spending and in controlling our debt. However, the special interest control of the politicians prevents real reform. In a *Market Democracy*, narrow interests can easily prevail over the general welfare. However, all governments, even a *Market Democracy*, ultimately depend on the consent of the governed.

It is possible to have honest, fair, and progressive government. If not that, instead of what we now have, we need politicians who can, at least, afford to be neutral. We must insure that things are kept fair, according to the unwritten agreement that allowed the formation of our society. We need political figures who would want people to make good choices. However, the way things are, politicians must remain bought to stay in office, and so have offered mostly false choices.

In summary: We have what it takes to be successful as a nation, a Constitution that is strong yet flexible and a diverse people who really want to do the right thing. We can overcome any obstacle if we are united and have good people to lead us. We are again in need of good people to become involved in politics, because since the 1960s participation in elections has declined. Being viewed as a *Market Democracy*, where politics and politicians are thought to be "for-sale" to the highest bidder may have played a big part in this decline.

The dynamic tension created by free and fair elections is what keeps us on track as a democracy. If elections can again be both free and fair, then we will once again be on the correct course for a brighter future. The dynamic tension of ideas that leads to good government, is also what brings progress and renewal in a free enterprise society. This civil discourse, this marketplace of ideas, was envisioned by the founders in the First Amendment Ideals. Free and fair debate between the two political extremes is encouraged because it promotes the development of good ideas. It is in this way that the balance of power will always be maintained between capital and labor, between buyers and sellers, and between big and small. Good ideas are what make them all work. In each working together, the total and each of them is enhanced.

There is one rule that the leadership of a free-enterprise society need always to remember: Always, keep people hoping for a profit. Never take away the freedom of the spirit by over-taxing or over-regulation, or worse, by allowing the level playing field of commerce to become corrupted by those anti-competitive elements of monopolies and trusts. The needs of those working together are important, but also are the needs of the individual who is working alone. The correct answer in all cases is not either/or; it is both.

We can have both, both industry and a clean environment, both a strong economy and low unemployment, both low inflation and economic growth, and both a higher standard and equal opportunity. The vision of the original patriots allows for both, because our government is the expression of our collective will. It allows for an unlimited future, but only when every individual is careful to look out for the rights of the others. An uncorrupted free market system will always find ways to do both, both to help the people and yet to stand out of their way. If True Patriots are involved, our America, our free enterprise system can and will always do both.

INDEX

AARP 199
Abraham Lincoln 17
Adolf Hitler 74, 75
AFDC 93
Affirmative Action 139
Africa 252
Agnew, Spero 54-55
Aid to Families with Dependent
                Children . 159
AIDS 40
America culture 17
American Express 83
American ideals 14,19,22,46, 85
American Revolution 51, 67
American society 17,32
Amtrak 147
Amway 119-122
Anti-trust laws 40,54,77,78
Arctic National Wildlife 29
Asia 15
AT&T 97
Bakker, Jim 121
Banking 16,48
Barbarianism 251
Bible 138
Big Brothers Big Sisters, Inc 240
Blacks 141
Block grants 159
Blue Cross 201
Bosnia 77
Browder, David 269
Buffett, Warren E 83
Burger, Sarah 185
Bush, George. 46,263
The Cabinet 146
The Civil War 70
California 167
Campaign
        campaign financing ... 11
        Negative Campaign .. 31
Canada 245
Capitol Hill 146
Carlson, Margaret 184
Carnegie Foundation 163
Cato Institute 154
China 148
Christ .. 41, 106, 115, 116, 122, 123
        Christianity 105
        Veil of Christ 118
Christian Coalition 109, 118, 123
Civil rights movement 61, 111
Church of England 82
Church, F. Forrester 118

Churchill, Winston 57
Civil Rights Movement 110
civilization 49,90,109, 118
Clean Water Act 242
Clinton health care plan 196
Clinton, Bill 28,128,157
Cohen, William 185
Collins, Gary 226
commerce 51, 52
        level playing field 33
        the conduct of trade ... 50
commercials
        "Harry and Louise" .. 27,36
Communism 38,7
community 22, 43-46, 50-52, 54
Cuomo, Mario 74
computer chips 96
Congress
53, 68, 73, 79,92, 99, 104,117,
        63,122,127,130
Congressional Airmail 146
Conservative
        politicians .. 18, 103, 120
        pundits 73
        administration 42
        capitalists 88
        business climate 104
        economic policies 76
        fiscal policies 13
        ideologues 130
        religious group 109
        tax policies 13
        conservative element . 125
        conservative elites ... 126
        conservative press ... 128
        "Revolution" 129
Constitution
..... 15, 58, 74, 77, 81, 82, 84, 102
Constitutional principles 13
Consumer Reports 217
cost shifting 38, 188
Craig, Larry 242
Crime 55,56,72
        criminal justice 70
Dark Ages 255
Darwin, Charles - theory 141
Dawkins, Richard 231
Debt 41, 107
        federal debt 42
decentralization of power 83, 130
Declaration of Independence
.... 67-69,82, 113
democracy
.... 58, 62,66, 67, 78, 80
        Democratic Republic . . 57
        American democracy . 71

279

American form 77
applied democracy ... 58
Market Democracy
...... 12, 20, 36, 55, 62
Democratic party .. 59-62, 65,99 101
Department of Education 126
Department of the Interior 28
Dewey, Thomas 140
Dutch 107
Dutch West Indies 108
Dynamic Tension ....
58-59 62-63 66,77 81
Easter Island 103
economy 14, 65
Dutch economy 107
economic growth 14
economic pie 56
entrepreneurial 14
Japanese government . 16
underlying problems .. 48
Egypt 171
Electronic town hall 62
Elites 18, 55 65, 93, 128
"Hollywood Elite" 75
communist elite 131
environment 29, 64
Environmental Protection Agency ....
244
Europe 60, 82
Falwell, Jerry 135
FBI 239
FDIC 87, 153
Federal Election Comm 79,122
Federal Reserve 133
Federal Reserve Board 148
Feme-Nazis 64
Ford Foundation 163
Ford, Henry 268
free enterprise 24, 49,119
system 14-16
Freidel. David 171
Gag rules 211
Gallop poll 29, 36
GDP 236
General Motors 132
Geneva Conventions, The 184
Germany 60,70,74
The Gilded Age 47
Gingrich, Newt 120
Speaker oftheHouse . 131
Global Commons 274
Golden Rule 217
GOPAC 120
Government
federal 53, 56
Gramm, Phil 253

Gramm-Rutman 130
Great Britain 67, 69
Harvard University 269
Hawes, Catherine 185
Hayes, Patrick 219
health care 11, 36
Clinton reforms 27
Helms, Jessie 34, 129
HMO 85
hospitals 38, 40
hospital bills 37
House Ways-MeansCommittee .. 189
Hoover, Herbert 16
Hutchison, Kay Bailey 242
IBM 94, 95
India 168
Indian Guides 240
Independent expenditures 32
Insurance
national health insurance 39
health insurance ... 38-40
Israel 60
Intel 95-96
interests 11
selfish interests 26
special interests 42
individual self-interest . 85
individual -interests ... 20
narrow 12, 26,35
opposing groups 19
powerful interst group . 12
self interest 11, 56
selfish interest 115
special interest .....
12, 15 21, 25, 26,31
special interest groups ....
60, 75, 89
"enlightened" 45
Italy 60
Iverson, Kenneth 100, 249
Japan 16
Jews 71, 75
Johnson, Andrew 182-183
Johnson, Lyndon 12, 187
Jordan, Michael 210
Justice Department, The 78
Kennedy, John 12
Kennedy, Ted 34
King George II 67, 69
Koester, Helmut 116
Labor 244
Labour party 59
Libertarian 61
Liberty 67, 70, 74, 75, 80
and justice for all .. 70, 73
maintaining liberty ... 74

280

Line Item Veto 164
Limbaugh, Rush 135
lobbying, "grassroots" 28
Machiavelli 267
Madrick, Jeffrey 149
Maine 185
Majority Rule 58, 80
market 15, 17, 50
    marketplace 33, 53
    marketplace of ideas .. 66
    bond market 16
    complex market 53
    free market ... 16, 87, 91
    government regulation of
        markets ... 16
    stock market crash ... 87
Marxist philosophy 136
media 12
Medicaid 93
Medicare reform 139
Medical Savings Accounts 216
Member of Congress 146
middle class 19, 24, 88, 106
    experiences 77
    strong middle class ... 52
Miller, Mary 171
Mills, Wilber 189
mob rule 62
Monarchy 58
Money magazine 263
Monopoly
    and trusts 54, 87
    Unfair monopolies 54
Moonies 120
Moral law 117
MSAs 216
Murdah Federal Building 65
Murdoch, Rupert 131
National Citizens Coalition for
    Nursing Home
    Reform .. 185
National Rifle Association 144
National Wildlife Refuge system . 28
Nazis 70, 71
NCR 97
Neo-Conservative 131
Neo-Nazi 143
New Deal 88, 99, 104, 111
New York City 109
New York Times 140
Nixon, Richard 54
    inflation controls 130
    President Nixon 46
Noblesse oblige 46
Non-Partisan League 61
North Carolina 135

Nucor Steel 100
Oklahoma City 65
OSHA 243
O'Neill, Tip 158
O'Rourke, P.J. 256
PAC 55
patriot 20, 81
    patriotic citizens 85
    original patriots 175
    Patriot Militias 142
    patriot groups 24
    patriot movement . 23, 80
Peirson, Paul 158
Perot, Ross 129
Pharisees 116
Pharmacists 52
Phillip Morris 217
Phillips, Kevin 47, 48, 87
physicians 227
Politics 34, 64
    politics of division 13
    balance of power 79
    political campaigns ... 79
    religion of America ... 17
    contemporary politics . 31
    crooked politician 98
    current political trends . 31
    highly partisan climate . 66
    level playing field for . 33
    narrow... position 25
    political arena 32
    political clout 99
    political debate 32
    political differences ... 77
    political discourse 77
    political parties 59
    Political power ... 84, 85
    political process 32
    political rhetoric 75
    politics "for sale" 32
    politics as a forum 32
    system of politics 42
    watershed change 47
pooled resources. 34
    community 39
prayer in schools 109
printing 258
profit motive 11
Prohibition 177
Project Relief 242
Purcells, Sarah 226
Putnam, Robert 269
Reform, election 19
Republican 47, 59, 60-63, 65
    budget cuts 127
    Candidate 121

National Committee . 120
strategy 101
Research Triangle Institute 185
Robertson, Pat 109, 119, 122
Rockefeller, John D. 194
Rome 115
  Roman army 115
  Roman Empire 105
  Roman law 115, 116
  Rome of Augustus . . . 105
Reagan, Ronald 13 28 46, 61
Russia
  the former USSR 131
  Russian communism . . 15
  USSR 19,132
Savings & Loan Association 107
scapegoat 15, 65
  scapegoating 13, 76
  broad groups 75
  tyrant's tools of 26
Schultz, George 147
Scouts 240
Secretary of State 148
Secretary of the Treasury 147
Securities ExchangeCommssion . . 87
Shell Oil 108
Sherman Anti-trust Act 87
Singapore 252
Simpson, O.J 73
Smith, Susan 247
Social Darwinism 130
Social Security 186
socialism 18, 49
  socialist state 57
society 50, 57, 74, 89, 129
  agricultural, rural and
    small town
  free society 49
  functioning society . . . 45
  orderly society . . 53, 55,56
  stable society 43
South Carolina Republican party 247
Spanish Empire 106
  Spanish Inquisition . . 106
Spiritual freedom
  . . . . 82, 93, 102, 117, 123
Standard Oil 194
Steelman, Deborah 192
Stein, Herbert 149
strong man 63
"Strong-Man" Rule 51-52, 56
Sutton, Willie 149
TB 241
Talk radio 23, 24
tax expendatures 153
taxes

raising taxes 76
lower taxes 76
who pays taxes 33
television ministry 122
Television 22, 113
  television tradition 24
  television advertising . 22
  television stations 54
term limits 11
Thatcher, Margaret 160
The Bolshevik revolution 256
The New Deal 48
The Progressive Era 48
The Stamp Act 67
The Supreme Court 110
The Ten Commandments 117
Think-tanks 157
Time magazine 127
Times Mirror poll 109
tribal instinct 24
Truman, Harry 89, 140
Trust
  trust in compromise . . . 25
  atmosphere of trust . . . 21
  breakdown of trust . . . 41
  national political trust . 41
  new trust 35
  special trust 67
  trust in our system 35
Tyson, Laura 127
Unfunded federal mandates 131
Union, South Carolina 247
United States 41, 47
University of Chicago 147
unwritten agreement 91
unwritten contract 37, 40
  unwritten rules 44-45
Vietnam War 110, 111
wages 11,16,76
wages kept artificially low 93
Wall Street 155
Wallace, George 55, 88
Walmart 163
Walton, Sam 163
Washington DC 109
Weiker, Lowell 190
welfare 55, 77
  Welfare mothers 141
  Welfare State 75
Whigs 61
White Supremeist 143
Wildlife Legislative Fund of America 28
Wise Use movement 29
"Willie M." children 239
Wilson, Pete 168, 171
Worth of the individual 82

ENDNOTES

1. John Naisbitt, *Megatrends-Asia,* (New York Simon & Schuster, 1996)
2. "Bank Alarms are Blaring, " Business Week, June 26, 1995, page 52.
3. Kevin Phillips on National Public Radio.
4. Sheriff LeRoy Russell.
5. David Herbert Donald, *Lincoln,* (New York-Simon & Schuster, 1995)
6. Mickey Kaus, New Republic, January 9, 1995, page 6.
7. Jane Bryant Quinn, "A Paycheck Revolt in '96, " Newsweek, February 19, 1996, page 52.
8. Ibid.
9. Steven Rattner, "Leaky Boats on the Rising Tide," New York Times, Tuesday August 29,1995 page 19
   (Calculated from this statistic: the average CEO salary is 150 times the average workers salary today vs. 35 times the average workers salary in 1973)
10. "Couch Potato Cronicles," WGHB-Boston.
11. Outdoor Life, volume 196, issue 4, October 1995.
12. "Inquiry into Sec. 73.1910 of FEC Rules and Regulation," 2 FCC.5272, paragraph 2, (1987)
13. John Steele Gordon, "The Federal Debt," American Heritage. November 1995, page 82.
14. Michael Duffy and Dan Goodgame, *Marching in Place, The Status Quo Presidency of George Bush*, (New York Simon & Schuster,1992) page 209.
15. Kevin Phillips, *The Politics of Rich and Poor,* (New York-Random House, 1990) from the liner notes.
16. Ibid, page 221.
17. David Walls, The Activist's Almanac, (New York Simon & Schuster, 1993) page 28.
18. B.J. Lossing, *Lives of the Signers*, (Philadelphia GG Evans, 1860) page 269.

19. Ibid, Page 259.
20. Ibid, Page 264.
21. To see how good a chance, see Yahoo: Government: Law: Legal Research: Cases: O.J. Simpson Case.
22. Michael Milken, 1990 Securities Fraud Trial.
23. Howard E. Kershner, *God Gold and Government*, (Englewood Cliffs, N.J. Prentice-Hall, 1957) page 31.
24. U.S. Congressional Budget Office, "The Economic Budget Outlook, Fiscal Years 1996-2000. G.P.O. Washington, DC
25. H.R. 1555
26. Al Gore
27. Computer Shopper, "'Intel Inside Now Means More Than Just the CPU," October 1995.
28. Ruy A. Teixeira and Joel Rogers, "Who Deserted the Democrats in 1994," American Prospect, Fall 1995.
29. Jared Diamond, "Easter's End," Discover, August 1995.
30. John Roseman
31. "Who was Jesus," Life Magazine, December 1994.
32. Kershner, op.cit., page 49.
33. Ibid, page 50.
34. "Who was Jesus," op.cit., page 82.
35. Robert Dreyfuss and Peter H. Stone, "Medikill," Mother Jones, Jan/Feb 1996, page 22.
36. Michael Isikoff and Mark Hosenball, "With God There's No Cap," Newsweek, October 3, 1994, page 42-43.
37. Untitled Chart, Time, November 6, 1995, page 36.
38. John Greenwald, "A Tilt Toward the Rich?" Time, October 30, 1995.
39. Nancy Gibbs, "Getting Nowhere," Time, July 3, 1995.
40. Barry Yeoman, The Nation, February 5, 1996, page 11
41. Howard Gleckman, "The Budget," Business Week, July 3, 1995, page 29
42. "For Murdoch, It's Business as Usual," Newsweek, January 30, 1995, page 32B.

43. "The Brown Lagoon," The Economist, September 2, 1995, page 24
44. Anthony Lewis, "Abroad at Home, Merchants of Hate," New York Times, Friday, July 15,1994, page 24.
45. MacNeil Lehrer News Hour
46. Scott Tucker, "Reaping the Whirlwing," The Humanist, January 1995, page 38.
47. Jeffrey Madrick, *The End of Affluence*, (New York Random House, 1995) page 7.
48. Ibid. Page 6.
49. Ibid. Page 9
50. Ibid. Page 118.
51. Gibbs, op.cit., page 18
52, Congressman David Obey, "Who is Downsizing the
53, American Dream," Speech to the Center for National
54. Policy, March 11, 1996.
55. Dreyfuss and Stone, op cit.
56. John A. Byrne, " How High Can CEO Pay Go?," Business Week, April 22, 1996, page 100.
57. Welfare Reform
58. Paul Pierson, *Dismantling the Welfare State?*, (New York: Cambridge University Press, 1995.)
59. Mary Beth Regan with Richard S. Dunham, "A Think Tank With One Idea,"Business Week, July 3, 1995, p 49.
60. Dreyfuss and Stone, op.cit.
61. Al Gore
62. Duffy and Goodgame, op. cit., page 223.
63. Joel E. Cohen, "Ten Myths of Population," Discover, April 1996, page 42.
64. Ibid. page 43
65. "An Interview with Linda Schele," Omni Magazine, February 1995, pages 73-77.
66. Ibid.
67. Robert J. Samuelson, "Corrupting the Constitution," Newsweek, January 30, 1995.

68. Ibid.
69. "A conservative hero surveys his heirs," U.S. News and World Report, December 26, 1994/ January 2, 1995.
70. William S. Powell, *North Carolina Through Four Centuries,* (Chapel Hill-UNC Press, 1989) page 380.
71. Ibid. page 385.
72. Margaret Carlson, "Back to the Dark Ages," Time October 30, 1995, page 63
73. "USA Profile," Scholastic Update, January 12,1996, page 28
74. Ed Rubenstein, "How Not to Cut," National Review, July 31, 1995, page 15.
75. The Twentieth Century Fund, "Medicare Reform," (New York: The Twentieth Century Fund Press-1996.)
76. Phillips, op.cit.
77. The Twentieth Century, op.cit.
78. Madrick, op. Cit., page 11
79. Alprazolam 0.5mg #124 priced on 8/5/95
80. Eric Schine and Catherine Yang, "From the folks who brought you Harry and Louise," Business Week, April 17, 1995, page 37.
82. Madrick, op. cit.
83. 1996 AP Polling data
84. Dreyfuss and Stone, op cit., page 22
85. Ibid.
86. Marc Levinson, "Profit Motive," Newsweek, April 22, 1996, page 56-57
87. only 1-2 % of total budget goes to pay for welfare
88. Duffy and Goodgame, op. cit.
89. Elizabeth Gleick, Time, January 29,1996, page 34
90. Robert C. Johnston, "Panel votes $300 million cut in school construction, job training," Education Week, February 22, 1995, page 14.
91. Barbara K. Huberman and Linda A. Berne, Reproductive Rights lecture, CWPC, March 2, 1994.

92. John Carey with Mary Beth Regan, "Are Regs Bleeding The Economy?," Business Week, July 17, 1995, page 75.
93. Ibid., page 76.
94. Dannye Romine Powell, "Class issues underlie the tensions that fed the Union, S.C. saga," The Charlotte Observer, July 24, 1995, page 6A.
95. Bill Clinton, speech, August 9, 1995.
96. Duffy and Goodgame, op. cit., page 225.